Druidism

The Ancient Faith of Britain

THE MASSACRE OF THE DRUIDS

Druidism

The Ancient Faith of Britain

BY

Dudley Wright

ARABI MANOR
A REBEL SATORI IMPRINT
New Orleans & New York

Published in the United States of America by
Arabi Manor
A Rebel Satori Imprint
www.rebelsatoripress.com

Originally published by Ed. J. Burrow & Co, Ltd, 1924.

Paperback ISBN: 978-1-60864-311-0

LIST OF ILLUSTRATIONS

N.B.—The Illustrations facing pp. 24, 48, 72, 96, 120 and Frontispiece are from the Fine Art Collection of Augustin Rischgitz.

The design for the chapter ending on p. 58 shows the comparative sizes of Druidical Stone Circles. The outer circle is that of Avebury, the intermediate that of Brogar, and the centre Stennis and Stonehenge; on p. 110 are represented the three circles referred to on p. 48; on p. 172 is given the Maiden Stone at Caldron, and on p. 183 the chambered structure at Callernish.

CONTENTS

The Druids now, while arms are heard no more,
Old mysteries and horrid rites restore ;
A tribe who singular religion love,
And haunt the lonely coverts of the grove ;
To these, and these of all mankind alone,
The gods are sure revealed, or sure unknown.
If dying mortals' doom they sing aright,
No ghosts descend to hell in dreadful night ;
No parting souls to grisly Pluto go,
Nor seek the dreary silent shades below :
But forth they fly immortal in their kind,
And other bodies in new worlds they find.
Thus life for ever runs its endless race,
And, like a line, death but divides the space :
A stop which can but for a moment last,
A point between the future and the past,
Thrice happy they beneath the northern skies,
Who that worst fate, the fear of death despise.
Hence they no cares for this frail being feel,
But rush undaunted on the pointed steel ;
Provoke approaching fate, and bravely scorn
To spare that life which must so soon return.

Rowe's *Lucan*.

CHAPTER I

THE ORIGIN OF DRUIDISM

It is problematical whether the question, asked so frequently both in the past and the present, as to what period in the history of the world witnessed the foundation of Druidism, will ever be answered with definiteness. Some writers have maintained that it was a development or offshoot of the Egyptian religion and, along with Freemasonry, originated in the sublime teachings of Ptah, which, by some, are believed to have been brought out of Egypt by Moses. Faber, in his *Pagan Idolatry*, expressed the opinion that the Druidical Bards were probably the founders of Freemasonry; certainly members of the Craft will be able to trace many analogies and similarities between Druidic and Masonic ceremonial and practices, but the extent, if any, to which the one has been drawn from, or is dependent upon, the other, must be more or less a matter of speculation.

Philology does not render much assistance in determining the origin of Druidism, the possible derivation of the various Druidical terms being very conflicting, although few modern scholars probably now maintain dogmatically the opinion, regarded seriously at one time, that the word *Druid* is derived from the Greek word *drus*, meaning " an oak," on which was founded, in part at any rate, the theory that the Druids had their original habitat among the oaks of Mamre, to which reference is made in the book of Genesis. Another derivation frequently given is that *derwydd* means " the body of an oak," that word being formed from two other words, *derw*, " oak," and *ydd*, a substantive terminal In like manner *Ovydd* (Ovate) was said to mean " sapling " or " unformed plant," from *ov*, " raw," and *ydd*; and *bardd* signified " branching, " being derived from *bar*, " a branch " or " the top." Pezron gives the derivation of *Druid* from the Celtic *deru*, " oak," and *hud*, " enchantment," and says that the name was given because the priests, sages, diviners, and magicians of the ancient Gauls practised their divination and enchantments in woods and especially under oaks. *Dryades*, the Greek word, he contends, is derived from the Celtic. The Celtic meaning of the word *Druid* is " to enclose within a circle " and the word was used in the sense of " prophet " or " one admitted into the mysteries of

the inner circle." Other writers give the derivation as from the Hebrew
derussim, or *drussim*, which means "contemplators." Vallancey ascribes
a Hebrew origin to the term, but traces it to the word *drush*, meaning
"an expounder" or "an interpreter." Another explanation given is
that it is an old Celtic word, *druis*, formed from *trowis*, or *truwis*, meaning
"a doctor of the faith." *Trowis*, in German, means "a revealer of
truth." *Trutis* was an ancient British name for the Deity, and the
first priests in Britain were called *Truti*. The celebrated philologist
Thurneysen derives *Druid* from *dru*, a prefix meaning "thorough" and
vid, meaning "know," so that, from this etymological reading, a Druid
was a man of great knowledge. The earliest mention of the name of
Druid is found in Diogenes Laertius's *Lives of the Philosophers*. The
Persian *duru* means "a good and holy man"; the Arabic *deri*, "an
absolver or remitter of sins." In Scotland, the Druids were called
Ducergli, and in Spain *Turduli* or *Turdutan*. The Oriental dervishes are
thought by some to derive their name from the same source as the Druids.
Mr. D. Delta Evans, who has devoted considerable time, attention, and
skill to the study of this subject, says that, according to the best information from Celtic scholars, it would appear beyond doubt that the word
derwydd is derived from *dar*, meaning "above," and *gwydd*, meaning
"understanding," "learning," or "knowledge."

Cynwal, an eminent Welsh poet of the sixteenth century, employs
the term in this foregoing meaning and thus apostrophises a well-known
Bard :

> *Dywed weithian dad ieithydd*
> *Dy feddwl ym, do foddawl wydd.*
> Declare thou then, thou father of languages,
> Thy mind, if of well-cultured knowledge.

Diogenes said that the Gaulish philosophers were known both as
Druids and as Semnothei, the latter word meaning "Venerable Deities."
All Hallows Day was known in Ireland as *La Samhna* and the month of
November as *Mi Saman*, but the derivation of these words is from *Samh*,
meaning "rest" or "repose from labour." The name *Saman* was one
of the titles of Buddha, who was regarded by the ancient Irish as the
lord of death and the judge of departed spirits. His festival, says Faber,
in *Pagan Idolatry*, occurred in the month of November, when sacrifices
of black sheep were offered to him for the souls of the deceased. The
festival of All Souls appears to have superseded the festival of Saman.
Among the Gymnosophists there was a sect of philosophers, women as
well as men, who, says Clement of Alexandria, made truth their study
and claimed ability to read into the future and to predict forthcoming
events. The female Semnes, he adds, always preserved their virginity.

The word really means " venerable," and it embodied an idea of antiquity and veneration and was applied only to persons worthy of respect for their morals, merits, prudence, and age ; it is probably the root of the words " Senatus," " Senatores," " Senex," " Senior," etc.

The Saxons called a sorcerer *dry ;* and sorcery or magic was known as *dry-craeft,* words not to be found in any dialects cognate to the British. From the word *dry,* the verb *bedrian,* " to bewitch " or " to fascinate " was formed. A disordered man was called *bedrida,* from which has descended the modern term " bedridden."

The antiquity of the Druidical system is not in doubt or question. It is indisputable that a highly-efficient organization such as Druidism was when it came first into historical view, could not have been of recent origin or foundation. According to Cæsar, who had no direct dealings or intercourse with the Druids and who had to depend upon other people for his information—Divitiacus, the arch-Druid of his time, in particular, and with whom, in all probability, he conversed through an interpreter— the Gauls boasted that they were descended from Dis as their father, this being a Druidical tradition. Dis, or Dives, according to mythology, was one of three brothers, Jupiter and Neptune being the two others. They are said to have had Saturn for their father and Minerva for their mother. Dives is the same word as the Hebrew Japheth, and this is probably the foundation of the tradition that Japheth was the progenitor of the Celts, who are claimed by some writers to have been the earliest inhabitants of Western Europe. Dr. Stukeley, referring to the temple planted by Abraham when he settled for a time at Beersheba (Genesis xxi, 33), speaks of it as " that famous oak-grove of Beersheba, planted by the illustrious parent and first Druid, Abraham, and from whom our celebrated British Druids came, who were of the same patriarchal reformed religion, and brought the use of sacred groves to Britain." There are, however, some subjects on which Dr. Stukeley must not be regarded too seriously. The positive statement is nevertheless made by other writers that Druidic colleges were in existence in the days of Hermio, a German prince, who is supposed to have flourished about the same time as Abraham.

Pococke, in *India in Greece,* claims that the Druids were of the Indu Vanes, or Lunar Race—hence the symbol of the crescent worn by them. Their chief settlement was in the Hi-Budh-des, or the land of the Hya-Bud'has, and their last refuge in Britain from the oppression of the Romans, the descendants of their own stock, was Mona, which should properly be Mooni. According to Wilson's *Sanskrit Lexicon,* the meaning of this word is " a holy sage," " a pious and learned person, endowed with more or less of a divine nature, or having attained it by rigid abstrac- tion and mortification." If this interpretation is correct, it explains the

amazing mechanical skill displayed in the construction of the massive
stone circles found throughout the country and it harmonises with the
industrious and enterprising characteristics of the Buddhists throughout
the world, for they were the same people that drained the valley of
Cashmir, and, in all probability, the plains of Thessaly.

Fergusson supposes the existence of two distinct races in the island
of Britain : the original inhabitants, who were of Turanian origin and
the more uncivilised, being driven by the other race, the Celtic, into the
fastnesses of the Welsh hills long previous to the Roman invasion. Among
the former he thinks that the religion of Druidism, consisting of tree and
serpent worship, may have been practised. Bertrand and Reinach both
maintain the pre-Celtic origin of Druidism, but Camille Julian inclines
to the opinion that it was of Gallic origin.

Possibly one reason why some writers have assigned a Gallic origin
to the primitive inhabitants of Britain, as well as to Druidism, is the
adoption of Gallic names by British tribes, a very insecure deduction.
There is greater reason for the assumption of an Asiatic origin, having
regard to the similarity of the Persian and Druidical forms of government
and religion, the use of military chariots, and the similarity in the names
of the leaders of the people in each of these countries. Pliny, however,
maintains that Druidism was taught to the Persians by the Britons and
not by the Persians to the Britons. According to the Triads (to which
fuller reference will be made later), however, the original colonists who
migrated to Britain were conducted thither by a leader named Huysgwyn
(Persian, *Hushang*), and the first settlers came by a long and devious
sea-voyage from the summer country (Asia) and inhabited Dyffro-banu
—presumably a corruption of Dyffryn-albanu, the name given to the
glens of Albania, a country situated between the Euxine and Caspian
Seas. Another triad states that the original inhabitants of Britain were
emigrants from a city called Gaf-fis, or the lower Gaf, a mountain
stretching between these seas. Schrader, in his *Reallexikon*, says that
the Celtic Druids are quite different from other priesthoods of ancient
Europe and that where the first beginnings of their origin started will
never be known.

The Celtic language, according to some authorities, is a dialect of
the Phœnician language, the Phœnician being a near relative of the
Hebrew. There is certainly a close resemblance in many details between
the Hebrew and Irish languages.

Vallancey, whose invaluable researches into the early history of
Britain and its inhabitants have placed all students under an eternal
debt of gratitude, says that the Druids were in existence at the time
Britain was peopled ; that they flourished in the east and were imported
by that great body of Persian Scythians, known to the Greeks under the

name of Phœnicians, that they invaded the Britannic islands, driving most of the original inhabitants into Gaul, retaining possession of the islands (as Welsh antiquarians also maintain) until the Cymmeri arrived, who, in their turn, expelled the Phœnico-Persico-Scythi to Ireland and Scotland. The Phœnician inhabitants of Tyre are said constantly to have visited the western parts of Britain between B.C. 1200 and B.C. 500, and to have carried on a considerable trade with the inhabitants in tin and other articles. Borlase is of opinion that the Druidical faith had its origin in Britain, whence it was transmitted to Gaul. Davies, in his *Celtic Researches*, says :

"The monuments we call Druidical must be appropriated, exclusively, to the aborigines of the midland and western divisions. They are found in such corners and fastnesses as have, in all ages and countries, been the last retreat of the conquered, and the last that are occupied by the victorious. In Wales and in Mona, they were used and venerated, until the aborigines were completely subjugated by the Roman arms. In the central countries, and in the west, they perpetually occur, from Cornwall to Cumberland ; whereas, comparatively, few traces of them are discovered in the eastern part of the island, which, therefore, appear to have been occupied by those people who did not construct buildings of this nature, and who obtained possession before the aborigines deeply impressed their character on the soil."

In Britain, the Druidical order is said to have numbered thirty-one seats of education, each being a Cyfiath, or City, the capital of a tribe. According to some writers there were three Arch-Druids in Britain, this official being peculiar to that country. Their seats are said to have been at Caer Troia, or London ; Caer Erroc, or York ; and Caer Leon, or Caerleon (Monmouthshire). Morgan, in *British Cymry*, gives the following list of Druidical seats in Britain : Caer Caint, Canterbury ; Caer Wyn, Winchester ; Caer Municip, St. Alban's ; Caer Sallwg, Old Sarum ; Caer Leil, Carlisle ; Caer Odor, Bristol ; Caer Llear, Leicester ; Caer Urnach, Wroxeter ; Caer Lleyn, Lincoln ; Caer Glou, Gloucester ; Caer Grawnt, Cambridge ; Caer Meini, Manchester ; Caer Ceol, Colchester ; Caerleon ar Dwy, Chester ; Caer Peris, Porchester ; Caer Don, Doncaster ; Caer Guorie, Warwick ; Caer Cei, Chichester ; Caer Ceri, Cirencester ; Caer Dur, Dorchester ; Caer Merddyn, Carmarthen ; Caer Ceiont, Carnarvon ; Caer Wyse, Exeter ; Caer Segont, Silchester ; Caer Baddon, Bath ; Caer Gorangon, Worcester. The students at these colleges are said to have numbered at times 60,000.

Mr. Akerman, in *Numismatic Journal* (I. p. 217), says that Druidical circles do appear on ancient British coins. "The coins of Adminius and Togodumnus," says Beale Poste, "are noticeable from the occurrence

B

of various symbols upon them, as bucrania, skulls of oxen ; circles of dots, cases of sacrificial knives, double circles, serpents, and loose horses. The upholding of the nationality of the Britons and of the Druidical religion is supposed to be implied in these emblems.

Whatever the origin of the inhabitants of Britain or of Druidism, few who have given any attention to the latter subject will venture to contest the statement of Theodore Watts-Dunton that, compared with Druidism—that mysterious, poetic religion, which, more than any other religion, expresses the very voice of nature—all other religions have a sort of commonplace and modern ring, even those which preceded it by centuries. Although the Druids are mentioned by Greek writers, the Greeks lay no claim to be the founders of the religion, and it is scarcely probable that it could have been derived from Judaism—although there are supporters of that theory—owing to the meagre intercourse of the Jews of those times with other nations.

The Druids are mentioned by name by the following pre-Christian writers : Aristotle, Sotion, Posidonius, Julius Cæsar, Cicero, Diodorus of Sicily, Timageneus ; and by the following writers of the Christian era : Strabo, Pomponius Mela, Lucian, Pliny, Tacitus, Suetonius, Dion Chrysostom, Clement of Alexandria, and St. Cyril, this last-named reproducing the opinion of a more ancient Greek historian, Polyhistor. Omitting Aristotle and Sotion, who knew of the Druids only by hearsay, there are some twelve writers contemporary with the Druids in the heyday of their existence and in their decline.

It may, however, be admitted that nothing precise is known with reference to the origin of Druidism ; that some, at any rate, of the statements made with regard even to its religious tenets are deductive only, and that even where there is anything approaching certitude, the source of information is invariably outside Britain. There is, however, no conflict in the testimony regarding the rites and ceremonies of the Druids among the numerous authorities and it is difficult to explain the many points of resemblance between the rites and institutions of the Druids of Britain and Gaul, the Magi of Persia, the Chaldeans of Babylon, the Brahmans of India, and the priests of Egypt, except upon the hypothesis that the rites and ceremonies of these various religions were derived from a common source, which would be a date anterior to the time when the Greeks and Romans produced those " elegant mythologies."

Britain appears to have been regarded as the principal home of Druidism, and, by some, is claimed to have held the faith in greater purity than any other country. The Gallic Druids appear to have been in the habit of journeying to Britain for the purpose of studying the religion, although Professor Rhys thinks they went more to Ireland than to Britain, in consequence of Druidism in Gaul having become corrupted

by reason of its contiguity to heathen forms of worship, by the admission
of strange gods into the calendar, and by the adoration of images. Cæsar
states in his *Commentaries* that the Druidical doctrine was evolved
(*inventa*) in the Isle of Britain, whence it was taken to Gaul, and, he
adds : " Those who wish to study it deeply usually go to the island and
stay there for a time." The Gallic Druids met annually in solemn
assembly or convocation in the territory of the Carnutes (Chartres and
Orleans) ; this country being chosen as it was considered to be the centre
of Gaul.

O'Curry, in his *Manners and Customs of the Ancient Irish*, says :
    " It must occur to everyone who has read of Zoroaster, or of
the Magi of Persia, and of the sorcerers of Egypt mentioned in the
seventh chapter of Exodus, that Druids and Druidism did not
originate in Britain any more than in Gaul or Erin. It is indeed
probable that, notwithstanding Pliny's high opinion of the power
of the British Druids, the European Druidical system was but the
offspring of the eastern augury, somewhat less complete, perhaps,
when transplanted to a new soil than in its ancient home."

Pliny was of opinion that the Druids were the Gaulish magi, and,
according to Porphyry, " the name *magi* in the east was most august
and venerable : they alone were skilled in divine matters and were the
ministers of the Deity." Higgins believed them to be Pythagoreans,
akin to the Essenes, whilst another writer holds to the opinion that they
were the descendants of the lost Atlanteans. Alexandre Bertrand maintains that Druidism was not an isolated institution, without analogy,
but that its parallel is to be looked for in the lamaseries which survive
still in Tartary and Thibet. Maurice contends that the Druids were the
immediate descendants of a tribe of Brahmans from the high northern
districts bordering on the vast range of the Caucasus. Polyhistor, in
his book on *Symbols*, declares that Pythagoras visited both the Brahmans
and the Celts. There are also other writers who affirm that the Druids
were initiated into their beliefs and practices by Zamolais, a sometime
slave of Pythagoras. If, however, we are to believe St. Clement of
Alexandria, the Druids took nothing from Pythagoras ; their reputation
drew Pythagoras to Gaul in order that he might be instructed in their
mysteries and Theology. This St. Clement is said to have learned from
Polyhistor. In fact, Pythagoras did not come into the world until the
forty-seventh Olympiad, four generations after Numa, while the philosophy of the Druids existed before the time of Homer.

Dr. Churchward, in *Signs and Symbols of Primordial Man*, holds that
the ancient Druids
    " were undoubtedly descendants of the ancient Egyptian priests,
who came over and landed in Ireland and the west of England, and

who brought with them their religious doctrines and taught and practised them here. The Tuathá-dè-Danann—the princes or descendants of Dia-tene-ion, the fire god, or the sun—who came to Ireland, were of the same race and spoke the same language as the Fir-Bolgs, or the Formarians, possessed ships, knew the art of navigation, had a compass or magnetic needle, worked in metals, had a large army thoroughly organised, a body of surgeons, and a Bardic or Druid class of priests. These Druids brought all their learning with them, believed and practised the eschatology of the solar doctrines, and came from Egypt. That their temples are older than those found in Uxmah, in Yucatan, in Mexico (which are stated to be 11,500 years old), those amongst the Incas in South America, and some of the Zimbabwe in South Africa, is clearly proved by their want of knowledge of building an arch, although we find in the oldest remains among the Zimbabwe lintels at Umnuk-wana, and no doubt there are others in South African ruins, but successive immigrants have obliterated most of the original, which was the old Egyptian, as can be proved by other facts.''

It would certainly be interesting to have further proofs of this arresting statement. Concerning the arrival of the Tuathá-dè-Danann in Ireland, Keating, in his *History of Ireland*, says that they journeyed to Erin after seven months' sojourn in the north of Scotland. They landed on the north coast of Ireland, but, in order that they should not be seen by any of the Fir Bolg, they, by means of the magical powers with which nearly all ancient writers invest them, raised a mist around their vessels until they reached Sliabh-an-iarainn (Slieve-an-ierin), the iron mountains in County Leitrim. Once landed, they made their departure impossible by burning their boats.

According to the traditional history of Ireland, the Tuathá-dè-Danann were the descendants of the followers of Faidh, the third son of a prince named Nemedius, when the Fomorians, an African tribe, made themselves masters of Ireland and enslaved its inhabitants. The Fomorians appear to have been civilised sufficiently to be able to teach the Tuathá-dè-Danann to build with stone and lime, but, according to Pomponius Mela, the latter emigrated to Achaia, a country of Greece bordering on Boetia, near the city of Thebes. It is said that while there they acquired that extraordinary skill in necromancy and enchantment which enabled them to work miracles and even to raise the dead. Rather than fall into the hands of the Assyrians, whose sorcerers and Druids were more powerful than their own, they migrated to Denmark and Norway. After a sojourn in those countries, they journeyed to Scotland, where they remained for seven years before removing to Ireland.

After the settlement of the Tuathá-dè-Danann, the Milesians

attempted to effect a landing in Ireland, but were for some time prevented by the Tuathá-dè-Danann, who, by the power of their enchantments and diabolical arts, cast such a cloud over the whole island that the Milesians were confounded. With much difficulty they effected a landing at Inohei Seeine, in the west of Munster. They proceeded to a mountain called Sliabh Mis, where they were met by Banba, the queen, who was accompanied by her Druids and soothsayers.

> " Banba they met, with all her princely train,
> On Sliabh Mis ; and on the fruitful plain
> Of Sliabh Eibhline, Fodhla next they spied,
> With priests and learned Druids for her guide,
> And all her charming court of ladies by her side ;
> Then virtuous Eire appeared in pomp and state,
> In Visneach's pleasant fields, majestically great."

Fodhla was a princess, who was also accompanied by a retinue of ladies and Druids. Eire, another princess, is said to have given her name to the country. These three ladies were married to the three sons of Cearmada, who ruled alternately over the whole of the kingdom :

> " Three Irish kings alternately reigned,
> And for their consorts chose three princesses,
> Fodhla, Banba, and Eire."

In the battles which ensued between the Tuathá-dè-Danann and the Milesians, Scota, Milesius's widow, as well as many learned Druids, are said to have been slain on both sides. Two of the Druids who lost their lives in this encounter were named Uar and Eithir, whose funeral rites were celebrated with great solemnity.

> " On Sliabh Mis our warlike squadrons stood,
> Eager of fight, and prodigal of blood ;
> Victorious arms our stout Gadelians bore,
> Ruin behind, and terror march'd before ;
> A thousand of th' enchanted host are slain,
> They try their charms and magic arts in vain,
> For with their mangled limbs they cover all the plain.
> Three hundred only of our troops are kill'd,
> Who bravely turned the fortune of the field.
> The learned Uar rush'd among the rest,
> But, with repeated blows and wounds oppress'd,
> He fell, and by his side expiring lay
> Eithir, a priest, and gasp'd his soul away.
> The victors then the funeral rites prepare,
> Due to their dead companions of the war."

The pedigree of Milesius is given in the old Irish Chronicles in the following words :

"Milesius, son of Bille, son of Breogan, son of Bratha, son of Deaghatha, son of Earchada, son of Alleid, son of Nyagath, son of Nannaille, son of Feithricglas, son of Heber Glunfionn, son of Heber Scotson of Sree, son of Easree, son of Gadelas, son of Niul, son of Feniusa Farsa, son of Baath, son of Magog, son of Japhet, son of Noah, son of Lamech."

It has been suggested that Ireland obtained her ancient name of "the sacred island" from the fact of the country having become the chosen depository of the Phœnician worship in that part of the world.

With reference to Ireland, the ground is more certain when dealing with Druidism than in the case of Britain or Gaul, inasmuch as the sole source of information relating to the Irish Druids is derived from Irish documents and writers, whereas the greater part of the information concerning British and Gallic Druidism is derived from Latin and Greek writers. According to some of the ancient Irish writers, Parthalonus made his advent into Erin about three hundred years after the date assigned to the Deluge. He came from Middle Greece, and brought with him three Druids : Fios, Eolus, and Fochmar, names which mean "Intelligence," "Knowledge," and "Inquiry." Three hundred and thirty years later there came another colony of immigrants, led by Nemid and his sons, who entered into a conflict with the Druidical forces they found established on the island. From that time there is some record or chronicle of the acts of the Druids in Ireland. They were referred to frequently as "men of science," and extraordinary powers were attributed to them. They were credited with the power to raise storms and atmospheric disturbances. The following translation of an incantation used by them is taken from the *Book of the Invasions of the O'Clerys* in the Royal Irish Academy :

"I pray that they reach the land of Erinn, those who are riding upon the great, productive, vast sea.

"That they may be distributed upon her plains, her mountains and her valleys ; upon her forests that shed showers of nuts and all other fruits ; upon her rivers and her cataracts ; upon her lakes and her great waters ; upon her spring-abounding hills.

"That we may hold our fairs and equestrian sports upon her territories.

"That there may be a king for us in Tara and that it may be the territory of many kings.

"That the sons of Milesius may be manifestly seen upon her territories.

"That noble Erinn may be the home of the ships and boats of the sons of Milesius.

" Erinn, which is now in darkness, it is for her that this oration is pronounced.

" Let the learned wives of Breas and Buagne pray that we may reach the noble woman, Great Erinn.

" Let Erinn pray and let Ir and Eber implore that we may reach Erinn."

The tempest is said to have ceased immediately upon the utterance of this incantation and the survivors were enabled to land without any trouble or difficulty.

There is an Irish tradition that the Druids first set foot in Ireland seven hundred years before the time of St. Patrick, or about B.C. 270. Certainly, it would appear from the evidence that the Druids settled at a date much earlier than they did in Britain. Connor is said to have been the name of the King of Ireland who was reigning at the time of the Crucifixion. Surprised, the legend runs, at the dreadful and super-normal eclipse which then took place, he consulted Bachrach, an eminent Druid of Leinster, for the purpose of ascertaining the meaning of the wonderful event. The Druid replied that a barbarous murder had that day been committed by the Jews, who had killed a divine and innocent person. The king immediately drew his sword, went to an adjacent grove, and, distracted almost to madness, hacked and cut away at the trees, protesting that if he were in the country of the Jews where this holy person had been executed, he would be avenged upon the murderers and chop them to pieces as he had done the trees. It is related that this Druid, Bachrach, prophesied to the people of Leinster that a most holy person should be born in a wonderful manner and be barbarously murdered by the great council of his own nation, notwithstanding his design of coming into the world for the happiness and salvation of the whole earth, and to redeem its inhabitants from the delusions and tyranny of infernal demons which had the power to torture them with insupportable pains in a future state. In this connection also it must be remembered that there is a legend to the effect that the Cup of the Holy Graal was a Druidic vase used in the most sacred rites. The Druids of Britain are said to have been mysteriously warned of the Passion of Jesus, as a result of which they sent the vase to Jerusalem, where it was used at the Last Supper. After the Crucifixion, it was entrusted to the care of Joseph of Arimathea, who conveyed it back to Britain, with which country he traded for tin, and whither, according to another legend among Cornish tin-workers, St. Joseph brought Jesus himself as a boy.

In A.D. 449 we find St. Patrick revising the Celtic laws, the work of the Druids, at the command of the King, whose confidence he had gained, in concert with three provincial kings, three Ollamhs or Druidical doctors, and three bishops, these last having replaced the Druids. The revolution had been rapid, since it had fallen on well-prepared soil. It would seem that Ireland had become Christian even before it bore that name. It is remarkable also to note the promptitude with which King Loegair, only a few years after his conversion, peopled the monasteries with faithful followers of the Christian faith, and this was done, not only in Ireland, but in Scotland and in England as well. These monasteries and abbeys, says Bertrand, would seem almost spontaneously to have risen from the earth at a time when Gaul possessed none. In A.D. 500, shortly after the death of St. Patrick, St. Findia (who died A.D. 582) founded an Abbey under the jurisdiction of the Archbishop of Armagh. In A.D. 520, there was in existence a very flourishing monastery in the Scottish isle of Iona. In the same century, while a large part of England, Ireland and Scotland was still pagan, were founded powerful abbeys at Bangor and in County Down. An event is narrated in ancient Irish history to the effect that Lughaid, son of the Loegair mentioned above, perished by lightning for his obstinate adherence to the Druidical superstition.

The Druidical faith survived in Ireland to a period much later than in Britain. Toland says that the Druidical college of Derry was converted into a Culdee monastery. About the year A.D. 561, Columba and twelve companions left Ireland to build the monastery of Icolmkill. So far as Wales is concerned, Druidism ceased to be practised, at least openly, by the end of the first century A.D., but long after the advent of St. Patrick, the chief monarchs of Ireland adhered to Druidism. Two of the daughters of King Laogorius, in whose reign St. Patrick expounded the tenets of the Christian faith, were educated by the Druids and maintained their ground in a dispute against the Christian religion. Laogorius and all the provincial kings of Ireland, however, granted to every man free liberty of preaching and professing the Christian religion if they wished to do so.

Ledwich tells us that in the sixth century Columba founded two celebrated monasteries, one in the oaken grove in the town of Derry, the other at Doire-magh, in the field of oaks in the King's County. Churches were also founded at Doire-macaidecain in Meath, Doire-melle in Leitrim, and those at Kildoire and Kilderry were constructed in groves of oaks. The Christians continued the Druidic notion of reverence for trees and consecrated trees to saints ; and so great was the veneration for these consecrated trees that the act of cutting or injuring them incurred severe penalty. Some archers who, in the twelfth century, destroyed some timber in the churchyard of Finglas, near Dublin, were said to have died of an unusual pestilence. Similarly, the holiness of groves was as firmly believed in as that of shrines. At Roscarbury, St. Fachnan very early founded a see and literary seminary. At Lismore is a Druidic cave and there was also a celebrated school and cathedral, and near the latter was the residence of an anchoret from the remotest time. Felibien, in his *Recueil historiq*, speaking of the caves under the church of Chartres, says that the grottos which are under this church are claimed to have been there in the time of the Druids. Over these caves, where probably the grand assembly of the Gaulish and British Druids was held, a Christian church was erected. In Brecknockshire is Ty Ilhtud, or St. Iltut's cell, which Camden says was made in the time of paganism and originally stood in a stone circle. Another sacred structure at Llantwit, in Glamorganshire, originally stood within a Druidic grove. In Ireland, not far from the church of Templebrien, is a stone circle with a central pyramidal pillar. Close by is an artificial cave which was the retreat of the Druid serving the pagan temple.

It was an established custom in the reign of Cormac, King of Ireland, A.D. 213–253, that every monarch of the kingdom should be attended by ten officers, one of whom was always a Druid, whose function it was to regulate the concerns of religion and worship, to offer sacrifices, to divine and foretell events for the use and advantage of the king and his dominions. The following is taken from a poem of great antiquity :

" Ten royal officers, for use and state,
    Attend the court, and on the monarch wait,
    A nobleman, whose virtuous actions grace
    His blood, and add new glories to his race.
    A judge, to fix the meaning of the laws,
    To save the poor, and right the injur'd cause.
    A grave physician, by his artful care,
    To ease the sick, and weakened health repair.
    A poet to applaud, and boldly blame,
    And justly to give infamy or fame ;
    For without him the freshest laurels fade,
    And vice to dark oblivion is betray'd.
    The next attendant was a faithful priest,
    Prophetic fury roll'd within his breast ;
    Full of his god, he tells the distant doom
    Of kings unborn and nations yet to come ;
    Daily he worships at the holy shrine,
    And pacifies his god with rites divine,
    With constant care the sacrifice renews,
    And anxiously the panting entrails views.
    To touch the harp, the sweet musician bends,
    And both his hands upon the strings extends ;
    The sweetest sound flows from each warbling string,
    Soft as the breezes of the breathing spring,

Music has pow'r the passions to control,
And tunes the harsh disorders of the soul.
The antiquary by his skill reveals
The race of kings, and all their offspring tells.
The spreading branches of the royal line,
Traced out by him in lasting records shine.
Three officers in lower order stand,
And, when he drives in state, attend the king's command."

Rowland gives it as his opinion that, when the Druids were expelled from Anglesey, they sought refuge in Ireland, the north of Scotland, and the Scottish Isles. Certainly, when Druidism was inhibited in Gaul, and the active persecution of the Druids began, they appear to have retired to Caledonia, there to practise and to teach their religion. About A.D. 76, Dothan, who is described as the eleventh king of Scotland, is said to have left his three sons in the Isle of Man, there to be educated by the Druids, as also was Corbed, son of Corbed, first king of Scotland, at a much earlier date. Sacheverell, in his *Survey of the Isle of Man*, is of opinion that the Isle of Man, rather than Anglesey, was the principal seat of the Druids, from the fact that it was called *Sedes Druidarum* and *Insula Druidarum*. " The original inhabitants of the Isle of Man," he says, " were undoubtedly the same with the rest of Britain, and their first government a sort of aristocracy under the Druids. I could almost venture to call it a theocracy, their notions of divinity were so lively and perfect ; their form of government so admirably adapted to the good of mankind ; in short, such an excellent mixture of prince and priest, that religion and the state had but one united interest."

According to Spotswood's *History of the Church of Scotland*, the Druids were in power in Scotland in the latter part of the third century. He writes :

" Cratylinth, king of Scotland, coming to the throne in the year 277, made it one of his first works to purge the kingdom of its heathenish superstition, and to expel the Druids, a sort of people held in those days in great reputation. They ruled their affairs very politely ; for being governed by a president who kept his residence in the Isle of Man, which was then under the dominion of the Scots, they did once every year in that place meet to take counsel together for the ordering of affairs, and carried things so politely and with such discretion that Cratylinth found it difficult enough to expel them, because of the favour they had amongst the people."

Huddleston says that it is established by the most unquestionable authorities that the Celts were the original inhabitants of Europe, that the Celtic language was a dialect of the primary language of Asia, and that the Celtæ had among them from the most remote antiquity an

Order of Literati, called Druids, to whom the Greeks and Romans ascribed a degree of philosophical celebrity, inferior to none of the ages of antiquity. With this view Pinkerton agrees, so far as admitting that the Celts were the aborigines of Europe and their language the original one. The presence of Irish words in the French language is accounted for by the Irish Druids, who travelled between the two countries and who were the instructors of the youth of each country.

According to another authority :

"The Druids of the first century B.C. affirmed that once there was a native population in Gaul : it was the population anterior to the Celtic conquests, that which was known in Ireland as the Fir-Bolg, Fir-Domann, and Galloir. A second group, named Druids, came thither from the most distant isles : in other words, from the Land of the Dead, the Isles of the Blest, or the All-Powerful of Greek mythology. This was the population that first crossed the Rhine and settled down in the western borders in pre-historic times, anterior to the fifth century B.C., and to the time of Hecatus of Miletus. When Timageus obtained this information from the Druids of the first century, B.C., the Celts of this first immigration had lost all recollection of their arrival in Gaul and had no other belief than the Druidical doctrine of the mythic origin of the Cult."

King Finnan, who succeeded to the throne of Man in B.C. 134, is said to have first established the Druids in the Isle of Man.

We learn from Origen that the Druids were not only well known to the Roman philosophers, but that they were held up by them as examples of wisdom and models for imitation on account of pre-eminent merit of some kind ; and Clement of Alexandria called Druidism "a religion of philosophers," like that of the primitive Persians.

By some the Druids were known as Saronides, a name given also to groves of oaks or sacred trees. Saronides is an ancient Greek appellation for the oak :

"When Rhea felt for Jove a mother's throes
By deep Iaon's streams the tall Saronides rose."

Callim, Jov. 22.

"She to the stiff Saronid's branch applied
Her sons, and in the noose her neck she tied."

Ap Rhod. ap Parthen, 11.

The word is derived from the root *sar*, meaning originally "a rock," but it came afterwards to be adopted as a mark of high honour. It is the root of the name "Sarah." In course of time high groves or hills with woods of oak were named "Saron," because they were sacred to the Deity. Davis in his *Celtic Researches*, insists that "Saronides'

is a British word, compounded from *ser*, " stars," and *honydd*, " one who
discriminates or points out," so that, according to his contention, the
Saronides were Seronyddion, or astronomers. Diogenes Laertius gives
the name of Semnotheist to the Druid ascetic and a Semnotheus seems
to have been a solitary religious who, in a secret cell, gave himself up to
the contemplation of heavenly things.

From the language of the Triads and other ancient poems, there
appears to be ground for the inference that during the Roman occupation
there was a Druidical seminary in the isle of Britain, or in an adjacent
island, and probably beyond the limits of the Empire, where the doctrine
and discipline were cultivated without interference ; that there the
Druids persisted in the sacrifices of human beings ; that certain devotees
from the southern provinces repaired thither to their solemn festivals ;
that upon the departure of the Romans they repaired to Mona and Wales ;
and that this northern seminary was not entirely suppressed until the
end of the sixth century. It is intimated in some works that the Britons
regarded this northern establishment with great respect and that they
made frequent pilgrimages there, particularly at the time of the solemn
festivals.

Druidism, under that particular name, does not appear to have been
known outside Gaul, Britain, and Ireland, although similar teaching and
practices are to be found in countries outside those boundaries, but the
name appears to have belonged exclusively to those parts. The religion,
however, appears to have been established among the Germans, Danes,
Swedes, Norsemen, Muscovites, Russians, Pomeranians, Laplanders,
Scythians, Goths, Thracians, Lithuanians, Poles, Hungarians, and
Samogethians, with, of course, local variations.

Although, in Britain, the Romans issued stringent laws for the
suppression of the Druidical groves and altars, there is no proof of the
eradication of Druidism at that time. It had taken root too deeply not
to spring up again after the Romans had taken their departure from the
island. The suppression of Druidism was essential to the Roman conquest
of Britain : the two were incompatible. Augustus Cæsar recognised that
Druidism would be a source of danger unless it could be assimilated to
Roman ideas and practices, and so he prohibited Roman citizens from
seeking initiation into the Druidical mysteries, a step also forbidden by
the Druids themselves. Tiberius went a step further and made a determined effort to destroy it. Suetonius states that Claudius Cæsar entirely
abolished the dreadfully atrocious religion of the Druids among the
Gauls, which Augustus had merely prohibited to the Roman citizens.
However, on the rebellion of the Gaulish tribes, which occurred during
the struggles of Vitellius and Vespasian, when the capital was burnt,
Tacitus says that " the Druids sang with vain superstition that the Gauls

had anciently taken Rome, but, since the seat of Jove had remained intact, her empire had also remained." Now the gods had given a sign of their wrath by a fatal conflagration and portended to the nations north of the Alps the supremacy over human affairs. According to Strabo, the Gauls held to the opinion that as the number of Druids increases the earth produces its fruits in greater abundance. In all probability when Claudius decided to exterminate Druidism it was because it seemed to contain within itself in a concentrated form the surviving national feeling of the Gaulish tribes which, in view of the annexation of Britain, might appear a real danger to the peace of the Western provinces.

The imperial measures taken to arrest Druidism and to abolish it were in vain. It is certain that the Druids were in existence at the time of St. Eloi, who died towards the end of the seventh century, and even for some time after. Eloi Eligius was Bishop of Noyon and patron saint of goldsmiths. Long passages could be quoted from the writings of this saint showing that Paganism still triumphed over Christianity in many parts of France in his day, and there is no reason to doubt from his statements that the mysterious rites, with which the Druids had always honoured their divinities, were then still practised. It may even be assumed that Druidism alone retarded the free passage of Christianity to all parts of France.

Pliny, in his *Natural History* (xxx., 4, 13) says that Tiberius Cæsar caused the Druids to disappear, yet he admits in another passage that they were still in existence and superintended the religious ceremonies in the time of Vespasian. His language leads to the assumption that all that was accomplished in the reign of Tiberius Cæsar was the temporary suppression of the outward observances of Druidism, or, particularly, the practice of human sacrifices.

In many parts of Britain, moreover, the Romans permitted the natives to retain many of their laws and customs and to be governed by their own princes, and here, in all probability, they would continue the performance of their ancient and sacred mystical rites. According to Strabo, the Druids still acted as arbiters in public and private matters, though, presumably, they had not the power to deal with murder indictments, as formerly they had. Thus, on the introduction of the civil law by the Romans, the principle of secular justice between man and man, priestly domination among the Britons passed away.

Cormac, who, about the middle of the third century, ascended the throne of Ireland, attempted to reform the religion of the Druids by divesting it of the polytheism into which it had degenerated, but, in consequence of his efforts, his subjects rebelled against him. In one of the battles which ensued he lost an eye, which compelled him, in accordance with the law then prevailing in Ireland, to resign the crown.

Celtic and Gaulish Druids are mentioned in the third century as being connected with events in the lives of Aurelian and Diocletian. They are mentioned by Ammianus Marcellinus and Ausenius and in the fourth century by Procopius. Gibbon epitomises the history of the Druids in the Christian era in the following words :

"Under the specious pretext of abolishing human sacrifices, the Emperors Tiberius and Claudius suppressed the dangerous power of the Druids ; but the priests themselves, their gods, and their altars, subsisted in peaceful obscurity till the final destruction of Paganism."

Eighteen years after Aulus Plautius first landed, there was a merciless massacre of the Druidical priests and their very devoted adherents in the Isle of Anglesey, and, although the religion may have been, and, in all probability, was practised, yet so far as it was a regularly organized system of religious belief, culture, and ritual, Druidism perished then by the edge of the sword wielded by the Romans. The foundation of the great Roman schools, such as that at Autun, deprived the Druids of many of their pupils. In Ireland, Druidism did not, however, disappear until about A.D. 560, after the abandonment of Tara, the capital of the supreme king of Ireland. In A.D. 452, the Council of Arles decreed that "if, in any diocese, any infidel lighted torches or worshipped trees, fountains, or stones, he should be guilty of sacrilege." In A.D. 658, the Council of Nantes ordered the destruction of all Druidical monuments, and, later, the capitularies also condemned the religion. Welsh historians assert that Christianity was accepted in a national council held by King Lucius, A.D. 155, when the Arch-Druids of Europe, Lud and Leon, became archbishops and the chief Druids of twenty-eight cities became bishops. Dom Pitra, in *St. Leger*, says : " The two thousand Brothers of Sletty, who sing day and night, divided into seven choirs of three hundred voices, reply across the seas to the sons of St. Martin, being, according to legend, children of the converted Druid Fiek." The Rev. W. L. Alexander, writing on Iona, says that while the Roman armies were harrying the Druids at Anglesey, there was a college of them in the Scottish islands, situate 56° 59′ N. designated Innis-nan-Druidneach, or " the isle of the Druids," and that the priesthood prevailed over all the other islands until A.D. 563-4, when Colum or Columba arrived with twelve companions who were continued in that number till after ages. The Druids remained after human sacrifices were abolished, for Mela, after speaking of the abolition of human sacrifices, goes on to say : " They still have their elegant speech and the Druids as their teachers of wisdom." Aurelius Victor (*De Cæsiribus*, iv, 2) refers to Druidism as an extinct superstition, but one of celebrity in his day. Druidism is said to have found an asylum in Armorica some ages after it had been proscribed and suppressed in the rest of Gaul. An attempt was made after its extirpation in Britain to revive it, particularly by one of the warlike remnant, named Dearg, but the attempt was a futile one. T. Taylor, in the *Celtic Christianity of Cornwall*, says that " Druidism prevailed among the Continental Celts just as it prevailed among those of Britain and Ireland. When the original home of the Celt has been determined it may be possible to discover the home of his religion." On this point Bertrand writes :

"The more deeply we study the question of the Druids, the more it enlarges, and the greater becomes its importance. We arrive at the firm conviction that behind the community of Gaulish or Celtic priests, of which Cæsar, Diodorus, and Strabo have popularised the name, is hidden an old social institution, which, from the highest antiquity, made its civilising influence felt, outside of Gaul, Ireland, and Scotland, in Wales, Scandinavia, Germany, among the Aestiens, the Celts of the Upper Danube, the Getes, and more particularly in Thrace. . . . The Pythagorean brotherhoods and the institutions of Numa constitute, we believe, one of the unrecognized aspects of these ancient cenobitic communities, of which our convents, monasteries, and abbeys became the successors, a new spirit animating these old bodies. The dominating idea of these monastic and conventual institutions is not, in point of fact, an idea emanating from, but is long anterior to, the gospel. If we wish to look for a precedent less removed from the Christian origin, it must be searched for among the Essenes or in Egypt. It does not originate with papal Rome. We believe that its origin will be found in Chaldea or Media, on which the western monks, as well as the Irish and Scottish Druids, founded their model. Montalembert recognizes that cenobitism is long anterior to the Christian era."

Like Mithraism, however, Druidism as a distinctive institution eventually was swept from off the face of the earth. But the fact must not be overlooked, when speaking of the supplanting of Druidism by Christianity, that the Druids held many of the tenets inculcated in Christianity and the practices and customs of the Christians. The doctrine of the immortality of the soul, the belief in miracles, the doctrine of reincarnation, all, in those days, articles of the Christian faith, had already been imparted to the Britons by their own priests. They were also no strangers to the rite of baptism, which every Christian neophyte had to undergo. Unhappily, Druidism has left behind no literature, no art : existing monuments, claimed to be Druidical, afford no clue to the social habits of the people and prove nothing beyond the fact that the people of the period when that religion held sway had no taste for the æsthetic arts.

This alleged succession of and similarity of Christianity to Druidism has been commented upon by several writers, and J. W. Arch, in *Written Records of the Cymri*, says :

"When a Druid instructor was persuaded of the general truth of Christianity, he had fewer prejudices to surmount than any other civilized heathen of the ancient world, and would willingly, while avowing his new faith, submit, not only to be baptized, but also to receive from his new superiors a commission to resume his functions as an authorized teacher and instructor in the doctrines of his new faith."

Similar testimony is borne by Hughes, who writes :

"Neither the Roman power, nor the superiority of the Christian religion, would easily overcome the attachment of the people to the superstitions of their ancestors. But if it be true, what some have affirmed, that the Christian clergy were selected from among the Bards, then we may easily conceive that their former notions, in many respects, would give a strong tincture to their new religion."

Smiddy gives an interesting account, adapted from Himerius, of a visit paid to Greece by a renowned Druid philosopher. He writes :

"About six hundred years before the birth of Christ, a Druid from one of the western islands visited Greece, and the description given of his person and dress by some of the Greek writers is very interesting. The name of this Druid traveller was Abaris, a word which signifies ' the father ' or ' the master of knowledge.' This title was something like that of ' Rabbi ' among the Jews, and even in sound it resembles it somewhat. This priest of the sun, as he is called, went to Greece for the purpose of study and observation ; and also to renew, by his personal presence and his gifts, the old friendship which, it appears, had existed for ages between the Greeks and the Celts. By the Greeks, he was called a Hyperborean, that is ' a northener,' a term which they applied to the Celtic nations bordering on the Euxine, and also to the colonies or peoples springing from them and inhabiting northern latitudes. The Greek writer, Strabo, says that Abaris was much admired by even the learned men of Greece, for his politeness, justice, and integrity. ' He came to Athens,' says Himerius, another Greek writer, ' not clad in skins, like a Scythian, but with a bow in his hand, and a quiver hanging on his shoulder, and a plaid wrapped round his body, a gilded belt encircling his loins, and trousers reaching from his waist down to the soles of his feet. He was easy in his address, agreeable in his conversation, active in the despatch, and secret in the management of great affairs; quick in judging of present occurrences, and ready to take his part in any sudden emergency; provident without inguarding against futurity; diligent in quest of wisdom; fond of friendship; trusting very little to fortune; yet having the entire confidence of others, and trusted with everything for his prudence. He spoke Greek with so much fluency that you would have thought that he had been bred or brought up in the Lyceum, and had conversed all his life with the academy of Athens.'

"Such is the singularly flattering character which the Greek writers give of this Druid traveller from the Hyperborean island. They also state that he had frequent interviews with Pythagoras, whom he astonished by the variety and extent of his knowledge. Now, to which of these northern Celtic, or Hyperborean, islands did Abaris belong ? The place of his abode is thus described by Greek writers, whose imperfect knowledge of geography, however, rendered it impossible for them to be very accurate in all particulars. It is the place where Latona was born, lying far north of Celtica and as big as Sicily, the inhabitants of which enjoy a temperate air and a very fruitful soil. They adore Apollo and the sun, preferably to all other deities, paying him the highest honours, and singing his praises so continually that they all seem to be priests appropriated to his service, and their town itself dedicated to his worship. There was a fine grove and circular temple consecrated to him, in which choirs of his votaries say hymns, celebrating his actions, and set to music; whilst others, playing on the harp, which most of the inhabitants understood, answered to their voices and formed a delightful symphony. They had a peculiar dialect of their own and a singular regard for the Greeks, particularly the Athenian and Hellean, with whom they had, from ancient times, cultivated a friendship, confirmed by mutual visits, which, however, as they had been intermitted for some time, Abaris was sent by the Hyperboreans to renew; and, in return, several of the Greeks, passing to their island, left there several sacred presents to their deities, with inscriptions in Greek characters."

In France, the opening of schools at Marseilles, Lyons, and Autun accomplished the demise of Druidism in that country. The Druidical communities there ceased to be, and many of the members migrated to England, Scotland, and Ireland, where they lingered until the final eclipse of the religion.

c

CHAPTER II

THE CREED OF DRUIDISM

" The sacred oaks,
These awful shades among the Druids strayed,
To cut the hallowed mistletoe, and held
High converse with their gods."

SIR HUMPHREY DAVY.

The Druids professed a creed which appears to have been as inspiring as that of any ancient or modern system of religion or theology, and the fact that sectarianism was unknown to them, all believers of the faith professing the same creed without any variation, had a cohesive and unifying effect upon the various nations among whom it prevailed.

Although seemingly polytheistic in character, Druidism recognized and inculcated the belief in the unity of the Supreme Being, to whom alone the prayers of the people, through the priests, were addressed. The Ruler of the Universe, in the discharge of his office, was assisted by subordinate divinities, who were supposed to act rather as angels or messengers than as possessed of any inherent authority of their own. Origen is opposed to the idea of Druidism being polytheistic ; he affirms that they believed in one God only, which fact he considers was instrumental in leading the people to Christianity, although it may be regarded as undoubted that the simple tenets of early Druidism became debased by the admission of the polytheism of the East. No text, says Bertrand, authorises us to suppose that the Druids introduced to the Celts any foreign divinities or new rites to the countries where they were established or settled, and it may even legitimately be affirmed to the contrary.

Bouché says that the Druids had the primitive intuition and the good sense to teach a uniform and just doctrine and that far from seeking to personify the Eternal they devoted themselves to shewing Him in His manifestation through His works. Although they taught the adoration of spiritual and invisible divinities, they had a great veneration for the elements and for all the different parts of the invisible world, for fire, water, the wind, the earth, trees, rocks, etc. They did not, however, regard the elements in the light of divinities, unlike, according to several authorities, the ancient Persians. The real foundation, says Pelloutier, for the worship which the Celts rendered to the different parts of the

22

material world, was the opinion, which they held, that each element, each corporeal body, was the seat or temple of a subordinate divinity, who resided there and directed its operations and made it, so to speak, the instrument of its liberality towards mankind. It was really to this Intelligence, and not to the visible object, that the religious veneration was rendered. They held that whatever was effected by the laws of nature was the work of God, and not simply the result of mechanism. For instance, they held that the motions of the leaves of a tree, the direction and colour of flame, the fall of a thunderbolt, were the work of an intelligent Being—instructions given by God to the human race, to which a wise man should give attention and from which he should profit. The same law was applied to the actions of the lower animals which were not ascribed to instinct : the flight and song of birds, the barking of a dog, the neighing of a horse, the hissing of a serpent, and the running of a hare. In like manner they said that all that man did naturally, or mechanically, or involuntarily, without any intervening reflection, could not be attributed to himself, but ought to be regarded as the work of a divinity. Thus they found presages from the involuntary movements of the eyelid, in the motions of the pulse, or in sneezing. They did not adore several gods equal in power and dignity, but only one sovereign God, with a large number of subordinate divinities. They multiplied the number of those divinities by the creation of topical or local gods, giving to their sanctuaries the name of the god adored. A man, for example, who went to say his prayers in a forest dedicated to the god Teut, or to consult the priests who presided at that cult, would say that he went to find Teut. But this was only to distinguish the sanctuaries. Thus the god Penius was not a special divinity, but the god whose sanctuary was upon the Alps. In like manner the Apollon Grynaeus of the Messians, established in Asia, was not an exclusive god, but the name given to the sanctuary by the Messians, because they offered their sacrifices to the sun in a wood where the trees could not lose their verdure and where the earth was always covered with flowers. The Druids maintained that the Supreme had produced a number of intelligences which animated different parts of matter and conducted people to the destiny of the Eternal Will. They regarded these intelligences either as angels or spirits, acting only in accordance with the orders and under the direction of the Supreme God, whose ministers and instruments only they were, but, participating in the empire and power of the sovereign God, they were worthy of being associated with His glory and with the religious worship which He received from man. When a man was accused of a crime of which he could not be acquitted or convicted by the ordinary method he was thrown into a river, his judges being persuaded that the intelligences residing there would not fail to draw him to the bottom or raise him to the surface, according to his guilt or innocence, which would thus be established. The Celts held in their mythology that water and fire took the first rank among the divinities emanating from the god Teut and his wife, the earth. The violent agitations of the air, the force and rapidity of its action, the terrible ravages of rain, thunder, storms, and tempests led them to believe that the air was filled with an enormous number of spirits who were masters of the destiny of man, and who consequently merited receiving religious worship. The Celts did not render a religious worship to heroes, or place them in the ranks of gods, neither during their life nor after their death. They believed that the union of the active with the passive principles had produced not only men, but gods, the latter springing from matter as well as the visible and corporeal beings. Here is a contradiction, but it may well be that they believed that the spirits or genii residing in matter emanated from the first principle and that the earth had supplied the body to which they were united, or the element in which it resided. It may be that with the Stoics they recognized a living, active, invincible matter, the essence of Divinity, and a visible entity, incapable by itself of life and motion, which was the substance of the body. Although the Druids acknowledged a beginning to all things, they believed that the world would exist for all time, but they maintained that the earth would become purified and renovated by a universal fire, as once it had been by the deluge. They did not believe in the existence of an almighty and universal evil power, but held that God could be offended by sin, but that He was placable and could be appeased by sacrifices.

The Druidic conception of God had not, so far as can be ascertained, been degraded to the anthropomorphism current in other and later ages. The Supreme Being was represented to them in the sun, but the sun, as sun, was not worshipped : it was the great and grand symbol of the Living God, known as Esus, the supreme light, self-existent and invisible, but yet seeing, penetrating, and knowing all things. The sun was supposed to be the most noble type of the Godhead—the most glorious object of the material creation. The following is said to be an ancient hymn used by the Druids in their Mysteries. It is called *A Song of Dark Import*, and is said to have been composed by a distinguished Bard named Ogdoad :

"The heat of the sun shall be wasted : yet shall the Britons have an inclosure of great renown, and the heights of Snowdon shall receive inhabitants. Then will come the spotted cow, and procure a blessing. On the serene day will she bellow : on the eve of May shall she be boiled : and, on the spot where her boiling is completed, shall her consumer rest in peace. Let truth be ascribed

Stonehenge,
from a water-colour drawing
by J. M. W. Turner, R.A.

to Menwydd, the dragon chief of the world, who formed the curvatures of Kydd; which passed through the dale of grievous water, having the fore part stored with corn and mounting aloft with connected serpents."

To this was added a chant, or chorus:

"Alas, my covenant. The covenant it is of Nuh. The wood of Nuh is my witness. My covenant is the covenant of the ship besmeared. My witness, my witness, it is my friend."

Many of the localities where Druidical worship is said to have prevailed can still be identified through the names which those places bear. Such, for example, as Grenach (in Perthshire), which means "field of the sun"; Greenan (a stream in Perthshire), "river of the sun"; Balgreen (a town in Perthshire and other counties), "town of the sun"; Grian chnoux, or Greenock, which means "knoll of the sun"; and Granton, which means "sun's fire." Oxford, it is claimed, should be included in any such list. According to tradition, Oxford was founded by Membricius, who was destroyed by wolves when hunting at Wolvercote, three miles from the city; hence its Celtic title was Caer Membre, or "the city of Membricius." It was also known as Caer Bosca, probably from the Greek *Bosphorus*, Ox-ford. The latter name, possibly, was bestowed upon the city when the Greek philosophers, brought by Brutus to Britain, migrated from their original college at Cricklade farther up the Tain and set up their school at the suburb of the Bel-Mont (from which Beaumont Street takes its name), just outside the city boundary.

In short, the glory of Bel was manifested in the sun, and the Druids, in singing hymns to that luminous orb, gave expression to their worship of the Supreme, and not of the emblem, thus offering their adoration to the Supreme and Eternal Being. The words "Bel" and "Baal" were as common in the East for the name of the Deity as was "Jupiter" in the West.

The name *Baal* is an interesting one from a philological point of view. It is composed of three radicals, denominated in Hebrew, *Beth*, *Aleph*, and *Lamed*; which correspond with the Arabic letters, *Ba*, *Alif*, and *Lam*, and the Greek *Beta*, *Alpha*, and *Lambda*. Each of these letters has a numerical value. In Arabic, Phœnician, Hebrew and Greek, *B*, when it is used as a numeral, stands for 2; *A* for 1; and *L* for 10, thus making a total of 33. Each number is regarded as a mystical number. The Pythagoreans regarded the number 2 as representing Intellect or Wisdom, the Source of all things. It typified God. The figure 3 typified male and female, who, in conjunction, produce life: from the odd proceed both odd and even. The 0 added to complete the 30 of Lamed, might, from its shape, stand for the ovum—the world or the cosmos. Intellect stands first. Thus we read in the Gospel ascribed to St. John: "In the beginning was Wisdom. And Wisdom was with God, and Wisdom was God." The numerals for which *B*, *A*, and *L*, stand, written consecutively in Roman letters, run II, I, and XXX, producing a total of XXXIII, representing nine separate strokes. In connection with this the Nundinals of the Romans are worthy of attention. The days were divided into groups of eight, and on every ninth day the people left their pursuits and went to the town to market ; hence the Latin saying : *Tres Mulieres Nundinas faciunt.* The Romans also held a purification ceremony on male infants on the ninth day of life, the presiding genius at this rite being named Nundina. Nine was termed by the Pythagoreans the perfect square of the perfect number : nine reasons for praising God are given in Psalm 145 ; the Eleusinian Mysteries occupied nine days in performance. With regard to the figure 33, King David reigned in Jerusalem for 33 years ; Jesus lived on earth for 33 years ; there are 33 vertebræ in the human spinal column : the Muslim Rosary of the 99 Beautiful Names of Allah is divided into three sections, each containing 33 beads.

Many of the religious services of the Druids, which were conducted with a pomp and a ritual which could vie with the ornate ritual of later ecclesiastical organisations, began and ended with the ceremony of going thrice round in the course of the sun. As these circumvolutions began at the East point and followed the course of the sun, they were known in the Isle of Man as *deas-iul*, or " the way to the south." This ceremony was regarded by the Druids as signifying conformity to the will of God. To go round the circle in the opposite direction, or *cartuia-iul*, was to court disaster. *Widdershin* was another name for this opposite movement, which, it was said, upset all nature and rendered its performers liable to a charge of witchcraft, which might end in a sentence of capital punishment. Borlase says :

" In the Isle of Skye, after drinking the water of a famous well there, they made three sun-turns round the well there, as if some deity resided in it, to whom they were to pay proper respect before they left it. Weak and simple as these turns may seem, they have been used by the most ancient and most polite nations in the same manner as now practised by these uncultivated highlanders. They turn three times round their karns : round the persons they intend to bless three times ; three times they make round St. Barr's Church ; and three times round the well, so that the number three was a necessary part of the ceremony."

Maurice, in his *Indian Antiquities*, says of the Greek drama :

" In the Strophe they danced from the right hand to the left, by which motion Plutarch is of opinion they meant to indicate the apparent motion of the heavens from east to west ; in the Antistrophe they moved from the left to the right in allusion to the motion of the planets from west to east ; and by the slow or stationary motion before the altar, the permanent stability of the earth."

The same kind of astronomical dance was used by the Hindoos in their religious ceremonies and called the *Raas Jattra*, or " dance of the circle." This circular dance in honour of the heavenly bodies was in use among a number of ancient nations. The Romans during their public worship were accustomed to turn themselves round from left to right, sometimes in larger and sometimes in smaller circles, and they derived this practice, according to Plutarch, from their religious monarch, Numa, who was deeply skilled in the mysteries of the Samothracian Cabiri.

The ceremony of *deas-iul* is still used on many occasions in the Highlands of Scotland. Women with child go thrice in this direction round some chapels to procure an easy delivery. Sick persons do the same round some carns in order to charm back health. In Scotland also the old Masonic Lodge at Melrose either elected the new office-bearers, or had the installation on the eve of St. John's day in summer, when the brethren walked in procession three times round the market-cross. After dinner they again turned out, walked two abreast, each bearing a lighted torch. Preceded by their banners, the procession again walked three times round the cross, and then proceeded to the Abbey, round which it slowly marched thrice, making a complete circuit of the building. The order of procession was right-hand to the centre in both cases— round the Cross, and also at the Abbey, or *deas-iul*, or sun-wise. William Simpson, commenting on this, says : " In addition to the installation ceremony, let the craftsman also recall the point in the Lodge that marks the rising of the sun. From that he can move on to another point where the luminary is at its meridian, and then on to where it sets, and he will have a circular movement, which, if fully carried round, would undoubtedly mark the whole course of the sun, and be with the right hand to the centre." There is also the rule for the principal officers of the Lodge taking their seats and leaving them again, in relation to the pedestal : this is also *deas-iul*, or sunwise.

Hercatœus of Abdura, in his *History of the Hyperboreans*, says that there was an island about the bigness of Celtica, inhabited by a people called Hyperboreans, because they were beyond the north wind. " The climate is excellent, the soil is fertile, yielding double crops. The inhabitants are great worshippers of Apollo (the sun), to whom they sing many hymns. To this god they have consecrated a large territory, in the midst of which they have a magnificent round temple replenished with the richest offerings. This very city is dedicated to him, and is full of musicians and players of various instruments, who, every day, celebrate his benefits and perfections."

The sun, as the giver and vivifier of life, says Napier, in *Folk Lore*, was the primary god of antiquity, being worshipped by the Assyrians, Chaldeans, Phœnicians and Hebrews, under the name of *Baal*, or *Bel*, and by other nations under other names. In Hebrew the name for God is *El* ; in Semitic, *Al* ; in Chaldee, *Il*. The Welsh name for sun is *Haul* ; in Mæso-Gothic it is *Hil* ; while *Ell* is the Gothic for " fire." The priests of Baal always held a high position in the state. As the sun was the image or symbol on earth, hence all offerings made to Baal were burned or made to pass through the fire, or were presented before the sun.

The foregoing facts will account for the contention of many writers that Druidism was a branch of the worship of the sun, which at one time prevailed.

Next in point of rank to the Supreme Being, represented by the sun, came the lesser divinities, symbolised by the moon and stars, all the celestial bodies being accorded honours. This feature was not more marked in Druidism than in other religions where veneration was accorded to the elements. Many religions regarded as polytheistic taught that their multitudes of gods or divinities were but emanations from, or constituted really but one Being. It was, in all probability, this veneration of the celestial bodies and observance of their motions which laid the foundation of the knowledge of astronomical science possessed by the Druids, testimony to which has been borne by Cæsar and other writers. They were undoubtedly in possession of sufficient knowledge of the motion of the heavenly bodies to enable them to fix definite times for their festivals and religious ceremonies, all of which were regulated by the sun and moon, and to calculate a thirty-year cycle of lunar years, in which the month began at the sixth day. In common with Gauls, Teutons, and Hebrews, the Britons reckoned time from evening to morning. Their principal hours for devotion were midday and midnight, and their most important solemn functions were held at the new and full moons.

Maimonides says :

"In the days of Enos, the son of Seth, men fell into grievous errors, and even Enos himself partook of their infatuation. Their language was that since God had placed on high the heavenly bodies, and used them as His ministers, it was evidently His will that they should receive from men the same veneration as the servants of a great prince justly claims from the subject multitude. Impressed with this notion, they began to build themselves temples to the stars, to sacrifice to them, and to worship them in the vain expectation that they should thus please the Creator of all things.

At first, indeed, they did not suppose the stars to be the only deities, but adored in conjunction with them the Lord God Omnipotent. In process of time, however, that great and venerable name was totally forgotten and the whole human race retained no other religion than the idolatrous worship of the host of heaven."

The Druids observed a very pronounced reticence with regard to the articles of faith which they professed—with one exception only, that of immortality. They are said to have been great writers in other respects, but they committed none of their religious or philosophical tenets to writing, except in allegorical poems, the key to which was in the possession only of the initiated, to whom the poems and doctrines were taught orally and by them committed to memory. It was the common practice of the nations of antiquity to transmit their laws and doctrines from generation to generation merely by oral tuition. This was done by, among others, the ancient Greeks and Spartans, who permitted nothing to be written down. In the Isle of Man, even, many of the laws were traditionary, and were known by the name of " Breast Laws." One of the Druidic objections to the use of writing, except in instances where it was absolutely necessary, was that it caused deterioration of the powers of memory.

The Bardic, or Druidic, alphabet consisted of thirty-six letters, sixteen of which were radical and the remainder mutations. It contained all the Etruscan letters without the least deviation of form, except that four or five were Roman. They were as follows :

rh   mh   f   c   ch   ngh

t   ch   nh   d   dh   n

e   ll   r   rh   s   h

hw   g   ng

Each letter received its name from some tree or plant of a species which was regarded as being in some way or another descriptive of its power.

Vallancey, in his treatise, *On the Ogham Writing*, says that the Ogham tree was first the symbol of numerals and then from these numerals were formed literary characters, and he continues :

" The tree of knowledge of good and evil has been thought by many scholars to be the symbol of science, of wisdom, etc. The Egyptians adopted the Kadmis, or mulberry tree, as the symbol of wisdom, of science, and of numerals ; and the vine as the symbol of literary characters. Pownall, in his *Treatise on the Study of Antiquities*, says that the tree of knowledge of good and evil, mentioned in Genesis, was a mythic tree, a tree representing, in the luxuriance of its branches, the wildness of men's opinions and by its tempting and poisonous fruit, the mischievous effects of being seduced by the vanity of false learning. Rabbi Nahum, a Chaldean, speaks of ' the Great Tree in the Garden of Eden, whose leaves were letters and whose branches were words.' "

Egyptian history informs us that the author of letters, numeration, astronomy, geometry, music, and of science in general was named *Thoth*, who was also called *Phine*, and Jablonsky claims that Thoth was not the name of a man, but signified science in general. *Phine* certainly appears to be identical with the Irish *Fenius*, the author of letters.

The Chinese claim to have been the wisest and most learned people in the world from the remotest times. They say that Confulu, or Confulus, was the inventor of letters and arts. But this Confulu was identical with the Cann-faola of the ancient Irish, meaning the learned *Cann*, or the head of the learned. *Chon* was the Egyptian name of Hercules and *Canoc* the Egyptian name of Thoth or Mercury. The Chinese always carried with them the symbol of a tree as a literary character, this symbol being 木

There is a tradition among the Jews that the tree of knowledge was named *Dar* and this was supposed to be the oak, whence *Dar* in Irish means " an oak " ; it also implies " wisdom."

William Beauford, in *Druidism Revived*, sets forth his reasons for asserting that the Irish Druids had not only the method of committing their doctrines and learning to writing, but that the characters and letters made use of for this purpose bear not only a great affinity to those of the ancient Phœnicians, Carthaginians, and Egyptians, but, in several instances, are exactly the same, as may be seen on comparing them with the characters and inscriptions on the Bembine and Remessean tables. By these also, it appears that the Hibernian Druids, like the Egyptian priests, made use of both hieroglyphic and alphabetic characters. Their letters also, like those of the ancient Egyptians, were of two species, sacred and profane. The profane were those used in the common occurrences of life, public contracts, ordinances of state, poems, etc., and mentioned by antiquaries under the denomination of Boboloth characters and were the same, or nearly those, of the Punic and Phœnician. The sacred were those mentioned under the name of Ogham and Ogham Croabh. These letters were mixed with symbols and hieroglyphics, in their hiero-grammatic writings, or those which treated of their general philosophy and laws.

An interesting philological excursion might be made, as can be gathered from the following few illustrations. *Debesh* is the Arabic for " unbarking a tree," while *debistan* means " a school for writing." *Dubir* is the Persian for " a writer " ; *dibiriston* means " a school for writing," and *duib* is the Irish for " writing." *Dané* is the Persian for " feed of fruit, science, learning." In the Irish language, *dan* means " learning," *dana* " learned man " ; and *aosdána* " magi, Druids." *Akdet*, in the Arabic, means either " a thick plantation of trees," or " confused words," while *uchdach*, in Irish, means " delivery of speech." *Asek*, in Arabic, means " a tree," and *asec*, in Irish, means " a literary character." There was a proverb among the ancient Arabians, which ran : " I know the wood of his tree before his fruit is ripened," meaning " I know his learning, genius, or eloquence, before he has spoken." Libanus was a mountain, so called from its tall cedars. The Jews formed an alphabet called *Catab Libona*, or *scriptura libonica;* these letters were flourished at the tops with scrolls like the tendrils of a vine.

The Bardic legend of the origin of letters states that Einigan, the first man, beheld three pillars of light, having on them all demonstrable sciences that ever were or ever will be. He accordingly took three rods of the quicken tree and placed on them the forms and signs of all the sciences, so that they should be remembered. People, however, came in time to regard these rods as a god, although they only bore his name. When Einigan saw this he was greatly annoyed and distressed, and in his grief broke the three rods. His anguish was such that he burst asunder, and with his parting breath he prayed to God that there should be accurate sciences among men in the flesh and a correct understanding of them. At the end of a year and a day of his decease men beheld three rods growing out of the mouth of Einigan which exhibited the sciences of ten letters. These ten letters were derived from the creative name of God ⋔ Beli the Great made them into sixteen. In the Runic alphabet the symbol for the god Tyr was ↑ and that for a man was Y

In the *Collection of Bardism*, made by Llewellyn Sion of Llangewydd in the sixteenth century, the following account is given of the origin and progress of letters :

" Pray, my skilful and discreet teacher, if it be fair to ask, how was the knowledge of letters first obtained ? "

" I will exhibit the information of men of wisdom and profound knowledge, thus : When God pronounced His name, with the word sprang the light of life : for previously there was no life except God Himself. And the mode in which it was spoken was of God's direction. His name was pronounced and with the utterance was the springing of light and vitality, and man, and every other living thing ; that is to say, each and all sprang together. And Menw, the Aged, son of Menwyd (meaning the source of intellect and happiness, the mind or the soul, derived from men, an active principle), beheld the springing of the light and its form and appearance, not otherwise than thus, ⋀ in three columns, and in the rays of light the vocalisation for one were the hearing and seeing, one unitedly the form and sound ; and one unitedly with the form and sound was life ; and one unitedly with these three was power, which power was God. And since each of these was one unitedly, he understood that every voice, and hearing, and living, and being, and sight, and seeing, were one unitedly with God ; nor is the least thing other than God. And by seeing the form, and in it hearing the voice—not otherwise—he knew what form and appearance voice should have. And having obtained earth under him co-instantaneously with the light, he drew the form of the voice and light on the earth. And it was on hearing the sound of the voice, which had in it the kind and utterance of three notes, that he obtained the three letters, and knew the sign that was suitable to one and other of them. Thus he made in form and sign the Name of God, after the semblance of rays of light, and perceived that they were the figure and form and sign of life ; one also with them was life, and in life was God ; that is to say, God is one with life, and there is no life but God, and there is no God but life.

" It was from the understanding thus obtained in respect of this voice, that he was able to assimilate mutually every other voice as to kind, quality, and reason, and could make a letter suitable to the utterance of every sound and voice. Thus were obtained the Cymraeg and every other language. And it was from the three primary letters that was constructed every other letter—which is the principal secret of the Bards of the Isle of Britain, and from this secret comes every knowledge of letters that is possible.

" Thus was the voice that was heard placed on record in the symbol and meaning attached to each of the three notes :—the sense of O was given the first column ; the sense of I to the second or middle column ; and the sense of V to the third, whence the word OIV.

" That is to say, it was by means of this word that God declared His existence, life, knowledge, power, eternity, and universality. And in the declaration was His love, that is, co-instantaneously with it sprang like lightning all the universe into life and existence— vocally and co-jubilantly with the uttered name of God, in one united song of exultation and joy — then all the worlds to the extremity of Annwn. It was thus, then, that God made the worlds, namely, He declared His Name and Existence /I\ OIV "

" Q. Why is it not right that a man should commit the Name of God to vocalisation, and the sound of language and tongue ?

" A. Because it cannot be done without misnaming God, for no man ever heard the vocalization of His Name, and no one knows how to pronounce it ; but it is represented by letters, that it may be known what is meant, and for whom it stands. Formerly signs were employed, namely, the three elements of vocal letters. However, to prevent disrespect and dishonour to God, a Bard is forbidden to name Him, except inwardly and in thought."

In the Iolo MS. the following occurs :

"Q. When were the three letters formed ?

"A. God, in vocalising His Name, said /\ and with a word all words and animations sprang co-instantaneously into being and life from their non-existence ; shouting in ecstasy of joy ↑ and thus repeating the name of the Deity. Immediately with the utterance was light, and in the light the form of the name in three voices thrice uttered co-vocally, co-instantaneously, and in the vision three forms, and they were the figure and form of the light, and together with the utterance, and the figure and form of that utterance were the three first letters, and from a combination of their three utterances were formed by letter all other utterances whatsoever.

The inspirer of Cæsar's account of Druidism is acknowledged to have been Divitiacus, the Arch-Druid at the time of the Roman Invasion, and the intimate of Cæsar and Cicero. Discretion must, however, be exercised in accepting as authentic all the statements made by Cæsar as to Druidical belief and worship, for reasons that will be apparent, and, fortunately, he is not the only source of information. It was quite impossible for Cæsar, during the short period of time he was on the island, to conduct any personal investigation or research, if, indeed, he had been permitted to do so frequently, and the meagreness and occasionally proved inaccuracy of his statements have more than once provoked comment. He states emphatically that the Druids worshipped Mercury, which has led some writers to commit themselves to the statement that Mercury was the principal British Deity. In all probability Cæsar had observed among the Druidical symbols and emblems the winged rod with the serpents entwined around it, which, in Rome, was one of the emblems which adorned the statues of Mercury. This emblem may be found engraved in conspicuous characters upon Druidical remains on the plains of Avebury, in Wiltshire, as well as in the Thebais of ancient Egypt. Mercury, according to some authorities, is identical with the Celtic name, *Merch-ur*, " woman-man." The Druids had also a veneration for the cube, which they regarded as symbolical of truth, because it presented the same appearance whichever way it was turned. This, again, was one of the symbols of Mercury, and this fact is also mentioned by some writers as a proof of the affinity claimed to exist between Druidism and Freemasonry. According to Cæsar, the Druids represented Mercury as the inventor of all the arts. Hercules was regarded as the patron of eloquence, arts, and commerce, but they called him Ogimus, a word which has for its meaning, " the power of eloquence." One emblem—the Cross—is not mentioned by Cæsar, yet it was assigned a very important place in the Druidical ceremonial.

Helvetia Antiqua et Nova, a work published in the sixteenth century, gives the following list of Druidical deities or divinities : Theutates, or Taut ; Hesus ; Taranis ; Belinus ; Cisa ; and Penninus.

Theutates, or Taut, is asserted to have been the chief God, or Universal Father. Apparently, he combined the attributes of Jupiter with those of Mercury, as he is said to have been the inventor of arts and to have acted as a guide to travellers. The word *taut* is still preserved in Switzerland, and is given to a lofty rock near Montreux, thought by some to be one of the sites of ancient Druidical worship. In this connection it may be remembered that *tout* in some parts of England is still the name given to the highest point in a range of hills. The invention of writing has been attributed by legend to Taut, who was identical with the Baal Hermon worshipped in Sidon and the adjacent country. The name *Tat* or *Teth* was well known to the ancient Irish. *Tat* is the same as the Hindoo *Tat* or *Datta* and the Egyptian *Thoth* or *Taut*. This point is established, not merely by the identity of title, but by a curious coincidence of an arbitrary nature. The first month of the Egyptians, which commenced on the calends of August, was called *Thoth*, in honour of the deity of that name ; and the first day of August was, for a similar reason, called by the Irish, *la Tat*. This god was supposed to preside over the harvest. He was akin to the agricultural Jupiter, Bacchus, Osiris, and Deo-Naush ; or, as the prototype of all those kindred divinities, Noah, the husbandman.

Hesus, the strong and powerful, was the representative of Mars, the god of war, carnage, and bloodshed. In the German patois of Switzerland, *Hées* still means a violent and quarrelsome person. Some writers have stated that this divinity was pictured with the head of a dog. If so, it is probably identical with the barking Anubis of Egyptian mythology, who was claimed to be the son of Osiris and Nepthys, and to have had the nature and characteristics of a dog. This divinity had the special guardianship of the tropics. According to the Welsh triads, Heus, or Hesus, brought the people of Cymry into this isle from the summer country called Defrobanni, over the Hazy Sea of Fairies (the North Sea). Davies in his *Celtic Researches*, says that one commentator explains the situation of Defrobanni as " that on which Constantinople now stands." As, or Aes, the British Heus, is preserved in the name of the towns Aswardby and Asgardby. One writer says that Jehovah came from Aes, or Heus, a god of the Celts; As being a subordinate god of the Celtic Dhia, a name for the Supreme Being, and identical with the Hebrew *Jah*, the Latin *Deus* being derived from the same word. Another maintains that the name *Hesus* comes from the Syrian *Hizzus*, or *Haziz*, signifying " strong and powerful in war."

In the latter part of 1859, a curious discovery was made near Lille by workmen engaged in cutting trenches for new fortifications. In removing the soil they laid bare a stone tumulus, which, instead of bones, contained a large block of stone, covered with inscriptions, which indicated that it was an altar used by the Druids in their sacrifices. The names Hesus and Theutates were perfectly legible upon it. Near the stone, a sacred golden knife, as used by the Druids for cutting the mistletoe, was also found. The inscriptions on the stone corroborate the fact already known, that human sacrifices were made by Druids in times of national calamity. The knife was placed in the museum at Lille.

Taranus is a word derived from *taran*, thunder, and is identical with the Jupiter of Greece and Rome and the Thor of northern nations.

Belinus, known in Old Testament times as Baal, is identical with Apollo, the god of the sun. A wood in the neighbourhood of Lausanne is still known as Sauvebelin, *viz.*, Sylvia Bellini, and traces of the name are to be found in many parts of England. Belus is also a Babylonish title of Ham, whose descendants include the Cuthites and Cadmians. Both were zealous adorers of the sun and addicted to rites of fire. They were men of superior stature, adepts in every branch of science, and particularly famed for their skill in astronomy. Tradition says that they were the first navigators of the sea, and the division of time with the notification of the seasons is ascribed to them. According to Herodotus, all these arts took their rise in Babylonia, whence they were carried into Egypt, and from Egypt westward into other countries. Elius Schedius, in his book *De Diis Germanorum*, imagines that he found in the name *Belenus* the 365 days of the year, in like manner as the Basilideans formerly found them in Abrazas and Mithras, thus:

$$
\begin{array}{ccccccc}
B & H & \Lambda & E & N & o & \Sigma \\
2 & 8 & 30 & 5 & 50 & 70 & 200 = 365
\end{array}
$$

Belenus is an ancient Celtic word Latinised meaning "blond," "yellow." The Greeks, changing the initial *B* into *M*, wrote *melnos* for "yellow," "blond," and "golden colour," though in certain quarters of Greece, *Bela* signified "splendour," "light," "sun." In this connection, attention should be drawn to the discovery in November, 1897, near Lyons, of the Coligny Calendar, which demonstrates that the priests of Gaul, in the first century of the Christian era—the ascertained date of the Calendar—possessed a belief in lucky and unlucky days. The Calendar divided up the year as follows:

Cantlos (May)	..	..	29 days	unlucky
Samos (June)	..	..	30 „	lucky
Duman (July)	..	..	29 „	unlucky
Rivios (August)	..	..	30 „	lucky

Anaculios (September)	.. 29	,,	unlucky
Ogrion (October)	.. 30	,,	lucky
Granion (December)	.. 29	,,	unlucky
Simivis (January)	.. 30	,,	lucky
Equos (February)	.. 30	,,	unlucky
Elembin (March)	.. 29	,,	unlucky
Edrin (April) ..	.. 30	,,	lucky

Cias was worshipped more particularly in the Grisons or Rhœtian Alps. Tuesday in some of the German cantons of Switzerland is called Cistag, or Zistag.

With regard to Penninus, *Pen*, which, in Celtic, means " summit " or " head," is applied to the mountainous region of the Apennines, and the monastery of St. Bernard stands on the site of the temple of the Pennine Jupiter. The prefix *Pen* is found in various parts of Wales, *e.g.*, Penmaenmawr, Pen-y-gwint, etc., and, of course, in many Cornish names of people and places.

Iau was one of the names which the Cymry gave to the Supreme God. The following dialogue appears in the traditions of the Bards :

" *Disciple :* Why is the Iau (yoke) given as a name for God ?

" *Master :* Because the yoke is the measuring rod of country and nation in virtue of the authority of law, and is in possession of every head of family under the mark of the lord of the territory, and whoever violates it is liable to a penalty. Now God is the measuring rod of all truth, all justice, and all goodness ; therefore, He is the yoke on all, and all are under it, and woe to him who shall violate it."

A further development of the name of God ı ⁁ ⱱ signified preservation, creation, and destruction.

The Druids represented the world as an enormous animal issuing out of the abyss from the abode of an evil spirit. In common with most nations and religions, they had their Deluge tradition, but they represented the event as occurring in a lake called Llyn Llion, the waters of which burst forth and overwhelmed the face of the whole world. One vessel only escaped the catastrophe, and in this were a man and a woman and certain of the animal species. By these Britain was re-peopled with human beings and animals. The name given to the man thus miraculously preserved was Hu, the Mighty, but he is sometimes called Cadwaldr. He is frequently represented as the diluvial god, and as such is generally attended by a spotted cow. The woman preserved in the ark was called Ceridwen. She was regarded as the first of womankind, with the same attributes as Venus, in whom were personified the generative powers. She is mentioned in several of the poems of the Bards

D

who lived under the Welsh princes.   Cuhelyn, a Bard of the sixth century, refers to her as Ogyrven Ahmad, or " the goddess of the various seeds," and from this and other similar references, some authorities have connected her with the goddess Ceres, or Demeter.   Ceridwen's first-born was named Movrah, or " the raven of the sea."

Antiquity furnishes us with several eminent men of the name of Hu, or Hierocles.   There was Hierocles, the brother of Menecles, the first of the Asiatic orators in the time of Cicero.   Another was cited by Stephanus, who wrote of the most remarkable things he had seen and speaks of a nation of Hyperboreans, a people addicted to philosophy, and who ate no manner of flesh.   The third Hu Gadarn, or Hierocles the Mighty, is said by Iolo Goch to have been Emperor of Constantinople, to have held the plough and to eat no bread but from corn of his own raising.   This may have been Hierocles, the Grammarian, who wrote a treatise on the Empire of Constantinople.

The triads that relate to Hu Gadarn, or Hu the Mighty, are seven in number and six contain distinct notices of him.   We learn from them that he drew to land the crocodile of the lake of floods, so that the lake burst out no more ; and the names of these oxen, we are informed, were *Neinio* and *Peibis*.   Then the patriarch appears before us as the great benefactor of the Cymry, whom he is recorded to have instructed in the useful arts of agriculture, before their arrival in Britain, when they were conducted by him, and while they remained in the summer country, which an ancient commentator has described to be that part of the East now called Constantinople.   Then he divided the people into various tribes, but directing them to a unanimity of action.   He is said also to have been the first to adopt vocal song to the preservation of memorial and invention and thereby contributed to the foundation of Bardism. Hu, or the aspirated U, was anciently employed to denote the Supreme Being.

As an outcome of the British tradition of the Deluge, the Druids consecrated certain lakes as symbols of the event, and looked upon the small islands which rose to the surface as mystical sanctuaries, because they were emblems of the ark.   A rock, when discovered, was hailed as typifying the place of debarkation of Hu the Mighty, and here, on certain occasions, would be celebrated by the " Druids of the Circle," or the Druids of high or advanced degree, certain mystical rites believed to be in commemoration of the salvation of the race from the waters of the flood.   The Irish have a tradition that a great part of the north of Ireland was swallowed up by an inundation of the sea, but that the submerged regions often arise out of the waves and become visible to those who unite together the two indispensable qualifications of a strong sight and a strong faith.   These regions are sometimes esteemed an enchanted paradisiacal island and at other times are described as a wonderful city floating upon the waves.

Traditions of the submersion of cities beneath the various lakes of the country are still current throughout the whole of Wales. The annotator of Camden mentions the names of no fewer than six lakes, in which ancient cities are reported to have been submerged. One of these is Llyn Savaddan in Brecknockshire. Some of the incidents, as related by an old man in the town of Hay, are thus narrated by Davies :

"The site of the present lake was formerly occupied by a large city ; but the inhabitants were reported to be very wicked. The king of the country sent his servant to examine into the truth of the rumour, adding a threat that, in case it should prove to be well-founded, he would destroy the place as an example to his other subjects. The minister arrived at the town in the evening. All the inhabitants were engaged in riotous festivity and wallowing in excess. Not one of them regarded the stranger, or offered him the rites of hospitality. At last he saw the open door of a mean habitation, into which he entered. The family had deserted it to repair to the scene of tumult, all but one infant, who lay weeping in the cradle. The royal favourite sat down by the side of this cradle, soothed the little innocent, and was grieved at the thought that he, too, must perish in the destruction of his abandoned neighbours. In this situation the stranger passed the night, and whilst he was diverting the child, he accidentally dropped his glove into the cradle. The next morning he departed before it was light to carry his melancholy tidings to the king. He had but just left the town, when he heard a noise behind him like a tremendous crack of thunder, mixed with dismal shrieks and lamentations. He stopped to listen. It then sounded like the dashing of waves, and presently all was dead silence. He could not see what had happened, as it was dark, and he felt no inclination to return into the city ; so he pursued his journey until sunrise. The morning was cold. He searched for his gloves, and, finding but one of them, he presently recollected where he had left the other. These gloves had been a present to him from his sovereign. He determined to return for that which he had left behind. When he was come near to the town, he observed with surprise that none of the buildings presented themselves to his view as on the preceding day. He advanced a few steps. The whole plain was covered with a lake. Whilst he was gazing at this novel and terrific scene, he remarked a little spot in the middle of the water. The wind gently wafted it towards the bank where he stood. As it drew near he recognisd the identical cradle in which he had left his glove. His joy on receiving this pledge of royal favour was only heightened by the discovery that the little object of his compassion had reached the shore alive and unhurt. He carried the infant to the king, and told him that this was all he had been able to save out of that wretched place."

The greatest similarity among Deluge legends to the Druidical is, perhaps, that of the Incas, who believed that no living thing survived except a man and a woman, who were preserved from the flood by being enclosed in a box. Then the Creator began to raise up peoples and nations by making clay figures with the kind of garments they were to wear. He then gave life and soul to each, and commanded them to multiply. The first of each nation were transformed into stones, which became objects of adoration. In some parts of Peru there are great blocks of stone, some of which are nearly the size of giants.

The following is said to have been the Druidical Hymn of the Deluge :

" The inundation will surround us, the chief priests of Ked (the ship-goddess Ceridwen). Yet complete is my chair in Caer Sidi. Neither disorder nor age will oppress him that is within it. It is known to Manawya [Menu-Ida, the Arkite or mundane Menu] and Pryderi [Wisdom, or Intellect, a title of Noah, and equivalent to the Greek *nous*, the Sanscrit *menu*, and the Latin *mens*, or *menes*], that three loud strains round the fire will be sung before it ; whilst the currents of the sea are round its borders and the copious fountain is open from above, the liquor within it is sweeter than delicious wine.

" O thou proprietor of heaven and earth, to whom great wisdom is attributed, a holy sanctuary there is on the surface of the ocean. May its chief be joyful in the splendid festival and at the time when the sea rises with expanding energy. Frequently does the surge assail the Bards over their vessels of mead ; and on the day when the billows come beyond the green spot from the region of the Picts. A holy sanctuary there is on the wide lake, a city not protected with walls ; the sea surrounds it. Demandest thou, O Britain, to what this can be meetly applied ? Before the lake of the son of Erbin let thy ox be stationed. A holy sanctuary there is upon the ninth wave. Holy are its inhabitants in preserving themselves. They will not associate in the bonds of Pollution. A holy sanctuary there is : it is rendered complete by the rehearsal, the hymn, and the birds of the mountain. Smooth are its lays in its periodical festival ; and my lord [the hierophant, or one initiated into the Mysteries] duly observant of the splendid mover [the sun], before he entered his earthly cell in the border of the circle, gave me mead and wine out of the deep crystal cup. A holy sanctuary there is within the gulf : there every one is kindly presented with his portion.

A holy sanctuary there is with its productions of the vessels of Ked [the cauldron of inspiration]. The writings of Prydain [Hu, the Gallo-Arkite Noah] are the first objects of anxious regard ; should the waves disturb their foundation ; I would again, if necessary, conceal them deep in the cell. A holy sanctuary there is upon the margin of the flood ; there shall every one be kindly presented with his wishes.

" Disturbed is the island of the praise of Hu, the island of the severe remunerator [Noah] ; even Mona of the generous bowls which animate vigour, the island whose barrier is the Mena [the firth between Anglesea and Wales, so called from Menu]. Deplorable is the fate of the ark of Aeddon [or Adonis, a title of Hu], since it is perceived that there neither has been nor will be his equal in the hour of perturbation. When Aeddon came from the land of Gwydion into Seon of the strong door [the Ark], a pure poison diffused itself for four successive nights, whilst the season was as yet severe. His contemporaries fell. The woods afforded them no shelter, when the winds arose in their skirts. Then Math and Eunydd, masters of the magic wand, set the elements at large ; but in the living Gwydion and Amaethon there was a resource of counsel to impress the front of his shield with a prevalent form, a form irresistible. Thus the mighty combination of his chosen rank was not overwhelmed by the sea. Disturbed is the island of the praise of Hu, the island of the severe inspector. Before Buddwas [a title of Hu] may the community of the Cymry remain in tranquillity ; he being the dragon chief, the proprietor, the rightful claimant, in Britain. What shall consume a ruler of the illustrious circle ? The four damsels, having ended their lamentation, have performed their last office. But the just ones toiled ; on the sea, which had no land, long did they dwell : of their integrity it was, that they did not endure the extremity of distress.

" Am I not called Gorlassar, the ethereal ? My belt has been a rainbow enveloping my foe. Am I not a protecting prince in darkness to him, who presents my form at both ends of the hive ? Am I not a Plougher ? Have I not protected my sanctuary, and with the aid of my friends caused the wrathful ones to vanish ? Have I not shed the blood of the indignant in bold warfare against the sons of the giant Nur ? Have not I imparted of my guardian power a ninth portion in the prowess of Arthur ? Did not I give to Henpen the tremendous sword of the enchanter ? Did not I perform the rites of purification, when Hearndor [*i.e.*, Iron-door, a title of the ark] moved with toil to the top of the hill ? I was subjected to the yoke for my affliction ; but commensurate was my confidence; the world had no existence, were it not for my progeny. Privileged on the covered mount, O Hu with the expanded wings, has been thy son, thy bardic proclaimer, thy deputy, O father Deon; my voice has recited the death-song, where the mound representing the world is constructed of stone-work. Let the countenance of Prydain, let the glancing Hu, attend to me.

" The birds of wrath securely went to Mona to demand a sudden shower of the sorceress : but the goddess of the silver wheel of auspicious mien, the dawn of serenity, the greatest restrainer of sadness, in behalf of the Britons, speedily threw round his hall the stream of the rainbow; a stream which scares away violence from the earth, and causes the bane of its former state round the circle of the world to subside. The books of the ruler of the mount record no falsehood. The chair of the preserver remains here : and, till the doom, shall it continue in Europe."

Hu was described by Iolo Goch, a learned Bard, who wrote in the fourteenth century, in the following language :

" Hu, the Mighty, the Sovereign, the Ready Protector, a King, the Giver of Wine and Renown, the Emperor of the Land and the Seas, and the Life of all that are in the world was he. After the Deluge he held the strong-beamed plough, active and excellent; this did our Lord's stimulating genius that he might show to the proud man, and to the humble wise, the art which was most approved by the Faithful Father; nor is the sentiment false."

Another poet has written :

" The mighty Hu, who lived for ever,
Of mead and wine to men the giver,
The emperor of land and sea,
And of all things that living be,
Did hold a plough with his good hand,
Soon as the Deluge left the land,
To show to men both strong and weak,
The haughty-hearted and the meek,
Of all the arts to heaven below
The noblest is to guide the plough."

Ceridwen is described by the Bards who lived under the Welsh princes as having presided over the most hidden mysteries of the religion, and as a personage from whom also the secrets of the priesthood were to be obtained in purity and perfection. They also intimate that it was requisite for those who aspired to the chair of presidency to have tasted the waters of inspiration from her sacred cauldron—or, in other words, to have been initiated fully and completely into the mysteries over which she presided.

It was a Druidical belief that water was the first principle of all things and existed before the creation of the world in unsullied purity, but that its qualities deteriorated when it became blended with the earth. Water was venerated, therefore, because it afforded a symbol, by its inexhaustible resources, of the continuous and successive benefits bestowed upon the human race and because of the mystical sympathy existing between the soul of man and the purity of water. The air was regarded as the residence of beings of a more refined and spiritual nature than humans, and fire was looked upon as a vital principle brought into action at the creation. Ceres, the goddess of agriculture, was originally a fire deity, and one of her early names was Cura, a title of the sun. In her towers the sacred fires were perpetually kept alight ; the storage of corn was a secondary use made of them. According to Strabo and Pliny, fire rites were practised in ancient Latium, and a custom, which remained even to the time of Augustus, consisted of a ceremony in which the priests used to walk barefooted over burning coals. This city stood at the foot of Mount Soracte, sacred to Apollo, and the priests were styled Hirpi. The earth was venerated by the Druids because it was the mother of mankind, and particular honour was paid to trees because they afforded a proof of the immense productive power of the earth. For many centuries the Druids refused to construct enclosed temples, regarding it as an outrage to suggest that the Deity could be confined within any limits, and the vault of the sky and the depths of the forest were originally their only sanctuary.

In Druidical lore the clouds were composed of the souls of men who had recently quitted their earthly abode, and their influence either inspired courage or struck terror into armies and people. Their souls were capable of terrifying mortals with howlings, cries, apparitions, and luminous phantoms. Their agency was seen in dreams and nightmares. They vainly endeavoured to soar above the atmosphere, but an irresistible force impeded their flight into the purer spheres where they waited until a new body was formed. Not having attained that high purity which would unite them to the sun, they were compelled to wander in the form of various birds, animals, and fishes, or, as they said, " creatures that peopled the air, earth, and seas." Millions of higher souls are said to have occupied vast ice-planes in the moon, where they lost all perception, save that of simple existence. They forgot even the kind of life they had lived, but on bridges, or, more correctly, " tubes " or tunnels caused by eclipses, they returned to earth where, revived by a particle of light from the sun, they began a new life career. The sun consisted of an assemblage of pure souls " floating on an ocean of bliss."

This glorious orb contained the souls of good, brave and wise people who had been the friends and defenders of mankind. These souls, when thrice purified in the sun, ascended to a succession of still higher spheres, from which they could not again descend to those stars which occupied a less pure atmosphere. Souls sullied by earthly impurities were refined by repeated changes and probations until the last stain of evil was worn away, and they were ultimately ripened for immortal bliss in a higher sphere. A meteor was supposed to be a vehicle for carrying to Paradise the soul of some departed Druid. Even to the present day the appearance of a ball of fire, a meteor, or what are called " falling stars," creates among the more credulous Highlanders a belief that some illustrious spirit has taken its flight into the great Beyond. *Dreug* is the Gaelic for " meteor," and is supposed by Dr. Smith to be a contraction of *Druidh-eug* or " Druid's death."

The Druids had a bold and remarkable aphorism : *Nid Dim ond Duw, nid Duw ond Dim*—" God cannot be matter and what is not matter must be God." They taught that the world was to be of permanent duration, but subject to a succession of violent revolutions, which would be produced, sometimes by the predominating power of the elements of water, and sometimes by that of fire. The doctrine of a succession of worlds and of continuous incarnations was held also by the Mexicans, who doubtless brought it out of Eastern Asia.

Pomponius Mela tells us that the immortality of the soul was a Druidical doctrine which the Druids only permitted to be published for political reasons. " There is one thing," he said, " which they teach their disciples, which hath been made known to the common people, in order to render them more brave and fearless, namely, that souls are immortal and that there is another life after the present." They held also to the belief that communication with the departed by the living was possible and really took place. The precise character of this after-life has been the occasion of debate between some writers. Some have held that the Druidical belief in life after death involved the tenet of transmigration, similar to the Buddhistic, but differing from the Theosophical belief : that is to say, they believed in the possibility of the descent of the human into the animal species. Lucan wrote :

> " Forth they fly immortal in their kind,
> And other bodies in new worlds they find ;
> Thus life for ever runs its endless race,
> And like a line death but divides the space.
> Thrice happy they beneath their northern skies,
> Who that worst fear—the fear of death—despise.
> Hence they no cares for this frail being feel,

But rush undaunted on the pointed steel ;
Provoke approaching death and bravely scorn
To spare that life which must so soon return."

Diodorus Siculus says that they held that " the souls of men are
undying, and after completing their term of existence they pass into
another body." Edward Williams declares that this doctrine of metempsychosis is that which, of all others, most clearly vindicates the ways of
God to men, is countenanced by many passages in the New Testament,
believed in by many, if not all, the early Christians, and by the Essenes,
at least, among the Jews. In Irish tradition, Find MacCumall, the
celebrated Irish hero, is described as being killed at the Battle of D'Athbrea
in A.D. 273, and being reborn in A.D. 601, and again later still as King
of Ireland. D'Arbois de Jubainville states that the belief in reincarnation
went back to ancient times in Ireland. Long before our era, Eochaid
Airem, supreme King of Ireland, espoused Elain, daughter of Etar.
Elain had several centuries before been born in Celtic lands as Aihill,
wife of Mider, and she was deified after her death. The Celtic doctrine,
after being lost for centuries, made its reappearance in modern France,
where it was reconstructed and sustained by a pleiades of brilliant
writers : Charles Bonnet, Dupont de Nemours, Ballanche, Jean Reynaud,
Henri Martin, Pierre Larouy, Victor Hugo, Flammarion, and many
others.

The Druids, apparently, were believers in a kind of evolution,
maintaining that the soul began its course in the lowest water animalculæ
and passed through several successive graduated bodies until it reached
the human species. This belief laid a restraint upon them in their
choice of animals for food, and though no restriction was placed upon
the choice of animals for sacrifice, they abstained from killing for domestic
purposes all animals except those which might directly or indirectly
eventually cause the death of man. According to some writers, the
Druids believed that the whole of the animated creation was in a state
of gradual transmigration from the animal to the human, but that the
soul was immortal and must be perfected for a higher state of existence.
In the human state it was in a condition of liberty, good and evil being
held to be equally balanced. Some writers maintain that, at death, if
the good qualities preponderated over the evil, the soul would pass into
Gwynvyd, or the state of bliss, but that if the evil qualities preponderated,
then the soul would pass into an animal displaying the characteristics
exhibited by the human being while on earth, though it would have
further opportunities of re-ascent to the human and of ultimate translation to Gwynvyd, even though repeated falls should postpone the latter
step for ages. Other writers, again, have maintained that the Druids
endeavoured to persuade their followers that death was but an interlude

to a succession of progressive human existences, and that in this or some other world the soul would find a new body and live another human life, and so onwards in an innumerable cycle of lives. It seems very probable that this was really the belief held by the Druids, particularly when it is remembered that one of their maxims was that money lent in this world would be repaid by the individual in the next, and that they also believed that letters given to dying persons or thrown upon the funeral pyre would be faithfully delivered in the next world.

> " Like money by the Druids borrowed
> In t'other world to be restored."
> *Hudibras.*

In some way the fear of death was removed, and the people were instilled with courage in battle and warfare. There is a Cornish saying of the present day which runs : *Ni fhuil an sablas athraghadh death*, " there is nothing in death but a change or alteration of life."

Jean Brantius, in his *Commentary on Julius Cæsar*, says that the Druids did not believe that the soul of a rational being could be degraded and debased, so as to pass from the body of a man into a brute beast, and Escalopier and Brucker maintain the same opinion.

D'Arbois de Jubainville, in *The Irish Mythological Circle*, says :

" If the Celtic theories on the survival of the personality after death resemble somewhat those of Pythagoras, they are not, however, identical. In the system of the Greek philosopher, to be born again and to lead one or more new lives in this world, in the bodies of animals or of men, is the punishment and common lot of the wicked : it is thus that they expiate their faults. The souls of the just are not encumbered with a body : pure spirits, they live in the atmosphere around, free, happy, immortal.

" Quite other is the Celtic doctrine. To be born again in this world, and to put on a new body has been the privilege of two heroes, Tuan mac Cairill, called at first Tuan mac Stairn, and Mongan, known in the first existence as Find mac Cumaill. For them it was a privilege and not a punishment. The common law, according to Celtic doctrine, was, that after death men find in another world the new life and new body which their religion holds out to them. This new life is a continuation of that led in the world, with all its ups and downs, all the social relations that are incident to it. The dead chief's favourite slaves and dependents are burned with him on his tomb, along with his chariot horses ; they followed their master into the other world to continue the services they rendered him in this. The debtor who dies without having acquitted his debt will find himself in the other world in exactly the same position towards his creditor. His obligations will follow him into the land of the dead, and he will have to fulfil all engagements he contracted in the land of the living.

"The Celt, then, did not conceive of the other life as a compensation for the ills which one suffers here, or as a place of punishment for those who have abused the pleasures of this world. The life of the dead in the mysterious region beyond the ocean is for each a continuation of that led here."

The Druidical teachings with regard to the persistence of life have been summarised in the following lines:

> "Let no mean thoughts of dissolution fright,
> Or damp your spirits with the dews of night:
> The soul's immortal and can never die:
> Then death and all his dreadful train defy.
> Another world is ready to receive
> Immortal souls that earthly bodies leave;
> To dust the perishable parts return,
> But at the grave eternal spirits spurn,
> And if in virtue's paths they trod below,
> In heavenly mansions 'tis their fate to glow;
> But, if by vice enslav'd, their doom's to roam
> Without a heavenly or an earthly home."

Lucan, fifty years after Christ, and after the withdrawal of the Romans, thus addressed the Druids:

"And ye, ye Druids, now that the sword is removed, begin once more your barbaric rites and weird solemnities. To you only is given knowledge, or ignorance, whichever it be—of the gods and the power of heaven: your dwelling is in the laire heart of the forest. From you we learn that the bourne of man's ghost is not the senseless grave, nor the pale realm of the monarch below: in another world his spirit survives still; death, if your lore be true, is but the passage to enduring life."

Several writers assert that in combats with the Romans, the Druids remained immobile as statues, receiving their wounds without fleeing or defending themselves. They knew themselves immortal, and counted on finding in another world a new and always young body.

In Martini Hamconii's *Frisia seu de viris rebusque Frisiæ illustribus*, published in 1620, it is set forth that Barco, *Pontifex seu Præfectus Druidum*, who lived in Holland in the fourth century, wrote on the immortality of the soul, and that another Dutchman, Poppa, "the most distinguished heathen author of the eighth century," left, along with other works, the treatises: *De officiis Druidum* and *De ritu sacrificorum*,

also that Occo, " a ferocious fellow," the last of the Frisian Druids, wrote
on the doctrines and lives of the chief Druidical priests.   These books,
however, are not available in England, and are referred to in the barest
terms in Seelan's *Selecta Litteraria*, which was printed at Lubec in 1726.
The Druids, it is ascertained from these and other works, apart from any
speculation as to their belief or dis-belief in the doctrine of reincarnation,
were non-believers in the doctrine of eternal punishment, maintaining
that " a state of eternal punishment is in itself impossible, and the
infliction of such a punishment is the only act which the Deity cannot
commit."   They, however, taught that the punishment of the wicked
after death might be cancelled or lessened by sacrifices to the Supreme
Deity, and they accordingly offered up black sheep for the sins of the
departed.   Lucan wrote :

> " If dying mortals' doom they sing aright,
> No ghosts descend to dwell in dreadful night.
> No parting souls to grisly Pluto go,
> Nor seek the dreary silent shades below."

The Druids believed in three circles of existence : the Circle of
Infinity, which was traversed only by God ; the Circle of Felicity, sometimes called Gwynvyd, or Happiness, through which men have to travel
after they have passed through their terrestrial changes ; and the Circle
of Abred, or Evil, through which humans pass in their varying states
of existence, necessary to be undergone before they are fit to inhabit
the Circle of Felicity.   In the third circle, man began in the lower state
of existence, which contained a mixture of good and evil, of which man
could make his choice or balance his propensities.   Thence man passed
through the Gate of Mortality, into the Circle of Happiness, where there
would be neither want nor adversity, sorrow nor death.   If there he
permitted evil affections and passions to govern him, he would sink from
the Circle of Happiness, and Death would return him to the lower circle,
where he would suffer punishment in proportion to his offences, the soul
doing penance in the form of a beast or reptile, or in several of these
successively.   From this degradation the soul would again arise and
resume human form, until repeated probations and corrections would
ultimately subdue all evil propensities.   Such is the generally accepted
statement of the Druidical belief in life after death as expounded by
the principal authorities.

Another topic which has formed the subject of much debate is the
question as to whether human sacrifices were offered by the Druids,
although it seems scarcely open to question in view of the categorical
statement of Cæsar.   Divitiacus is scarcely likely to have consented to
the publication of the statement if it had not been accurate.   Possibly,

however, the explanation of the divergent view may be found in the assertion of some writers that the practice of human sacrifices was the perpetuation of a pre-Druidic custom. Superstitions connected with the mystical power of human sacrifices are of scytho-medique origin. Doubtless, the practice of immolating human victims to superior persons or powers comes from an instinct common to all primitive people. This barbarous custom is found among the yellow tribes of America, the black tribes of Africa, as well as among the Gauls. Humanity has everywhere, in a greater or lesser pronounced degree, the same native instincts. There seems no doubt but that the practice must be admitted, always remembering, however, that it was not peculiar to the Druids, and that the Greeks and Romans, amongst others, had their sacrifices of men and women. Bertrand says that it is impossible to deny, after a close examination of texts, that human sacrifices, up to the time of the Roman Conquest, were very popular and were regarded as an ordinary practice in several parts of Gaul and Germany. He also arrives at the conclusion that they were established in Gaul anterior to the introduction of Druidism in that country. It is doubtful, however, whether these sacrifices took place in the vicinity of the temples. The religion of the Druids, apart from this custom, seems to have been spiritual and refined, without statues, enclosed temples, and the like. Tacitus calls one of their temples *castum nemus*, " the chaste wood." Chastity implies freedom from every kind of pollution, and so exact a writer as Tacitus would scarcely have applied the epithet " chaste " to a grove stained with human gore.

These Druidical sacrifices appear, however, to have been legal executions, and an interval of five years generally elapsed between sentence and execution. There is no evidence that the human sacrifices of the Druids consisted of aught save the capital punishment meted out to criminals ; but it is necessary to observe that, according to Bardic law, even murderers seldom expiated their crimes with death, except when these were proved to be premeditated and perpetrated deliberately, and the victims subjected to ill-usage and cruelty before being despatched. The Bardic teaching was that " a man having been guilty of crimes that are punishable with death must be so punished ; and, by giving himself up as a voluntary victim, being conscious of deserving death, a man does all that is in his power to expiate his crimes."

There is no proof that the Druids ever offered sacrifices in the sense of substitution or atonement. Although some writers have ventured to censure the Druids for their alleged inhumanity in regard to this practice, they have never brought the charge of immorality, either in public or private, against the Druids, and it is generally admitted by all writers that no obscene or improper language was permitted in the celebration of the Druidical rites and mysteries. The candidates, indeed, were for ever disgraced if they " uttered one word of unseemly import." It is also worthy of note that Druidism was free from that spirit of intolerance which has marred other faiths, and there is no record of any Christian missionary undergoing martyrdom at the hands of the Druids. Diodorus said of them : " They are of much sincerity and integrity, far from the craft and knavery of men amongst us ; contented with homely fare, strangers to excess and luxury," while Strabo states that they were remarkable for justice, moral and religious doctrines.

Some writers maintain that human sacrifices were offered only on solemn occasions, such as when the people feared a famine, when they were hard pressed by the enemy, or when they were about to enter on some arduous undertaking. It was then that they sacrificed malefactors, felons, or captives of war. The Druids believed that those who killed themselves to accompany their friends into the next world would live with them there, so that there was no lack of victims who, in time of trouble, came forward as volunteers to submit to death with this object in view. Eager to rejoin their dear departed in the happier sphere, eager to ascend into the Circle of Felicity, the Celts mounted gladly the sacrificial stone, and death came to them in the midst of a song of joy. The old Mosaic law of " a life for a life " was also required by the laws of Cymry, and the capital punishment inflicted by the executioner was regarded as the requital of the debt due to God and man. The object of the sacrifices was to remit to an offended Deity a reprobate spirit to suffer the judgment of heaven. According to the laws of Dyonwal Moelmund, the three forms of capital punishment practised in Britain, were beheading, hanging, and burning. It is possible that the practice of burning was derived from Phœnicia, where the annual sacrifice of human beings by fire, which was part of the worship of Moloch, may have given rise to the custom of burning malefactors and prisoners taken in war, and other immolations in vogue amongst the Druids.

Dr. Milner, in his *History of Winchester*, says that at Douay and Dunkirk, there was an immemorial custom of constructing huge figures of wickerwork and canvas that were filled with men and women and moved about to represent a giant who was killed by their patron saint. Columba, when beginning the erection of his church at Iona, addressed his followers in words which point clearly to human sacrifice : " It is good for us that our roots should go under the earth here ; it is permitted that one of you should go under the clay of this island to hallow it." The story runs that Odran rose readily and said : " If thou shouldst take me, I am ready for that." Columba readily accepted the offer, Odran went to heaven, and Columba founded the church of Hi. Adamnan mentions that the church founded by Columba was a *Duirthech*, or oak building.

The Romans issued stringent laws forbidding the retention of the practice of human sacrifices, although they were by no means free from the guilt of such practices themselves, even in their most civilized ages. Adam, in his *Roman Antiquities*, says that by an ancient law of Romulus, persons guilty of certain crimes, such as treachery or sedition, were devoted to Pluto and the infernal gods. In after times, a consul, dictator, or prætor might devote not only himself, but any of the legion, and slay him as an expiatory victim. In the first ages of the Republic, human sacrifices appear to have been offered annually, and it was not until the year of the city 657 that a decree of the senate was made to prohibit them. Boys used to be put to a cruel death in the time of Cicero and Horace for magical purposes. Augustus ordered three hundred senators and equites, who had sided with Anthony, to be sacrificed on the altar of Julius Cæsar. Gibbon tells us that " under the specious pretext of abolishing human sacrifices, the Emperors Tiberius and Claudius suppressed the dangerous power of the Druids." The Romans, however, regarded human sacrifices as pleasing to the gods. Even at so late a period as the Second Punic War a man was buried alive for the purpose of conciliating the divine favour, and when the soldiers of Julius Cæsar attempted an insurrection at Rome, two of them were sacrificed to Mars in the Campius Martius, and their heads were stuck up in the Regia. The Egyptians carried the practice to such a monstrous excess, says Carte, in his *History of England*, that, at Heliopolis, they offered every day three men to Juno, till Amosis abolished the custom, substituting images of wax instead of men ; as the Laodiceans of Syria did in lieu of the virgin they yearly offered to Minerva. The aborigines of Italy offered their victims to Jove and Apollo.

Ireland is said by some writers, particularly d'Arbois de Jubainville, to have been free from the taint of human sacrifices, but this is because, wherever possible, all mention of this practice has been suppressed by partial writers. Marcus Keane, in *Towers and Temples of Ancient Ireland*, says :

> " I have no doubt of the custom of human sacrifices having prevailed in Ireland also. Several writers upon Ireland have asserted the fact ; and the Celtic Druids are stated to have sacrificed children at Meagh Sleachth, in Cavan, shortly before the coming of St. Patrick. I believe this charge to be an anachronism, so far as the Druids are concerned, as no such sanguinary rites could have prevailed during the age immediately preceding the introduction of Christianity, without receiving some particular notice from the early Christian writers. But the slight notices of such sacrificial

rites, which have survived, I believe to be due to traditions of the antecedent Cuthites."

In the Latin *Life of St. Patrick*, however, it is stated that, on the festival of Tara, not only princes and heads and chiefs of provinces, but also the *druidum magistri*, assembled for the purpose of offering human sacrifices to idols. The following poem is found in the Books of Leinster, of Ballymote, of Lecan, and in the Rennes MS. The translation was made by Dr. Kuno Meyer, and it appears as an appendix to Nutt's *Voyage of Bran*:

> " Here used to be
> A high idol with many fights,
> Which was named the Cromm Cruaich ;
> It made every tribe to be without peace.
>
> 'Twas a sad evil !
> Brave Gæls used to worship it.
> From it they would not without tribute ask
> To be satisfied as to their portion of the hard world.
>
> He was their god,
> The withered Cromm with many mists,
> The people whom he shook over every host,
> The everlasting kingdom they shall not have.
>
> To him without glory
> They would kill their piteous, wretched offspring
> With much wailing and peril,
> To pour their blood around Cromm Cruaich.
>
> Milk and corn
> They would ask from him speedily
> In return for one-third of their healthy issue :
> Great was the horror and the scare of him.
>
> To him
> Noble Gæls would prostrate themselves,
> From the worship of him with many manslaughters,
> The plain is called ' Mag Slecht.'
>
> There came
> Tigernmas, the prince of Tara yonder,
> On Hallowe'en with many hosts,
> A cause of grief to them was the deed.

They did evil,
They beat their palms, they pounded their bodies,
Wailing to the demon who enslaved them,
They shed falling showers of tears.

Dead were the men
Of Banba's host, without happy strength,
Around Tigernmas, the destructive man in the North,
From the worship of Cromm Cruaich—'twas no luck
    for them.

For I have learnt,
Except one-fourth of the keen Gaels
Not a man alive—lasting the snare !
Escaped without death in his mouth.

Around Cromm Cruaich
There the hosts would prostrate themselves ;
Though he put them under deadly disgrace,
Their name clings to the noble plain.

In their ranks stood
Four times three stone idols ;
To bitterly beguile the hosts,
The figure of the Cromm was made of gold.

Since the rule
Of Herimon, the noble man of grace,
There was worshipping of stones
Until the coming of good Patrick of Macha.

A sledge-hammer to the Cromm
He applied from crown to sole,
He destroyed without lack of valour
The feeble idol which was there."

The animals of a chief also were killed on his grave at the time of his funeral in the same manner as in Gaul in the time of Cæsar.

It is improbable that the religious instruction of the populace was limited absolutely to the teaching of the doctrine of the immortality of the soul. It is more likely that the Druids followed the practice of the Gymnosophists of India, the Magi of Persia, the Chaldeans of Assyria, and other priests of antiquity, by having two sets of doctrine, one being communicated to the initiated only, admitted after certain ceremonies and rites and sworn to secrecy, and the other taught freely and openly to the uninitiated. No verses or poems whatsoever relating to the system or creed were permitted to be issued unless previously examined and publicly approved at a Gorsedd. For this purpose they were first recited by the Dageiniaid, or reciters, in the hearing of all.

Diodorus states that the Britons paid great regard to the exhortations of the Druids, not only in times of peace, but also in the time of war. " They sometimes," he says, " step in between two hostile armies, who are standing with their swords drawn and their spears extended, ready to engage ; and, by their eloquence, as by an irresistible enchantment, they prevent an effusion of blood." Tacitus also says that " the British chieftains, before a battle, fly from rank to rank and address the men with animating speeches tending to inflame their courage, increase their hopes, and dispel their fears."

According to Justin, the Druids declared that in times of public calamity the people could not be rid of pestilence or trouble until they had dipped the gold and silver secured to them during a time of war into a lake. He gives the following description of this ceremony :

> " Many persons resorted to a lake at the foot of the Gevaudan mountains, consecrated to the moon under the name of Helanus, and thither cast, some the entire human habits, linen, cloth, and entire fleeces ; others cast in cheese, wax, bread, and other things, everyone according to his ability ; they then sacrificed for several days."

Strabo also states that the Gauls consecrated their gold in certain lakes.

The old metrical *Life of St. Patrick*, ascribed to Fiacc of Sleibthe, says : " The Tuatha adored the Sidhe. According to the *Book of Armagh*, the Sidhe were supernatural beings supposed to dwell in the earth, the sea, the rivers, in valleys and hills, in fountains, wells, and trees. Both they and the natural objects in which they were supposed to dwell were invoked or conciliated. They were supposed to be conciliated by the spells and incantations of a sacred caste called Druada or Magi. The Banshee is just the *bean-sidh*, or female sprite or fairy. Mullaghshee, the hill on which the church stands in Ballyshannon, is the hill of the *sidh* or *shee*, or fairy palace."

Cæsar says that the Druids were the judges on all points of law and equity, and were the distributors of all punishments and rewards. They had the power of excommunication against all who did not submit to their decrees, of excluding persons of all ranks from the benefits of Society, and even from Society itself ; of deposing princes, and even of condemning them to death, a power not infrequently exercised, and of declaring war and peace. The Druids themselves were exempt from bearing arms and paying taxes. Divitiacus, the Arch Druid, however, we learn from Cæsar, was permitted to carry arms, and was entrusted even with the command of a corps in one of Cæsar's battalions.

Cæsar gives the following account of the effect of the sentence of excommunication :

" If any person, either private or public, does not acquiesce in their decisions, they interdict him from their sacrifices. That is, among them, the severest punishment. They who are thus interdicted are reckoned impious and accursed ; all men depart from them ; all shun their company and conversation, lest they should sustain some misfortune from their contagion ; the administration of justice and the protection of the laws is denied to them and no honour is conferred upon them."

The sentence consigned the miserable defaulter to a lingering death from cold and hunger, says George Jones. He had no fire to cheer his home or dress food for his subsistence or to warm himself in the depth of winter, while surrounded with frosts and snows. No friend, kinsman, or neighbour was permitted to supply him with it under pain of incurring the like cruel sentence. The excommunicated had also to walk with bare feet and wear black garments for the remainder of their lives.

Repentance and purification were regarded by the Druids as necessary duties. They observed one day in seven as peculiarly sanctified and made holy by the Great Creator, and they were wont to dedicate one-tenth of all their substance to religious purposes.

Geometrical figures, such as lines, angles, squares, and perpendiculars were ranked amongst the symbols of Druidism.

" As the Druids had no enclosed temples," says Borlase, " thinking them inconsistent with the majesty of the gods, so neither had they any carved images to represent them, and for the same reason ; but, instead thereof, rude stones were erected in their places of worship at some mystic, significant distance, and in some emblematic manner, situation, and plan ; sometimes in triangles, sometimes in squares, sometimes in both ; now single and fifty paces distant or more from the circles ; or eminently taller than the rest in the circular line, and making a part of it like portals, not only to shape the entrance, but also to hallow those that entered : it appearing by many monuments that the Druids attributed great virtue to these passages between rocks."

The Druidical philosophy and religion, even in their corrupted state, were certainly equal, if not superior, to any of the philosophies and religions current in other parts of the world in their day and time. Manxmen ascribe to the Druids the excellent laws by which their island has always been governed, and the ancient Greeks, on their own admission, learned part of their philosophy and many of their fables from the Gallic

Druids. The power of the Druidical priesthood was tremendous, all the moral force of the country was in the hands of the priests, who were accountable to no other superior human power. At one time their authority appears to have extended over France, Flanders, the Alpine Regions, Lombardy, and the British Isles, but was ultimately confined within the narrow limits of the Isle of Man, where the blood of the last victim was shed and where the last temple was overthrown.

The knowledge of the Druids astonished the Fathers of the Church. St. Augustine declared that their philosophy almost approached that of Christian monotheism. Their studies embraced those elevated objects which had engaged the attention of the whole world—the nature of the Deity, the nature of the human soul, the future state, the heavenly bodies, the terrestrial globe, and its various productions. Their conceptions were great and sublime, their speculations comprehensive in their sphere, pervading most of the arts and sciences which had interested the earliest peoples. M. J. P. Megnin, in his work, *De l'origine de la Ferrure du Cheval*, says that the Druids taught the structure of the horse's foot by the enormous sacrifices they made of this animal, and accustomed to the manipulation of metals, and their intelligence continually cultivated by study, were marvellously disposed to be the inventors of shoeing by nails. " When we also look to the rational form they gave to their work," he continues, " how wisely they placed the nail holes, and how skilfully they made the nail heads to form so many cages to assist travelling in rocky and mountainous regions, we cannot but be astonished at the perfection which the sacred smiths had attained in defending and assisting nature two thousand years ago." Perhaps, also, there was no order of men among the pagans who preserved the philosophical opinions of mankind in the early state with greater simplicity or integrity. The ceremonies of their religion were performed with a solemnity that deeply affected the spectator, and it is said that even the Romans "stood astonished and trembled." They were monogamists and of the highest morality, but followed the Phœnician custom of giving a widow to her husband's brother. No idol or graven image has ever been discovered among Druidical remains, despite Cæsar's statement that the countries of the Druids were full of idols. Under a variety of names and characters the Druids acknowledged one God, the Maker of all things, and the Lord of all the earth. They taught the superintendency of Divine Providence, of moral responsibility, and of recompense after death. As a consequence of these principles they observed, as well as enjoined, the most rigid justice in their decisions and in their dealings with their fellow-men.

According to Banier : " Although the memoirs of our Druids are extremely short, yet we can very evidently discover from them that the Druids were of Abraham's religion entirely, at least in the earliest times, and worshipped the Supreme Being in the same manner as he did, and probably according to his example, or the example of his and their common ancestors." Certainly, when the teachings of the Druids are examined—the creation of the world, the formation of man, his primitive innocence and felicity, and his fall into guilt and misery, the creation of angels, their rebellion and expulsion from heaven, the universal deluge, the final salvation of humanity, it will be seen that there was no great divergence from those teachings contained in the writings of Moses and other parts of the Jewish scriptures. Their worship consisted in rites of sacrifice, prayer, and praise : the people knew their institutes, believed and practised them. Sermons appear generally to have been absent from their services.

In its primitive state, Druidism may be regarded as an edifice raised upon the same basis as the patriarchal religion. Its ostensible design was to enlighten the understanding, to promote harmony, and to encourage virtue. As a religion, it undoubtedly deteriorated in the course of its history, possibly under the influence of commerce, and probably by the contaminating influence of the Carthaginians and the Phœnicians. From them possibly were derived those cruel and abominable rites of human sacrifices and the burning of infants. Deterioration, however, is a factor common to all religions. The East to-day is losing its former deservedly high reputation as the home of mysticism and high spiritual culture under the advance of commerce, and the art of meditation, even among Buddhist priests, is becoming a lost accomplishment, whenever and wherever such come into contact with western ideas and customs. There seems to be much truth in what Taliesin describes as " the oppression of the metal-workers."

A note to Lord Lytton's *King Arthur* says :

" The testimony to be found in classical writers as to the original purity of the Druid worship, before it was corrupted into the idolatry which existed in Britain at the time of the Roman conquest, is strongly corroborated by the Welsh triads. These triads, indeed, are of various dates, but some bear the mark of a very remote antiquity—wholly distinct alike from the philosophy of the Romans and the mode of thought prevalent in the earlier ages of the Christian era ; in short, anterior to all the recorded conquests of the Cymrian people. These, like proverbs, appear the wrecks and fragments of some primeval ethics or philosophical religion. Nor are such remarkable alone for the purity of the notions they inculcate relative to the Deity ; they have often, upon matters less spiritual, the delicate observation, as well as the profound thought of reflective wisdom. Nor were the Druids of Britain inferior to those with whom the Sages of the Western and Eastern worlds came into contact. On the contrary, even to the time of Cæsar, the Druids of Britain excelled in science and repute those of Gaul, and to their schools the neophytes of the Continent were sent."

Hutchinson, in his *History of Cumberland*, bears similar testimony when he says :

"We do not find that the Britons, from the first account of them in this part of the island, were enveloped in that dreadful darkness of mind in which most other nations, on their first discovery by Europeans, have been described to us : on the contrary, they were not ignorant of the Deity and had not corrupted their religion with idolatry."

The Druidical teaching concerning man's spiritual nature is comprised in the following Triad :

"In every person there is a soul : In every soul there is intelligence : In every intelligence there is thought. In every thought there is good and evil : In every evil there is death : In every good there is life : In every life there is God."

Another utterance shows the spiritual character of the Druidical teaching :

"Let God be praised in the beginning and the end ;
Who supplicates Him, He will neither despise nor refuse ;
God above us, God before us, God possessing all things,
May the Father of Heaven grant us a portion of mercy ! "

In Ireland, the Druids left more solid traces of their domination and their teaching. Ireland has never been subject to the influence of foreign civilizations. Only one influence has effected any sensible modification in that island—the triumph of Christianity, which has been exclusively moral.

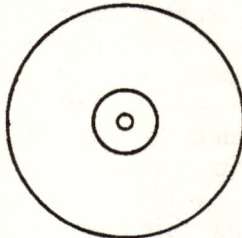

CHAPTER III

THE INITIATORY CEREMONIES AND PRIESTHOOD

"Hark ! 'twas the voice of harps that poured along
The hollow vale, the floating tide of song.
I see the glittering train in long array,
Gleam through the shades, and snowy splendours play ;
I see them now with measured steps and slow,
'Mid arching groves the white-robed sages go.
The oaken wreath with braided fillet drest—
The Crescent beaming on the holy breast—
The silver hair which waves above the lyre,
And shrouds the strings, proclaim the Druid's quire.
They halt, and all is hushed."
                                        WORDSWORTH.

". . . . The Sages skill'd in Nature's lore ;
The changeful universe, its numbers, powers,
Studious they measure, save when meditation
Gives place to holy rites : then in the grove
Each hath his rank and function."
                                MASON. *Caractacus.*

The mode of life adopted by the Druidical priests made easy the transition from Pagan to Christian monasticism. To all intents and purposes the Druids formed a Church, and their ecclesiastical system seems to have been as complete as any other system of which records have been preserved, whether Christian or non-Christian. The word "Church," it is interesting to note, is by many etymologists derived from the Greek word *kirkos*, meaning " a circle." It appears in varied, though similar forms in different languages : Welsh, *cyrch ;* Scotch, *kirk ;* Old English, *chirche, cherche,* or *chireche ;* Anglo-Saxon, *circe* or *cyrice ;* Dutch, *kerk ;* Icelandic, *kirkja ;* Swedish, *kyrka ;* Danish, *kirke ;* German, *kirche ;* Old High German, *chirihha.*

The rank of the Arch, or Chief, Druid was that of *pontifex maximus,* and, apparently, he held his position until death or resignation, when his successor appears to have been elected in a manner similar to that in which the Pope of the present day is elected, although some writers assert that the Arch Druid was elected annually. Cæsar states that " when the presulary dignity becomes vacant by the head Druid's death, the next in dignity succeeds ; but, when there are equals in competition, election carries it."

Many Druids appear to have retired from the world and lived a hermit existence, in order that they might acquire a reputation for sanctity. Martin, in his *Description of the Western Isles*, has pointed out that, in his time, in the most unfrequented places of the Western Isles of Scotland, there were still remaining the foundations of small circular houses, intended evidently for the abode of one person only, to which were given the name of "Druids' Houses" by the people of the country. The Druids were great lovers of silence, and if any one was found prattling during their assemblies or sacrifices he was admonished ; if, after the third admonition, he did not cease talking, a large piece of his garment was cut off ; and if, after that, he again offended, he was punished in a more rigorous manner.

The majority of the Druids, however, appear to have lived a communal life, uniting together in fraternities and dwelling near the temples which they served ; each temple requiring the services of several priests, except, perhaps, in isolated districts. In Wales, one Druid resided in every *Cwmwd* to offer sacrifices and to instruct the people. In addition to the portion of land to which every freeborn Cymro was entitled, and the immunities and privileges belonging to his class, this local priest could claim a contribution from every plough used in the hamlets of his Cwmwd. Ammianus of Marseilles describes these early priests of Britain in the following words :

"The Druids, men of polished parts, as the authority of Pythagoras has decreed, affecting formed societies and sodalities, gave themselves wholly to the contemplation of divine and hidden things, despising all worldly enjoyments, and confidently affirmed the souls of men to be immortal."

Not a few, however, lived in a more public and secular manner, attaching themselves to kingly courts and the residences of the noble and wealthy. The Druids have thus a close affinity with both the monastic orders and religious congregations of the Church of Rome, known as the regular clergy ; and those living unrestricted by special vows, known as the secular clergy.

The period of novitiate and the character of the training of an aspirant to the Druidical priesthood was as lengthy and as rigorous as that of an aspirant to membership of the Society of Jesus, better known as the Jesuit Society. It lasted for twenty years and, although the candidates were, in general, enlisted from the families of nobles, many youths in other ranks of life also entered voluntarily upon the novitiate, and very frequently boys were dedicated to the priestly life by their parents from an early age. None but freemen were admitted as aspirants, so that a slave seeking admission into the Order had first to obtain his freedom from his master.

The ceremony of initiation, so far as can be gathered from the records, was solemn and arduous. The candidate first took an oath not to reveal the mysteries into which he was about to be initiated. He was then divested of his ordinary clothing, crowned with ivy, and vested with a tri-coloured robe of white, blue, and green—colours emblematical of light, truth, and hope. Over this was placed a white tunic. Both were made with full-length openings in the front and, before the ceremony of initiation began, the candidate had to throw open both tunic and robe, in order that the officiating priest might be assured that he was a male. This divesture was also to symbolise his extreme poverty, which was supposed to be his characteristic prior to initiation.

The tonsure was one of the ceremonies connected with initiation. As practised in the Roman Church the tonsure, the first of the four minor orders conferred upon aspirants to the priesthood, is undoubtedly a Druidical survival. There is evidence of its practice in Ireland in A.D. 630, but it does not appear to have become a custom in England until the latter part of the eighth century. The tonsure was referred to by St. Patrick as " the diabolical mark," although, according to Druidical lore, St. Patrick himself was tonsured ; and in Ireland it was known as " the tonsure of Simon the Druid." The Druidical differed greatly from both the modern monastic and secular form. All the hair in front of a line drawn over the crown from ear to ear was shaved or clipped. All Druids wore short hair, the laymen long ; the Druids wore long beards, the laymen shaved the whole of the face, with the exception of the upper lip. The tonsure was known also in Wales as a sign of service in a kingly or noble family. In the Welsh romance known as the *Mabinogion*, we find among the Brythons a youth who wished to become one of Arthur's knights, whose allegiance was signified by the king cutting off the youth's hair with his own hand.

The initiation took place in a cave, because of the legend which existed that Enoch had deposited certain invaluable secrets in a consecrated cavern deep in the bowels of the earth. There is still to be seen in Denbighshire one of the caves in which Druidical initiations are said to have taken place. The caves in which the various ceremonies were performed were, like the over-ground Druidical temples, circular in form. The underground rooms of the Red Indians, where their secret councils were held, were also circular in form, with a divan running around them. After taking the oath the candidate had to pass through the Tolmen, or perforated stone, an act held to be the means of purging from sin and conveying purity. Captain Wilford, in *Asiatic Researches*, says that perforated stones are not uncommon in India, and that devout people pass through them, when the opening will admit it, in order to be regenerated. If the hole be too small to permit of the passage of the entire body, they put either the hand or foot through the hole ; and, with a sufficient degree of faith, this answers nearly the same purpose. Among the Namburi of the Travancore State a man is made a Brahman by being passed through the body of a golden cow, or being placed in a colossal golden lotus flower, which article then becomes the property of the priests. The individual is, by this act, said to acquire a new birth of the soul, or have become twice-born. Passing persons through holed stones is also practised in other parts of India, as it is in the East Indies. In some parts of the north of England children are drawn through a hole in the " Groaning Cheese " on the day on which they are christened. All rocks containing an aperture, whether natural or artificial, were held to possess the means of transmitting purification to the person passing through the hole. At Bayons Manor, near Market Rasen, Lincolnshire, there is a *petra ambrosiæ*, consisting of a gigantic upright stone resting upon another stone and hollowed out so as to form an aperture sufficiently large for a man to pass through. This stone is believed to have been used by the Druids in the performance of their sacred rites. The celebrated Purgatory of St. Patrick, at Lough Derg, in Ireland, is also thought to have been a place of Druidical initiation, and even in ante-Druidical times no person was permitted to enter the enclosure without first undergoing all the ceremonies of preparation and purification. Some writers have conjectured that the prophet Isaiah was referring to a practice similar to this when he wrote (i, 19) : " And they shall go into the holes of the rocks and into the caves of the earth for fear of the Lord, and for the glory of His majesty, when He ariseth to shake terribly the earth." All such orifices were consecrated with holy oil and dedicated to religious uses, hence the distinguishing name of *lapis ambrosius* which was given to each.

Forlong, in *Rivers of Life*, throws much light upon this custom. In one passage he says :

" The superstition of passing through natural, or even artificial, clefts in trees and rocks, or, failing them, caves and holes, has scarcely yet left the most civilized parts of Europe, and is firmly maintained throughout the rest of the world, and, in India, takes the thoroughly literal aspect of the question, *viz.*, of being really ' born again,' the person to be regenerated being actually passed through the mouth and organ of a properly constructed cow—if the sinner be very rich, of a gold or silver cow, which is then broken up and divided among the purifying priests. A wooden or lithic perforation, that is an *I Oni*, is, for ordinary men, however, a sufficient 'baptism of grace,' and in these islands the holy ash, or Ygdrasil, is the proper tree to regenerate one. Major Moor describes his gardener in Suffolk as splitting a young ash longitudinally (the oak is its equivalent) and passing a naked child through it three times, 'always head foremost for rickets and rupture.' The tree is bound up again, and if it heals, all goes well with the child. The operation is called *drawing* in Suffolk, and, in 1834, seems to have gone beyond the spiritual and passed into the sphere of a medical luxury. In England the ash is for *drawing* preferred to the oak ; it should be split for about five feet, as closely as possible east and west, and in the Spring, or fertilising season of the year, before vegetation has set in, and just as the sun is rising. The child must then be stripped quite naked, and some say passed feet, and not head, foremost, through the tree three times, and it should then be carefully turned round, or, as the Celts say, *deasil-ways*, that is with the sun, after which, the cleft of the tree must be bound up carefully. Here we see the tree as a *thing of life*, and forming the very *IOni-ish*, 'door of life,' and in the presence of Siva, or the Sun, without whom regeneration of old, or the giving of new life is known by all to be impossible.

Bottrell, also, in his *Traditions of West Cornwall*, says that children were at one time brought to Madron Well to be cured of shingles, wild fires, tetters, and various skin diseases, as well as to fortify them against witchcraft and other mysterious ailments. The child was stripped naked, then it was plunged or popped three times through the water against the sun ; next it was passed quickly nine times round the spring, going from east to west, or with the sun ; then dressed, rolled up in something warm, and made to sleep near the water ; if the child slept and plenty of bubbles rose in the water, it was a good sign.

The candidate was next placed in a chest or coffin, in which he remained enclosed—apertures being made for the circulation of air—for three days, to represent death. From this chest he was liberated on the third day to symbolise his restoration to life. The Bard, in describing the initiation of Arthur, says that at his (mystical) death, the " three nights was he placed under the flat stone of Echemeint." When the aspirant emerged from the tomb in which he had been immured he was pronounced regenerated, or born again. Dr. George Oliver, in *Signs and Symbols*, says that in all ancient Mysteries before an aspirant could claim to participate in the higher secrets of the Institution he was placed within the Pastos, or Bed, or Coffin ; or, in other words, was subject to a solitary confinement for a prescribed period of time, that he might reflect seriously, in seclusion and darkness, on what he was about to undertake, and be reduced to a proper state of mind for the reception of great and important truths, by a course of fasting and mortification. This was symbolical death and his deliverance from confinement was the act of regeneration, or being born again. The candidate was made to undergo these changes in scenic representation and was placed under the Pastos in perfect darkness.

The sanctuary was then prepared for the further ceremonies in connection with the initiation, and the candidate, blindfolded, was introduced to the assembled company during the chanting of a hymn to the sun and placed in the charge of a professed Druid, another Druid, at the same time, kindling the sacred fire. It is said that we still retain in some old English choruses the odes which those Phallo-Solar worshippers used to chant. Thus : " Heydown, down derry down," is held to be *Hai down ir deri danno*, signifying : " Come, let us haste to the oaken grove " ; or, if taken from the Celtic, *Dun dun daragan dun*, it would mean, " To the hill, to the hill, to the oaks, to the hill." Another chant : " High trolollie, lollie loi, or lee," is said to come from the Celtic *Ai tra la, la, li*," which would be an address to the rising sun as " Hail ! early day."

Still blindfolded, the candidate was taken on a circumnambulation nine times round the sanctuary in circles from East to West, starting at the South. The procession was made to the accompaniment of a tumultuous clanging of musical instruments and of shouting and screaming, and was followed by the administration of a second oath, the violation of which rendered the individual liable to the penalty of death.

Then followed a number of other ceremonies, which typified the confinement of Noah in the Ark and the death of that patriarch, the candidate passing eventually through a narrow avenue, which was guarded by angry beasts, after which he was seized and borne to the waters, symbolical of the waters on which the Ark of Noah floated. He was completely immersed in this water, and, on emerging from the water on the bank opposite to that from which he had entered, he found himself in a blaze of light. The most dismal howlings, shrieks, and lamentations are said to have been heard during the progress of this ceremony, the barking of dogs, the blowing of horns, and the voices of men uttering discordant cries. These were made partly for the purpose of intimidating the candidate, and partly with the design of inspiring with terror any uninitiated persons who might be within earshot, and so deter them from prying into the secrets. Some writers assert that the sound of thunder was heard, which is not improbable : the art of making artificial thunder was known to the priests of Delphos. The candidate, on arriving at the opposite bank, was presented to the Arch Druid, who, seated on his throne or official chair, explained to the initiate the symbolical meaning of the various ceremonies in which he had just taken an active part.

Taliesin, in his account of his initiation, says :

" I was first modelled into the form of a pure man in the hall of Ceridwen, who subjected me to penance. Though small within my ark and modest in my deportment, I was great. A sanctuary carried me above the surface of the earth. Whilst I was inclosed within its ribs, the sweet Awen rendered me complete ; and my law, without audible language, was imparted to me by the old giantess darkly smiling in her wrath ; but her claim was not regretted, when she set sail. I fled in the form of a fair grain of pure wheat ; upon the edge of a covering cloth she caught me in her fangs. In appearance she was as large as a proud mare, which she also resembled : then was she swelling out, like a ship upon the waters. Into a dark receptacle she cast me. She carried me back into the sea of Dylan. It was an auspicious omen to me, when she happily suffocated me. God, the Lord, freely set me at large."

The ceremony of initiation was similar to that of the Egyptian rites of Osiris, which were regarded as a descent into hell, a passage through the infernal lake, followed by a landing on the Egyptian Isle of the Blessed. By this means men were held to become more holy, just, and pure, and to be delivered from all hazards which would otherwise be impending. The cave in which the aspirant was placed for the purpose of meditation before he was permitted to participate in the sacred Mysteries was guarded by a representation of the terrible divinity Busnawr, who was armed with a naked sword, and whose vindictive wrath, when aroused, was said to be such as to make earth, hell and even heaven itself, tremble.

Dionysius tells us that when the Druidesses celebrated the mysteries of the great god, Hu, the Mighty, they passed over an arm of the sea in the dead of the night to certain smaller contiguous islets. The ship or vessel in which they made the passage represented the Ark of the Deluge ; the arm of the sea that of the waters of the Flood ; and the fabled Elysian island, where the passage terminated, shadowed out the Lunar White Island of the ocean-girt summit of the Paradisiacal Ararat.

After the initiation was completed the novice retired into the forest, where the period of his novitiate was spent, his time being devoted to study and gymnastic exercises. The Druids encouraged learning, and candidates for the priesthood passed first through the courses assigned to those who were to become Ovates or Bards. Four degrees were conferred during the long novitiate ; the first being given after three years' study in the arts of poetry and music, if the candidate, by his capacity and diligence, merited the honour. The second was conferred after six years' further study, if merited ; the third after a further nine years' study ; and the final degree, equal to a doctorate, was bestowed two years later, on the completion of the twenty years' course.

The *Book of the Ollamhs* gives the following as the course of study for the first twelve years. The Druids, it may be remarked, have been claimed as the originators of the collegiate system of education.

First year.—Fifty oghams, the Araicecht, or grammar, twenty tales, and some poems.

Second year.—Fifty more oghams, six minor lessons in philosophy, thirty tales, and some poems.

Third year.—Learning the correct diphthongal combinations, the six major lessons of philosophy, forty tales, and various poems.

Fourth year.—Fifty tales, Brèthà Nemidh, or law of privileges, twenty poems called " Enan."

Fifth year.—Sixty tales, critical knowledge of adverbs, articles, and other niceties of grammar.

Sixth year.—Twenty-four great Naths, twenty-four small Naths (this was a name given to a certain kind of poems), the secret language of the poets, and seventy tales.

Seventh year.—The Brosnacha of the Sai (professor) and the Bardesy of the Bards.

Eighth year.—Prosody or Versification of the poets, meaning of obscure words (or glosses), the various kinds of poetry, the Druidical or incantatory compositions called Teinm Laeghdha, Imbas Forosnai, Dichetal di channaibh, the knowledge of Dinnseanchus or topography, and all the chief historical tales of Ireland, such as were to be recited in the presence of kings, chiefs, and goodmen.

Ninth and tenth years.—Forty Sennats, fifteen Luascas, seven Nenas, an Eochraid of sixty words with their appropriate verses, seven Truths, and six Duili Fedha.

Eleventh year.—Fifty great Anamains, fifty minor Anamains. The great Anamain was a species of poem which contained four different measures of composition, *viz.*, the Nath, the Anair, Laidh, and Eman, and was composed by an Ollamg only.

Twelfth year. Six score great Ceatals (measured addresses or Orations) and the four arts of poetry, *viz.*, Laidcuin Mac Barceda's art ; Ua Crotta's art, O'Briene's art, and Beg's art.

J. W. Arch, in *Written Records of the Cwmry*, says that the Druids, unlike the hereditary priest castes of the Eastern world, owed their sacro-sanct character, not to blood and race, but to a long continued course of instruction, from which they were supposed to emerge a wiser, more sober, a better informed, and a more learned class than any other portion of the community.

The presiding officers in all Druidical ceremonies and Mysteries were three in number. They were named Cadeiriaith, the Principal, who was stationed in the East ; Goronwy, who represented the moon, and occupied a position in the West ; and Fleidwr Flam, the representative of the meridian sun, and was stationed in the South. Other subordinate officers were necessary for the due celebration of the mysteries. The principal of these were Sywedyad, or the mystagogue, who assisted the Arch-Druid in the illustration, and Ys yw wedydd, the revealer of secrets, who communicated to the initiated the mysterious tokens of the Order and their meaning. The two great lights of heaven were of no little importance in these rites and ceremonies. The Sun was a symbol of the superior god Hu, because he is the great source of light and the ruler of the day. The mild sovereign of the night typified the supreme goddess Ceridwen, in whose sacred cauldron were involved all the mysteries of this religion.

The Druids ascribed the origin of all things to three principles, therefore during the initiation ceremony three hymns were chanted to the Deity. These hymns were called by the name of Trigaranos, or " the triple crane."

"The Druids," says Hollinshead, "applied themselves as earnestly to the study of philosophy, as well natural as moral, that they were held in no small reverence of the people, as they were both accounted and known to be men of the most perfect life and innocence, by means whereof their authority daily so far increased that, finally, judgments in the most doubtful matters were committed unto their determination, offenders by their discretion punished, and such as had well deserved accordingly by their appointments rewarded. Moreover, such as refused to obey their decrees and ordinances were by them excommunicated, so that no creature durst once keep company with such till they were reconciled again and by the same Druids absolved."

Rowlands, in *Mona Antiqua*, bears testimony to the nature of the studies pursued : "The Druids considered nature in her largest extent ; in her systems and in her motions ; in her magnitude and powers ; in all which they seemed to cabbalize. Their philosophy was so comprehensive as to take in, with the theory of nature, astronomy, geometry, medicine, and natural magic, and all this upon the corpuscularian hypothesis."

They were very studious of the virtues of plants and herbs, and were exceedingly partial to the vervaine, which they used in casting lots and foretelling events. This was gathered at the rise of the Dog-star, and, before digging it up, they described a circle around it. It was gathered with the left hand into a clean, new napkin, the right hand being covered with a sacred vestment kept specially for that purpose. The plant was waved aloft after it was separated from the ground. It was infused in wine and then used as an antidote to the bite of serpents. It was also supposed to possess the virtue of fascination. Medea, in Sophocles, it will be remembered, is described as gathering her magic herbs with a brazen hook. In gathering the selago, a kind of hedge hyssop, the Chief Druid had to be clothed in white, as an emblem of internal purity, after bathing himself in clean water. The herb was gathered in bare feet and the gathering was preceded by participation in a sacrament of bread and wine. The Druids looked upon this herb as a preservative against all misfortune, and the smoke of it was regarded as an excellent cure for, as also a preservative against, sore eyes. The act of going with naked feet was always considered to be a token of humility and reverence, and the priests in the temple worship always officiated with feet uncovered, although frequently it was regarded as inimical to their health. The command thus given to Moses did not represent the civil and legal ceremony of putting off the shoes, as the Israelites were subsequently directed to do, when they renounced any bargain or contract (Deut. xxv, 9; Ruth iv, 3); nor yet the sign of grief and sorrow, as when David entered into Jerusalem barefooted (II Samuel xii, 30); but it was enjoined that Moses might approach that sacred place with reverence and godly fear, as if it had been a temple consecrated to divine worship. There was another herb, called by the Gauls " samolus," which grew in moist places and had to be gathered with the left hand while fasting. He who gathered it must not look upon it before it was plucked, and he was not allowed to place it anywhere save in the canals or places where beasts drank, bruising it before depositing it. It was held to be a prevention of disease among swine and oxen.

The three degrees of Ovate, Bard, and Druid were regarded as equal in importance, though not in privilege, and they were distinct in purpose. There is little doubt that knowledge was confined mainly, if not altogether, to the professed Druids, and it was one of their tenets that the Arcana of the Sciences must not be committed to writing, but to the memory. Cæsar says that the Druids disputed largely upon subjects of natural philosophy and instructed the youth of the land in the rudiments of learning. By some writers the Druids are credited with a knowledge of the telescope, though this opinion is based mainly upon the statement of Diodorus Siculus, who says that in an island west of Celtæ the Druids brought the sun and moon near to them. Hecatæus, however, informs us that they taught the existence of the lunar mountains. The fact that the Milky Way consisted of small stars was known to the ancients is often adduced in support of the claim to the antiquity of the telescope.

Idris the giant, a pre-Christian astronomer, is said to have pursued his study of the science of astronomy from the apex of one of the loftiest mountains in North Wales, which, in consequence, received the name which it now bears—Cader Idris, or the Chair of Idris. The Druids encouraged the study of Anatomy to such an extent that one of their doctors named Herophilus is said to have delivered lectures on the bodies of more than seven hundred men in order to reveal the secrets and wonders of the human frame. Diodorus Siculus is responsible for the statement that the Druids were the Gaulish philosophers and divines, and were held in great veneration, and that it was not lawful to perform any sacrifices except in the presence of at least one of these philosophers.

Sir Norman Lockyer writes :

"The people who honoured us with their presence here in Britain some four thousand years ago had evidently, some way or other, had communicated to them a very complete Egyptian culture, and they determined their time of night just in the same way that the Egyptians did, only of course, there was a great difference between the latitude of 25° in Egypt and 50° in Cornwall. They could not observe the same stars for the same purpose. They observed the stars which served their purpose for one thousand years or so. These stars were Capella and Arcturus."

P. W. Joyce, in his *Social History of Ancient Ireland*, says that in pagan times the Druids were the exclusive possessors of whatever learning was then known, and combined in themselves all the learned professions, being " not only Druids, or priests, but judges, prophets, historians, poets, and even physicians." He might have added " and instructors of youth," since education was entirely in their hands. No one was capable of public employment who had not been educated under a Druid. Children were brought up and educated away from their parents until they reached the age of fourteen. Even St. Columba began his education under a Druid, and so great was the veneration paid to the Druids for the knowledge they possessed that it became a kind of adage with respect to anything that was deemed mysterious or beyond ordinary ken : " No one knows but God and the holy Druids."

There is a legend concerning St. Columba and a Druid which runs : " Now when the time for reading came to him, the clerk went to a certain prophet (*faidh*, or Druid) who abode in the land to ask him when the boy ought to begin. When the prophet had scanned the sky, he said : ' Write an alphabet for him now.' The alphabet was written on a cake, and St. Columba consumed the cake on this wise, half to the east of a water and half to the west of a water. Said the prophet : ' So shall this child's territory be, half to the east of the sea and half to the west of the sea.' " This is claimed to have reference to Columba's work in Iona and among the Picts, *i.e.*, one half in Ireland and the other half in Scotland.

The Druids were the intermediaries between the people and the spiritual world, and the people believed that their priests could protect them from the malice of evilly-disposed spirits of every kind. The authority possessed by the Druids is easily understood when it is remembered that they were possessed of more knowledge and learning than any other class of men in the country. " They were," says Rowlands, in *Mona Antiqua Restorata*, " men of thought and speculation, whose chief province was to enlarge the bounds of knowledge, as their fellows were to do those of empire into what country or climate soever they came."

Kings had each ever about them a Druid for prayer and sacrifice, who was also a judge for determining controversies, although each king had a civil judge besides. At the court of Conchobar, king of Ulster, no one had the right to speak before the Druid had spoken. Cathbu, or Cathbad, a Druid once attached to that court, was accompanied by a hundred youths, students of his art. After the introduction and adoption of Christianity, the Druid was succeeded by a bishop or priest, just as the Druidesses at Kildare were succeeded by the Briggintine Nuns. Martin, who wrote his *Description of the Western Islands of Scotland* in 1703, tells us that :

" Every great family of the Western Islands had a Chief Druid who foretold future events and decided all causes, civil and ecclesiastical. It is reported of them that they wrought in the night time and rested all day. Before the Britons engaged in battle the Chief Druid harangued the army to excite their courage. He was placed on an eminence whence he addressed himself to all standing about him, putting them in mind of all great things that were performed by the valour of their ancestors, raised their hopes with the noble rewards of honour and victory, and dispelled their fears by all the topics that natural courage could suggest. After this harangue the army gave a general shout and then charged the enemy stoutly."

In the time of Tacitus the Gallic Druids prophesied that the burning of the Capitol signified the approaching fall of the Roman Empire.

The position of Arch Druid was, as already stated, at one time held by Divitiacus, the Eduan, the intimate acquaintance and friend of Cæsar, who is believed to have inspired the account of Druidism given by Cæsar in *De Bello Gallico*. The British Arch Druid is said to have had his residence in the Isle of Anglesey, in or near to Llaniden. There the name of Tre'r Dryw, or Druidstown, is still preserved, and there are also still there some of the massive stone structures which are associated invariably with Druidism. The courts of the Arch Druids were held at Drewson or Druidstown. A short distance from the road leading from Killiney to Bray there stands a chair formed of large blocks of granite, which is called " The Druid's Judgment Seat." On occasions of ceremony the Arch Druid's head was surrounded by an oaken garland, surmounted by a tiara composed of adder stones encased in gold. When at the altar he wore a white surplice, fastened on the shoulder by a golden brooch. In Ireland there appears to have been no chief Druid, nor even a Druidical hierarchy or corporation. The Druids acted singly or in twos and threes. They were married and each lived with his family in his own house.

The principal seat of the French Druids was at Chartres, the residence of the Gallic Arch Druid, at which place also the annual convention of Gallic—and some say the British—Druids was held. There was also a large Druidic settlement at Marseilles. It was here that Cæsar, in order to put an end to Druidism in Gaul, ordered the trees to be felled.

Dr. John Jamieson, in his *Historical Account of the Ancient Culdees of Iona*, published in 1870, says that twenty years previously there was living in the parish of Moulin an old man who, although very regular in his devotions, never addressed the Supreme Being by any other title than that of Arch Druid. He quotes this as an illustration of the firm hold which ancient superstition takes of the mind.

Druids had the privilege of wearing six colours in their robes, and their tunics reached to their heels, while the tunics of others reached only to the knee. Kings and queens reserved to themselves the right of wearing robes of seven colours ; lords and ladies five colours ; governors of fortresses, four ; young gentlemen of quality, three ; soldiers, two ; and the common people, one colour. When the Druids were officiating in their official capacity they each wore a white robe, emblematic of holiness as well as of the sun. When officiating as a judge the Druid wore two white robes, fastened with a girdle, surmounted by his Druid's egg encased in gold, and wore round his neck the breastplate of judgment, which was supposed to press upon his breast should he give utterance to a false or corrupt judgment. One is reminded by this breastplate of the wonderful collar referred to in Irish lore and legend, known as the Jadh Morain. This collar was attended with a very surprising virtue, for if it was placed on the neck of a judge who intended to pronounce a false judgment it would immediately shrink and almost stop the breath ; but if the person that wore it changed his resolution and resolved to be just in his sentence, it would instantly enlarge itself and hang loose about the neck. This miraculous collar was also used to prove the integrity of the witnesses and if it were tied about the neck of a person who designed to give false testimony it would shrink close and extort the truth or continue contracting until it had throttled him. From this practice arose the custom, in the judicature of the kingdom, for the judge, when he suspected the veracity of a witness, to charge him solemnly to speak the truth, for his life was in danger if he did not, because the fatal collar, the Jadh Morain, was about his neck and would inevitably proceed to execution.

Vallancey, in *Collect. de Reb. Hibern.* tells of one of the Druidical breastplates found twelve feet deep in a turf bog in the county of Limerick. It was made of thin plated gold chased in a neat and workmanlike manner : the breast plate was single but the hemispherical ornaments at the top were lined throughout with another thin plate of pure gold ; they were less exposed to injury when on the breast than when on the lower part. About the centre of each was a small hole in the lining to receive the ring of a chain that suspended it around the neck, and in the centre in front were two small conical pillars of solid gold, highly polished. The whole weighed twenty-two golden guineas. Another was also found in County Longford and sold for twenty-six guineas.

The Druid sitting as judge also wore a golden tiara upon his head and two official rings on his right hand fingers. On ordinary occasions the cap worn by the Druid had on the front a golden representation of the sun under a half moon of silver, supported by two Druids, one at each cusp, in an inclined position. The Irish Druid wore a long crimson robe over which was a shorter one, and suspended at his side was his Druid's knife. He wore a white cap, in shape and appearance like a fan : it was ornamented with a gold plate. The British Arch-Druid wore over his ordinary robes a white mantle edged with gold ; around his neck was a golden chain from which was suspended a golden plate, inscribed with the words : " The gods require sacrifice." J. C. Walker, in his *Historical Essay on the Dress of the Irish*, says that when the Druids were employed in sacrifice and other solemn ceremonies they wore, behind an oak-leaved crown, a golden crescent, with buttons at the extremities, through which a string was drawn that served to fasten it behind. Several of these crescents have been found in Irish bogs. The dress of the Druids was uniformly and universally a white garment, emblematic of the affected purity of their mind. In order to render their appearance more venerable and imposing they encouraged their beards to flow on their breasts.

> " His seemly beard, to grace his form bestow'd,
> Descending decent, on his bosom flow'd ;
> His robe of purest white, though rudely join'd
> Yet showed an emblem of the purest mind ;
> Stern virtue, beaming in his eye, controul'd
> Each wayward purpose, and o'eraw'd the bold."

It is also established that in many instances priesthood was hereditary and that a special name was given to a priestly family. Thus the following was written by Ausonius, in honour of Attius Patera.

Stonehenge,
from a water-colour drawing by Constable
(Victoria and Albert Museum).

" Tu Bajocassis stirpe Druidarum satus
    (Si fama non fallit fidem)
BELENI sacratum ducis e Templo genus :
    Et inde vobis nomina ;
Tibi PATERAE (sic Ministros nuncupant
    Apollinaris Mistyci.)
Fratri-Patrique nomen à Phœbo datum
    Natoque de Delphis tuo."

From this verse it is clear that all the family of Attius had a particular name, owing to their deriving their origin from the Druids of
Bayeux, and that they were also devoted to the Mysteries of Belenus.
The new name of Attius was Patera : that of his father and brother
was derived from Phæbus. The name of the son of Attius was Delphidus,
as we read later :

" Facunde, docte, lingua et ingenio celer,
    Jocis amæne, Delphidi."

Here is another verse from Ausonius in confirmation :

" Nec reticedo senem
    Nominie Phœbtium,
    Qui Beleni ædituus
    Nil opis inde tulit :
    Sed tamen, ut placitum,
    Stirpe satus Druidum,
    Gentis Aremoricæ,
    Burdigalæ Cathedram
    Nati opera obtinuit.
    Et tu Concordi,
    Qui profugus patria
    Mutasti sterilem
    Urbe alia cathedram,
    Et libertina, etc."

The following interesting narrative appears in Wilson's *Prehistoric
Annals of Scotland :*

" In the museum of the Phrenological Society of Edinburgh
may be found an interesting group of six skulls brought from the
sacred isle of Iona, and each marked as the " skull of a Druid from
the Hebrides." They were presented to the society by Mr. Donald
Gregory, secretary of the Society of Antiquaries of Scotland and of
the Iona Club, who procured them under the following circumstances.
The institution of a Scottish Club, specially established for the
investigation of the history, antiquities, and early literature of the
Highlands of Scotland, was celebrated at a meeting held on the
island of Iona, upon the 7th September, 1833, when the sepulchres

of the Scottish kings were explored. The results were detailed by Mr. Gregory in the following letter addressed to Mr. Robert Cox, ot the Edinburgh Philological Society.

" ' Along with this you will receive six ancient skulls procured under the following circumstances. There is a place here called *Cladh na Druineach*, *i.e.*, the burial place of the Druids, in which I have caused some deep cuts to be made. An incredible quantity of human bones has been found : and as it is perfectly certain that this place has never been used as a Christian churchyard, or as a place of interment at all, since the establishment of Christianity here by St. Columba, there can be no doubt of the antiquity of the skulls now sent. They are by every one here firmly believed to be the skulls of the Druids, who were probably interred here from distant parts as well as from the neighbourhood, on account of the sanctity of the island, which formerly bore the name of *Innis na Druineach*, or the Druids' Isle. The six skulls herewith sent were selected with care by myself from a much larger number. One you will observe is higher in the forehead than the rest. But this is an exception : for I am satisfied—and others whose attention I directed to the matter agree with me—that the general character of the skulls is a low forehead, and a considerable breadth in the upper and posterior parts of the head, which you will undoubtedly readily perceive. Although, with the exception mentioned, these skulls have the same general character (as far as I can judge), yet there are sufficient differences in the individuals to make them of considerable interest to the phrenologist. I must not omit to mention that the present race in the islands appear to have much better foreheads than the Druids, and independent of intellect and intelligence, are perhaps above the average of the Highlanders and islanders. Some of the skulls did not present such strong individual character as those sent and were more quickly developed. But as I was limited in the number to be taken, I preferred choosing well-marked skulls, particularly as the general character of the whole was so much the same."

The mode of excommunication from the community was to expose the erring member to a naked weapon. The Bards had a special ceremony for the degradation of their convicted brethren. It took place at a Gorsedd, when the assembled Bards placed their caps on their heads. One deputed for the office unsheathed his sword, uplifted it, and named the delinquent aloud three times, adding on the last occasion the words : " The sword is naked against him." After these words were pronounced the offender was expelled, never to be re-admitted, and he became known as " a man deprived of privilege and exposed to warfare."

CHAPTER IV

BARDS AND VATES

" You, too, ye bards, whom sacred raptures fire
To chant your heroes in your country's lyre—
Who consecrate in your immortal strain
Brave patient souls, in righteous battle slain—
Securely now the tuneful task renew,
And noblest themes in deathless songs pursue."
                                LUCAN. *Pharsalia*.

                                " Yonder grots
Are tenanted by Bards, who nightly thence,
Rob'd in their flowing vests of innocent white,
Descend, with harps that glitter to the moon,
Hymning immortal strains. The spirits of air,
Of earth, of water, nay of heav'n itself,
Do listen to their lay : and oft, 'tis said,
In visible shapes dance they a magic round
To the high minstrelsy."
                                MASON. *Caractacus*.

Before an aspirant to the priesthood could attain to that exalted rank, he had to pass through the two preliminary and definite degrees of Bard and Vate, or Ovate. Many of the youth of the land, however, who entered the service of the temple, did so with the express intention of remaining in the ranks of one or other of these two Orders. It is said that originally there was but one rank, which went by the name of Gwyddoniaeth, with no legal privileges or immunities. Vallancey is of opinion that the Bards were the original Celtic priests, so called from their chanting to the deities in their sacred office. This opinion is also held by Borlase. The division into Druids, Bards, and Ovates came later, when each had its peculiar honours and duties, and all were equally endowed and protected by the state. The term " Bard " is said by some to have been derived from one Bardus, the fifth king of Britain, *circa* 2082, A.M., and who was a man famous for the invention of verses and music. Verse was anciently the principal vehicle for conveying information. The Hindoo Arithmetic is in verse. The most ancient of the Cambrian Bards taught in verse and preserved the records of transactions through the medium of rhyme and measure, and when laws were to be enacted and historic facts preserved, they were thrown into triadic form. Toland asserts that the Bards did not belong to the body of the Druids. But against his opinion must be placed the categorical statements of Cæsar, Strabo, and others. Irish history also relates that the same Amergin, who, at the Milesian invasion, assumed the dignity of Arch Druid, took upon him also the office of Ard-Filea, or Chief Bard.

The initial step for aspirants to any of the three Orders or Degrees was to enrol among the Awenyddion, or Disciples—a preliminary, or fourth class. The first requisite for admission as a disciple was unimpeachable moral character, for it was indispensably necessary that the candidate, above all things, should be above any criticism as to character and conduct. Nor was it permitted for one to be admitted to the possession of any of the secrets of the various degrees until his understanding, affections, morals, and principles had undergone severe trials. His passions and tendencies were watched closely and tested when he was least aware of the fact. At all times, in all places, and on every possible occasion, there was an eye, unknown to him, fixed continually upon his actions, and from the knowledge thus obtained of his head and heart, indeed, of his very soul, an estimate was made of his inclinations and mental and spiritual abilities, and agreeable to the approbation given, and in the manner and degree most suitable, he was initiated by graduating steps into the mysteries and instructed in the doctrine and practices of Druidism.

Poseidonius, the Stoic of Rhodes, who travelled in Gaul about B.C. 100, was the first to mention the Bards. He describes them as " parasites," who attended the Celtic warriors, even on their warlike expeditions, to celebrate their praises. The Bards, however, he says, were not barbarians among barbarians : they were men of letters.

Vallancey says that the Vates, or Prophets, were called Baidh, Vaith, Vaithoir, or Phattoir. The name was written *Vaedh* by the Arabs, and *Outeis* by the Greeks. The word is thought to be derived from the Persian word *Bach*, which means " holy." *Baid* is the Chaldean *bada*. The Irish *Faithoir* is the Hebrew *ptr*, meaning " to solve an enigma." Pezron says that the word *baid* in the Gaelic language means " poet." *Barth* comes probably from the Hebrew or Chaldee word *brt*, " to sing." *Bar* is the root of the Irish *Bear la*, " speech," traces of which are found in the words " parole," " parler," " parliament."

The first Bards were called by the triad names of *Plennyd*, *Alawn*, *Gwron*, meaning " light," " harmony," and " energy." Afterwards their calling came to be held in such high esteem that they were maintained at the expense of the state, but their pride became so overbearing, their demands so extortionate, and their members so numerous that they deservedly earned, in the course of time, the mistrust and indifference even of their friends, although they retained their position after the extinction of Druidism.

Mason, in his *Caractacus*, speaks of the three Orders. After referring to the Arch Druid, he proceeds :

> " His brotherhood
> Possess the neighb'ring cliffs :
> On the left
> Reside the sage Ovades ; yonder grots
> Are tenanted by Bards."

No sacerdotal functions were performed by the Bards : these were reserved exclusively for the Derwyddon, or Druids, who were set apart for, and employed solely in the exercise of peculiarly religious functions ; and long after the conversion of the Britons to the Christian faith, the ministers of religion were called by this term.

From Anewydd, the postulate rose to the degree of Inceptor, thence to Inchoate Bard, or Bardd ; Caw, when, for the first time, he wore the band of the Order, together with a white mantle and a blue cap, ornamented with a gold crescent. When he became a fully-fledged Bard, he received the faculties to proclaim and hold a Gorsedd, admit disciples, and instruct others in the principles of religion and morality. In Ireland, the Bard wore a white mantle and a blue cap ornamented with a gold crescent. In Britain the Bard wore a uni-coloured robe of sky blue, the emblem of peace and truth. Blue was the favourite colour among the Britons from the earliest times. An old Welsh proverb runs : " True blue keeps its hue."

The Laws of Howel Dda (Howe, the good) have been published by the Record Commission, in the *Ancient Laws and Institutes of Wales*. In editing the volume, Mr. Aneurin Owen is careful to indicate on the title page the uncertainty connected with the authorship and codification of these laws. He places the oldest manuscript in the twelfth century. The laws relating to the Bards are given as follows :

> " Three branches of the art of Bardism. First, the primitive bard, or a bard licensed by privilege, having his degree and his privilege by discipleship, from an authorised teacher, who is a presiding bard ; and upon him depends every memorial of art and science, so far as they may be in his department ; as being an authorised bard of degree and privilege ; and, likewise, every memorial and record of country and kindred, in respect to marriages, and kins, and arms, and territorial divisions, and the privileges of the country and kindred of the Cymry. Second, the Ovate, having his degree under the privilege of genius and commendable sciences, which he shall exhibit authenticated, and for which he shall be able approvingly to answer before a customary and legitimate session of

bards; or, where that shall not be, before a lawful and authorised congress, under the patronage of the lord of the territory, or twelve of his judges of court, or of twelve justices of court where that is customary; and discipleship shall not be required in respect to him, nor other claim than as to authorised sciences. And this is for the purpose of protecting sciences, lest there should not be found customary teachers, and, consequently, that the sciences and art of record and wisdom should pass into oblivion, from a deficiency of systematic teachers and disciples. And, likewise, for the purpose of improving and increasing the sciences of art, by adding everything new to them, by the judgment of teachers and wise men, and thence to establish and give them authorized privilege, and also against precluding sciences of wisdom, which might spring from the natural burst of genius and intuitive invention. Third, the Druid Bard, who is to be a presiding Bard, graduated and warranted as to wisdom and sciences, and of elocution to demonstrate judgment and reason in respect to sciences; and his function is to be under the privilege of a grant by the direction and induction of a customary session, authenticated by the vote of session by ballot. And his function is to diffuse instruction and to demonstrate the sciences of wisdom and religion in the session of the bards, and in court, and in church, and in the household wherein his office is performed. And it is right and law for each of these three to have his five free erws [an erw means 'what has been tilled.' It was a measure applied exclusively to arable lands: it appears to have contained about 4,320 yards] under the privilege of the function of his art, distinct from what is due to him otherwise by the privilege of an innate Cymro; for innate privilege extinguishes no art; nor any art innate privilege."

Malkin says that the laws of Howel Dha were enacted by him and his senatorial assembly in the open air. The place where they met is as highly venerated to this day as is Runymede, near Windsor. By those laws it appears that the courts of justice, especially the supreme courts, were always held in the open air; and the king, or prince, who was accustomed to sit as supreme judge, was placed on the leeward side of a large stone fixed up for the purpose. It is very clear, from the oldest historical documents, that the early Welsh Christians, from the middle of the first to the middle of the fifth century, always met for religious worship in the open air.

Before a Bard was regarded as fully qualified to exercise all the functions of Bardism, he had to preside at Gorseddau, when, if approved, he was classed as one of the Gorseddogion.

According to the triads, there was one special Gorsedd in each of the three principal provinces. The Gorsedd was a kind of national assembly to which the majority of residents in the respective provinces resorted at appointed times for the purpose of receiving instruction. The triads state :

"The three principal Gorsedds of the Bards of the Isle of Britain : the Gorsedd of Bryn Gwyddon at Caerleon-upon-Usk, the Gorsedd of Moel Evwr, and the Gorsedd of Beiscawen."

"The three Gorsedds of entire song of the Isle of Britain : the Gorsedd of Beiscawen in Dynwal, the Gorsedd of Caer Caradog in Lloegria, and the Gorsedd of Bryn Gwyddon in Cymru."

Further particulars of their constitution and formation are given by Meyryg of Glamorgan, who says :

"A Gorsedd of the Bards of the Isle of Britain must be held in a conspicuous place, in full view of hearing of country and aristocracy, and in the face of the sun and in the eye of light ; it being unlawful to hold such meetings under cover, at night, or under any circumstances otherwise than while the sun shall be visible in the sky. . . . It is an institutional usage to form a conventional circle of stones on the summit of some conspicuous ground, so as to enclose any requisite area of greensward ; the stones being so placed as to allow sufficient space for a man to stand between two of them, except that the two stones of the circle which most directly confront the eastern sun should be sufficiently apart to allow at least ample space for three men between them ; thus affording an easy ingress to the circle."

Nine years was generally sufficient for graduation as a Bard, but his education was not considered complete, for the purposes of this graduation, until he had committed to memory 20,000 verses containing, in allegorical language, the tenets of the Druidical faith. By the term *Bard* the Welsh did not understand merely poets, but persons regularly instructed in the institutes and mysteries of the ancient British religion. The name of Bard appears to have been common in various parts of the Celtic world. In septentrional Italy, near to Milan, there was a place known as Bardomague, *champ du barde*. In Helvetia, there was a part known as Bardus, and the same name is found in Carinthie, Vienna, Styria, and Misène (Italy).

Toland says that there were often at a time a thousand Ollaws, or graduate poets, in addition to a proportionable number of inferior rhymers, all of whom lived free of any cost to themselves or their families, being encouraged in their studies and supported by the great men and nobles.

Merddin, or Merlin, as he is generally known, a Caledonian, lived in the sixth century. He was among the last of the Druidical Bards, and, in allegorical language, bewailed the decline of his religion, the pollution and cutting down of the sacred groves, and the demolition of the circular temples by the Christian missionaries. Writing on the decline and fall of Druidism and the persistence of Bardism, Blair, in his *Dissertation on the Poems of Ossian,* says :

> " So strong was the attachment of the Celtic nations to their poetry and their Bards that amidst all the changes of their government and manners, even long after the order of the Druids was extinct, and the national religion altered, the Bards continued to flourish, not as a set of strolling songsters, like the Greek Rhapsodists, in Homer's time, but as an order of men highly respected in the state, and supported by a public establishment. We find them, according to testimonies of Strabo and Diodorus, before the age of Augustus Cæsar, and we find them remaining under the same name, and exercising the same functions as of old, in Ireland, and in the north of Scotland, almost down to our own times."

In his work, *Musical and Poetical Relics of the Welsh Bards,* Edward Jones gives a detailed description of the divisions of the Welsh Bards. He states that they were divided into three classes and that the subjects of which they treated were as follows. The duties of the Clêrŵyr were, To satirize, ridicule or taunt, to mimick, to sue for or intreat, to lampoon, and to reproach. Two Clêrŵyr usually stood before the company, one to give in rhyme at the other's extempore, to excite mirth and laughter with their witty quibbles. The duties of the Teulûwr, or family songster, or Bard of domestic eloquence, were to dwell with and solace his patron, to divert and enliven the time by mirth and pleasantry, to infuse liberality, to receive guests, and to solicit in a polite, becoming manner. The poets of this class composed extempore as well as in writing. They also sang love songs, or amatory verses, in every kind of metre, with delicacy and elegance. The duties of the Prydd were to teach aright, to sing aright, and to judge properly of all things. His three excellencies were to satirize without ribaldry, to commend a married woman without obscenity and to address men suitably to their calling. He was to commend a pleasant disposition of mind, to praise liberality, to celebrate the science of music and the art of poetry, to delight his hearers, to oppose the bitter invective of the Clêrŵyr and, in so doing, to avoid satirizing any other person, to be obedient, liberal, chaste, to make himself perfectly beloved, to avoid the seven deadly sins : extortion, theft, pride, fornication, gluttony, indolence, and envy, because these things destroy the genius, memory, and imagination of the poet.

Other writers classify the Bards as (1) Privardh, or Chronologers ; (2) Posvardh, or Heralds ; and (3) Aruyvardh, or Comic or Satirical Bards.

The Constitutions of the Irish Bards differed somewhat from those of the British, and Joseph Cooper Walker, in *Historical Memoirs of the Irish Bards*, gives a detailed account of the Irish organization. When the student had finished his course, an honorary cap called *Barred* (from which some think the name *Bard* was derived) and the degree of *Ollamh*, or Doctor, were conferred. The young Bard then decided his choice of a profession : whether he would pursue his studies and seek for admission into the Order of Druids, or whether he would remain as a Bard. If he decided upon the latter, he had to become a Filea, a Breitheamh, or a Seanacha, according to his birth.

The *Filidhe*, or *Ollamhain Re-Dan*, were the poets who turned the tenets of religion into verse, who animated the troops before and during engagements with martial odes, raised the war song, celebrated valorous deeds, and wrote the birthday odes and epithalamiums of the chieftains and princes. They were the heralds and constant attendants in the field of battles and the chiefs whom they served, marching at the head of their armies, arrayed in white flowing robes. The *Breitheamhain* (Brehons) or legislative Bards promulgated the laws in a kind of recitative chant. The *Seanachidhe* were antiquaries, genealogists, and historians. They recorded remarkable events and preserved the genealogies of their patrons in a kind of unpoetical stanza. Each province, prince, and chief had a Seancha. In addition to these three Orders of Bards, there was another of an inferior kind, known as *Oirfidigh*, comprising the Cleananaigh, Crutairigh, Ciotairigh, Tiompanach, and Cuilleannach, all of whom took their names from the instruments on which they played. The head of this Order was called Ollamh-le-Ceol. Their profession, as well as that of the higher classes of Bards, was hereditary, just as the office of piper in Scotland. When a prince or chief fell in battle, or died in the course of nature, " the stones of his fame " were raised amidst the voices of the Bards. The Druids having performed the rites prescribed by religion, and the pedigree of the deceased having been recited aloud by the Seanacha—the Caione, or funeral song, composed by the Filea of the departed and set to music by one of his Oirfidigh was sung in recitative over his grave by a Racaraide (or Rhapsodist), the symphonic parts being performed by minstrels, and the responses given by Oirfidigh. Macpherson gives an illustration of the Caione sung over Circullin's tomb, which was as follows :

> " By the dark rolling waves of Légo, they raised the hero's tomb—Luäth, at a distance, lies, the companions of Cuchullin, at the chance. Blest be thy soul, son of Semo : thou wert mighty in battle. Thy strength was the strength of a stream : thy speed like the eagle's wing. Thy path in the battle was terrible : the steps

of death were behind thy sword.   Blest be thy soul, son of Semo:
car-borne chief of Dunscaick!

"Thou has not fallen by the sword of the mighty, neither was
thy blood on the spear of the valiant.   The arrow came, like the
sting of death in a blast: nor did the feeble hand, which drew the
bow, perceive it.   Peace to thy soul in thy cave, chief of the isle
of Mist!"

Ollamh Fodhla, who became king of Ireland in A.M. 3236, made the
Order of Bards his peculiar care.   He ordained that none but young
men of genius and noble descent should be admitted to the Order;
that the profession should be hereditary, but when a Bard died, his
estate was to devolve, not to his eldest son, but to such of his family as
had displayed the most distinguished talents for poetry and music;
that every Ard-Filea might retain thirty inferior Bards as his attendants,
and a Bard of the second class be allowed a retinue of fifteen.   He also
furnished a university at Teamor, called Mur-Ollavan, where the powers
of verse and song, the mysteries of metrical cadence and vocal harmony
were taught.   Those bards on whom the highest degree in this seminary
was conferred preceded all others of the same rank in every part of the
kingdom.   He invited to his palace at Eamanis a representative gathering
of Bards where their laws were codified and the several *Filean graduatus*
were instituted.   They were as follows: 1, The Fochlucan; 2, Mac-
fuirmidh; 3, Doss; 4, Canaith; 5, Cli; 6, Anstruth; and 7, Ollamh.
In no Filean College from this period could a Bard obtain the diploma of
Ollamh, or Doctor, till he had passed through the first six of those degrees,
but when the honour was conferred upon him, he was considered as
qualified for any office in the state, and frequently became the minister,
friend, and confidant of princes.

The Brehon laws fixed the studies and obligations of each degree,
and according to these, the Fochluchan was to be able to repeat thirty
tales, if required, upon any of the festivals, or public meetings.   His
reward was two heifers or one large cow.   He was to be attended for one
day and supplied with all kinds of necessaries; and if on a journey, he
was to be attended by two men for five days.   He was also to be furnished
with a horse and a greyhound.   The Mac-Fuirmidh was to repeat forty
tales, if required, and his reward was forty milk cows.   He was also to
be attended for three days and supplied with all kinds of necessaries;
and to be waited on by three attendants on all festivals and public
meetings.   The Doss was to repeat fifty stories, if required.   His rewards
were variable, according to the nature of the poems or compositions, and
varied from one to five cows.   He was to be attended by four learned men
and he and his attendants supplied with all kinds of necessaries.   The
Canaith was rewarded in accordance with the nature of the compositions

he recited. He was attended by six men on all public occasions and
supplied with all necessaries for eight days ; and protected from all
accusations on account of debts or any other charge. The Cli was
rewarded with five cows and ten heifers. He was attended by eight
students in poetry and entertained for ten days, he and his attendants
being supplied with necessaries. The Anstruth was to repeat for the
Assembly half as many stories of times past as an Ollamh. His reward
was twenty kine. He was attended by twelve students in his own science,
entertained for fifteen days, and he and his attendants supplied with all
necessaries. The Ollamh, or Chief Doctor, was skilled in the four principal branches of poetry, in each of which he had to study for three years.
He was to have in memory 350 stories to entertain the Assembly. His
reward was twenty milk cows and he was attended by twenty-four men
on all occasions, whether at home or abroad, who were also to protect
him if occasion required. And he and all his attendants were to be
supplied with all kinds of necessaries for a month.

Ollamh Fodhla instituted a parliament to be held at Tara once in
every three years to revise the laws in accordance with the exigencies of
the times. This parliament was composed of the nobility, the Druids,
the poets, and the historiographers.

> " The learned Ollamh Fodhla first ordained
> The great assembly, where the nobles met,
> And priests, and poets, and philosophers,
> To make new laws, and to correct the old,
> And to advance the honour of his country."

Eochoid ô Flinn, a poet of the seventh century, composed the
following poem " On the Triennial Convention at Tara."

> " Once in three years the great convention sate,
> And for the public happiness debate ;
> The king was seated on a royal throne,
> And in his face majestic greatness shone.
> A monarch for heroic deeds design'd ;
> For noble acts become a noble mind ;
> About him, summon'd by his strict command,
> The peers, the priests, and commons of the land,
> In princely state and solemn order stand.
> The poets, likewise, are indulg'd a place,
> And men of learning the assembly grace.
> Here ev'ry member dares the truth assert,
> He scorns the false and double-dealing part,
> (For a true patriot's soul disdains the trimmer's art).
> Here love and union ev'ry look confess'd,
> And love and justice beat in ev'ry breast.

Justice by nothing bias'd or inclined,
Is deaf to pity, to temptation blind :
For here with stern and steady rule she sways,
And flagrant crimes with certain vengeance pays ;
The monarch, ever jealous of his state,
Inflexibly decrees th' offender's fate :
Tho' just, yet so indulgently severe,
Like heaven, he pities those he cannot spare."

It was here that the youth were instructed in poetry and music and initiated into the mysteries of " the hidden harmony of the universe." Tara was for centuries the great Irish stronghold of Druidism. At a National Assembly, or Parliament, at Drumoat, in Londonderry, in A.D. 597, under Aidus Animrens, a Christian king, it was decreed that for the better preservation of their genealogies and the purity of their language, the supreme monarch and the subordinate kings, with every lord of a cantred, should entertain a poet of his own, no more being allowed by the ancient law of the island, and that upon each of these and their posterity a portion of land free of duties should be settled for ever ; that for encouraging the learning these poets professed, public schools should be appointed and endowed under national inspection and that the monarch's own Bard should be arch-poet and have superintendency over the others. This office of domestic bard is one found in the earliest historic times among Indo-European nations : there are many items of evidence which show an intimate connection between singers, story-tellers, and the like, and the priesthoods in the early forms of religion. Many of these practised to a high degree the cultivation of the memory in order that the rites, formulæ, poems, and tales of their religion might be handed down from generation to generation.

The Bard was recognised as the sacred herald of peace, under the title of *Bardd Ynys Prudain*, or " Bard of the Isle of Britain." The members of the Order made hymns for the temple, but this was the extent of their temple duties. In Ireland, there were Bardic colleges at Clogher, Armagh, Lismore, and Tamar. Aithan, the son of Conachar, was the chief Bard, or laureate, of Arth, or Art, king of Ireland. On the death of that monarch, he accompanied his son and successor as Chief Bard. It is believed that originally the Bards were Celtic priests, and that it was not until their office was usurped by the Druids that they became mere poets, heralds, and chanters to the Drui.

The voice of the Bard caused instant attention if heard by armies in the heat of action, both sides immediately desisting from fighting, so that the appearance of a Bard operated as a modern flag of truce. His word was to be credited in preference to that of any other person whatever. According to the old Welsh laws, whoever even slightly injured a Bard was to be fined six sows and one hundred and twenty pence. A serious assault on a Bard was to be visited with severe punishment and a fine of one hundred and twenty cows. In Ireland, to kill a Bard was a crime of the highest degree, while to seize his estate was deemed an act of sacrilege.

Bardism inculcated free investigation of all matters contributing to the attainment of truth and wisdom, grounded upon the aphorism : " To believe nothing and to believe everything," that is, " to believe everything supported by reason and proof and nothing without." The Bard was, however, to be bold in the cause of truth, in accordance with his motto : " The Truth in opposition to the world."

From the Triads of Dynwal Moelmud, who is said to have written about four hundred years before the Christian era, we learn that :

" There are three distinguished characters of the art of Bardism. First, the chief Bard or the free privileged Bard, who obtains his dignity and privilege through discipline under a master duly author- ised, being a conventional bard. He must preserve every record of the arts and sciences whilst he should continue in his office of Bard regularly inducted in dignity and privilege. He must also keep every record and memorial of the country and tribe respecting marriage, pedigrees, arms, inheritances, and privileges of the country and tribe of the Cambrians. The second is the Ovate, who obtains his dignity according to the privilege of public genius and praise- worthy sciences, by fully proving that he understands them before the customary and honourable convention of the Bards, or where there is no such convention, before a legal sessions guaranteed by the tribe of the district ; or before twelve of the judges of his court, or before twelve juniors of the court in the customary manner. The Ovate is not to be interrogated respecting any regular discipline, through which he may have passed nor respecting anything else, except that his views of the sciences be strictly accurate. And this is done for the purpose of protecting the sciences where the regular instructions are not found, and where the sciences and arts of record and wisdom are in danger of being totally lost by the failure of organised teachers and skilful masters. Beside they are privileged for the purpose of improving and enlarging the arts by submitting every new experience respecting them to the judgment of masters and wise men, so that they may establish them and annex the common privileges ; and also lest the sciences of wisdom may be deprived of the knowledge that arises from the natural bursts of poetic genius and the energies of inventions. The third is the Druid-Bard, who must be a graduated conventional-Bard, and be inducted in wisdom and the sciences, and be able to communicate

G

his judgment and views respecting them.   He is raised to this office according to the privilege granted by reason and the tribe of the customary Convention and is elected by ballot, which election is guaranteed by the vote of the Convention.   His office is to impart instruction and to teach the sciences of wisdom and virtue in the Convention of the Bards, in the court, the sacred place, and in every family where he has his office in full privilege.   Each of these three is entitled by equity and law to five acres of free land according to his privilege as a professor of the authorised arts, besides what belongs to him by his privilege as a free-born Cambrian, for the privilege by the arts does not abrogate that by nature, nor that by nature what the arts produce."

The Triads contain a great number of memoranda of remarkable events which are said to have taken place among the Ancient Britons, but are entirely deficient in the matter of dates, as instanced in the following examples :

" There were three awful events in the Isle of Britain ; the first was the bursting of the Lake of Floods, and the rushing of an inundation over all the lands, until all persons were destroyed, except Dwyvan and Dwyvack, who escaped in an open vessel and from them the Isle of Britain was re-peopled."

In the most ancient songs of the Bards the naked vessel without sails by which the island of Britain was constantly alluded to was a ship preserving what was left of the inhabitants of the old world. *Dwyvan* and *Dwyvach* signify in the Welsh language, " the godlike man and woman."   The former was also called *Dyglan*, " son of the sea," and *Hu Gadarn*, " the mighty inspector."   He was thus described by one of the ancient Bards :

" Hu Gadarn, the sovereign, the ready protector,
    A King, distributing the wine, and the renown,
    The Emperor of the land and seas,
    And the life of all in the world was he,
    After the deluge, he held
    The strong beam'd plough, active and excellent :
    Thus did our Lord of stimulating genius,
    That he might show to the proud man, and to the humbly wise
    The most approv'd art, with the faithful father."

Another of these historical Triads runs :

" The three inventors of song and record of the Kymry nation : Gwyddon Genhedon, who was the first in the world that composed vocal song ; Hu the Mighty, who first applied vocal song to strengthen memory and record ; and Tydain, the father of poetic genius, who first conferred art on poetic song and made it the medium of record.

From what was done by these three men, originated Bards and Bardism; and the privileges and institutes of these things were organised by the three primary Bards, Plenydd, Alawn, and Gwron." There is another Triad which runs :

" There are three pillars of the nation of the Isle of Britain. The first was Hu, the Mighty, who brought the nation of the Kymry first to the Isle of Britain ; and they came over from the Hazy Sea to the Isle of Britain and to Armorica, where they settled. The second was Prydain, the son of Aedd, the Great, who first organised a social state and sovereignty in Britain ; for, before that time there was no justice but what was done by favour, nor any law except that of supreme force. The third was Dyvwall Moelmud, for he first made arrangements respecting the laws, maxims, customs, and privileges of the country and tribe. And on account of these three reasons they were called the three pillars of the nation of the Kymry." Two others of a similar character are :

" There were three social tribes of the Isle of Britain. The first was the tribe of the Kymry, who came to the Isle of Britain with Hu, the Mighty, because he would not possess a country and land by fighting and pursuit, but by justice and tranquillity. The second was the tribe of the Lloegrians, who came from Gascony, and they were descended from the primitive tribe of the Kymry. These were called the three peaceful tribes, because they came by mutual consent and tranquillity ; and these tribes were descended from the primitive tribe of the Kymry, and they had all three the same language and speech.

" There were three refuge-seeking tribes that came to the Isle of Britain ; and they came under the peace and permission of the tribe of the Kymry, without arms and without opposition. The first was the tribe of the Caledonians in the north. The second was the Irish tribe, who dwell in the Highlands of Scotland. The third were the people of Galedin, who when their country was drowned, came in naked vessels to the Isle of Wight, where they had land granted to them by the tribe of Kymry. They had no privilege of claim in the Isle of Britain, but they had land and protection assigned to them under certain limitations ; and it was stipulated that they should not possess the rank of native Kymry, until the ninth of their lineal descendants."

The Bards were in the habit of decorating their tribunals with plants and herbs suitable to the season and suggestive of some moral truth in religious doctrine. These were :

1. The trefoil for Alban Eilir, or the vernal equinox ;
2. The vervain for Alban Hervin, or the summer solstice ;

3. Ears of wheat for Alban Elved, or the autumnal equinox ;
4. Mistletoe for Alban Arthvan, or the winter equinox.

The principle of the Bardic *Memoria Technica* was the number three,
and religious, scientific, and historical facts were committed to memory
under this form of Triads, of which various discoveries have been made
and compiled, particularly of the tenth, twelfth, thirteenth, and fourteenth
centuries.   The Bards brought this system of acquiring knowledge to
the highest state of perfection, and it was applied to the purpose of
preserving every kind of knowledge and science.   The Triads, however,
must not be regarded as the production of any one individual, or of any
given period of time, but as an accumulation formed successively by
national concurrences, as the various events appeared and became
recognised in public observation.   The arrangement of classes, both in
civil and religious polity, partook of the ternary form.   Nothing could
be transacted by the British Druids without a reference to this figure.
On solemn occasions the processions moved three times round the sacred
enclosure ;   the invocations were thrice repeated, and the poetry was
composed in Triads.   The ternary *deiseal*, or procession from east to
west by the south, accompanied all the sacred rites, as well as secular,
and nothing was accounted holy without the performance of this preliminary ceremony.   In a word, the Triad formed the spirit of religion
among the forefathers of Britain : it was introduced into the poetry, it
pervaded the philosophy, politics, and morals ;   and, like the property
for which the number three was venerated by all antiquity, it formed the
beginning, middle and end of all their policy, whether civil, military, or
religious.

Speaking generally, the historical value of the Triads is accepted
by most authorities.   Edward Davies, in his *Celtic Researches*, says :

"We find among the oldest Welsh MSS. many historical notices
upon the model of the Druidical Triads and purporting to be the
remains of Druidical ages.   Their contents furnish, in my opinion,
strong evidence of their authenticity.   I cannot account for them
at all upon other grounds.   Many collections of these Triads are
preserved at this day, in old copies upon vellum."

The editors of *Welsh Archæology* say :

"The Triads may be considered amongst the most valuable
and curious productions preserved in the Welsh language ;   and
they contain a great number of memorials of the remarkable events
which took place among the ancient Britons.   Unfortunately,
however, they are entirely deficient with respect to dates ;   and,
considered singly, they are not well adapted to preserve the con-
nexion of history.   Yet a collection of Triads combined together, as
these are, condense more information into a small compass than is

to be accomplished, perhaps, by any other method ; and, conse-quently, such a mode of composition is superior to all others for the formation of a system of tradition."

The following Triads are submitted as proof of the nobility of the system of ethics and morals as taught and practised by the Druids, Bards, and Ovates :

The three primary principles of Wisdom : Obedience to the Laws of God ; Concern for the welfare of mankind ; and Suffering with fortitude all the accidents of life.

The three great laws of man's actions : What he forbids in another ; What he requires from another ; and What he cares not how it is done by another.

The three great ends of Knowledge : Duty, Utility, and Decorum.

Three things corrupt the world : Pride, Superfluity, and Indolence.

There are three things which God will not love him that delights to look at : Fighting, a monster, and the pomp of pride.

Diogenes Laertius, who died A.D. 222, gives as one of the Bardic Triads :

To worship the gods ; to do no evil ; and to exercise fortitude. Other Triads are :

The three foundations of Bardism : Peace, Love, and Justice.

For three reasons ought a man to hazard his life and to lose it, if necessary : In seeking for truth ; In clinging to justice ; and In performing mercy.

The following Triads are the Laws of Dyvnwal Moelmud, the cele-brated prince and legislator, who flourished in the fifth century B.C.

The three principles and protection of a social state : Security of life and person ; security of possession and dwelling ; security of national right.

Three things that confirm the social state : Effectual security of property ; just punishment where it is due ; and mercy tempering justice where the occasion requires it in equity.

The three elements of law are knowledge, national right, and conscientiousness.

The three ornaments of a social state : The learned scholar ; the ingenious artist ; and the just judge.

The three proofs of a judge : Knowledge of the law ; knowledge of the customs which the law does not supersede ; and knowledge of its times and the business thereto belonging.

Three things which a judge ought always to study : Equity

habitually ; mercy conscientiously ; and knowledge profoundly and accurately.

The Laws of Dynwal declared that there were :

Three persons who forfeit life, and who cannot be redeemed : A traitor to country and kindred ; one who shall kill another through ferocity ; and a proved thief for the worth of more than four byzants.

Some of the Welsh Triads bear witness to the Druidical belief in a Supreme Being :

There are three primary unities, and no more than one of each kind exist : One God ; one Truth ; and one Point of Liberty— and this is where all opposites equipreponderate.

Three things of which God necessarily consists : The greatest life ; the greatest knowledge ; and the greatest power—and of what is greatest there can be no more than one of any thing.

Three things it is impossible God should not do : Whatever perfect goodness should be ; whatever perfect goodness would desire to be ; and whatever goodness is able to perform.

Three things evince what God has done and will do : Infinite power ; Infinite wisdom ; and Infinite love—for there is nothing that these attributes want of power, of knowledge, or of will to perform.

Three things it is impossible God should not perform : What is most beneficial ; what is most wanted ; and what is most beautiful of all things.

The three grand attributes of God : Infinite plenitude of life ; Infinite knowledge ; and Infinite power.

Three things that none but God can do : Endure the eternities of the Circle of Infinity ; Participate of every state of existence without changing ; and Reform and renovate every thing without causing the loss of it.

Three causes that have produced rational beings : Divine love possessed of perfect knowledge ; Divine wisdom knowing all possible means ; and Divine power possessed by a joint will of divine love and divine wisdom.

Here are two further Triads worthy of quotation :

Three things which make a man equal to an angel : The love of every good ; the love of charity ; and the love of pleasing God.

There are three sorts of men : A man to God, who does good for evil ; a man to man, who does good for good and evil for evil ; and a man to the devil, who does evil for good.

The candidates for the degree of Ovate had to be well versed in science, letters, medicine, and language. Each had to be proposed by a Druid or Bard, to whom he was known personally, or by a judge or magistrate, or, failing these, by twelve respectable men. The British Ovates wore a green robe, that being the colour symbolical of learning, but the Irish Ovates wore a mantle of grey or sky-blue. The badge was a golden star, bearing the inscription : " The judgment of heaven will severely punish iniquity." The Ovates officiated as physicians and diviners, and are said to have been greatly proficient in natural philosophy and the secret workings of nature. Diodorus Siculus says that the Ovates from auspices and the entrails of victims predicted future events.

On the fall of Druidism, Bardism adapted itself to Christianity, for the Chair of Urien Rheged, that military chief who led the British against the Saxons at the memorable battle of Cattraeth, celebrated by Aneurin, in his immortal *Gododin*, was decidedly Christian.

CHAPTER V.

DRUIDISM AND MAGIC

One of the principal items in the curriculum of study of a Druidical initiate during his twenty years' novitiate, which was spent in the depths of the forest, was instruction in the art of magic.

Confused ideas are often held upon this subject of magic which does not mean deception, or cunning, or a skilful dexterity in hand-manipulation alone, though it is sometimes employed in one or other or all of these ways. Magic proper, however, means the understanding of nature, and it derived its name from the fact that this occult knowledge was supposed to be the exclusive possession of the Magi, or wise men. The founder of Magic is claimed by the mythologists to have been Chus, the reputed founder of the Cuthites, who is also accredited by tradition to be the first to venture upon the high seas. The Greeks, however, claim that magical arts were invented in Persia, in which country the Magi applied themselves to the study of philosophy and the assiduous search after the most curious works and mysteries of Nature. These men were chosen generally to superintend divine worship and all religious rites and ceremonies; they attended constantly upon kings to advise them in all affairs of moment and were chosen for the highest honours and places demanding the greatest trust and confidence. It was at a later stage in Persian history that their credit and esteem became diminished in consequence of their abandonment of the contemplation of nature and the betaking of themselves to the invocation of demons.

The magicians and sorcerers whom Pharaoh and Nebuchadnezzar summoned to their aid are referred to in the Gaelic Bible as *Draoitho*, Druids, the same name as is given to the wise men who are mentioned in the New Testament as travelling from the East to Bethlehem. The word *Druid* in Celtic signifies " a wizard," and the translators of the New Testament into that language have accordingly rendered the expression " Simon Magus " as " Simon the Druid."

Professor John Rhys, in his *Lectures on the Origin and Growth of Religion*, says :

" The appearance of Simon on Celtic ground is not very difficult to explain. He was known to the early Church as a notorious opponent of the apostles, and his name became identified with all that was pagan and anti-Christian : thus, the ancient Druidic tonsure usual among the clergy of the British Church till the latter half of the eighth century, and among those of the Irish Church not quite so late, was probably a Druidic tonsure continued. At any rate, it was described by those who had adopted the Roman tonsure as that of Simon Magus. As to Ireland, in particular, all the fiercest opposition there to Christianity is described as headed by the Druids, who competed with Patrick and other saints in working miracles. So it would be natural enough to Christian writers to liken the chief Druids of Ireland to Simon, especially seeing that when they used the Latin tongue the native word *drui*, " Druid," had to be rendered by *magus*, " a magician." Vice versa, Simon Magus became in Irish *Simon Drui*, or " Simon the Druid " : nay, he was at last claimed as an Irish ancestor and as such he appears as Simon Brec, or Simon the Freckled, son of Starn, or Stariath, of the family of Nemid, and as ancestor of the Fir Bolg, who, owing to Simon's eastern origin, are made to come from the east on one of the motiveless wanderings so common in the legendary history of Ireland.

" The mythical creation, known as *Roth Fail*, or Fáil's Wheel, and *Roth Ramach*, or the wheel with paddles, is said to have been made by Simon Magus, assisted by Mog Ruith, a celebrated Irish Druid from the island of Valencia, who, having learned all the Druidism or magic that could be learned in these islands, went with his daughter to take lessons from Simon Magus, in whose contest with St. Peter he is represented as taking a part. The wheel was to enable Simon to sail in the air ; but it met with an accident, and Mog Ruith's daughter brought certain fragments of it to Ireland, one of which she fixed as the rock or pillar stone of Cnámchoill, a place near Tipperary, the name of which has been Anglicised into Cleghile. The stone was believed to have produced blindness if looked at, and death if touched."

In Ireland the modern art of magic is known as Druidity and the magician's wand as the " Rod of Druidism." The Irish Druids of ancient times are said to have been a species of sorcerers, to have been in league with the demons of paganism, and to have been able, through their agency, to do good to their friends and to work mischief upon their enemies. They were credited by the people with the power of transforming men into stone pillars by magical means, and this credulity assisted in making the Druids as great as, if not greater than, any priesthood in ancient or modern times. They were held in such veneration by all classes that no public measures became operative unless and until they received their approbation.

The pre-Milesian races—the Nemedians and the Formarians—had their Druids, who worked mutual spells against each other. The Tuathá-dè-Danann had innumerable Druids among them who employed spells. The Tuathá-dè-Danann were descendants of those who followed the Nemedians out of Ireland when the Africans usurped that kingdom. They landed in Achaia, where they learned the arts of necromancy and enchantment and became experts in magical knowledge. It was said that when the country of Achaia and the city of Athens were invaded by the Assyrians, these sorcerers were enabled by means of their charms to revive the bodies of the dead Athenians and bring them again on to the field of battle The Assyrians resolved to take counsel of a learned Druid and discover, if possible, in what manner they could defeat the skill of those necromancers and break the power of their charms. The Druid told them that after a battle was over they should thrust a stake of wood through every one of the dead bodies : this would demonstrate whether the dead were brought to life by diabolical means or divine power. If the former, the bodies could not then be resuscitated ; but if the latter, they would find it futile to fight against an Almighty Power. The Assyrians are said to have acted upon the advice given, and the sorcerers were defeated. The Tuathá-dè-Danann then fled from Achaia and Greece and betook themselves to Norway and Denmark, afterwards migrating to Scotland and then back to their former home, Ireland.

Druids are mentioned in connection with all early Irish stories, from the first colonisation down to the time of the saints. At the time of the battle between the Milesians in Ireland and the invaders in the early days of the Christian era, some of the invaders, known by the name of Tuatha Fiodhga, poisoned the heads of their arrows, which had the effect of making the slightest wound mortal or incurable. Criomthan Sciathbeil, who was governor of Leinster at the time, was informed by a Milesian Druid, named Trosdane, of an antidote to such poisonous wounds. It was to procure one hundred and fifty white-faced cows and when he had digged a pit near to the place where he usually fought with his foe, to empty their milk into the hole, and when any of his soldiers were wounded by the enemy, they were to go immediately into the pit and bathe themselves in the milk, which would prove a sovereign antidote against the poison. Criomthan, it is said, followed the advice of the Druid ; and the Milesians, as a result, obtained a complete victory.

" The wandering Picts, after a tedious voyage
Around the British coasts, at length arrive
Upon the Irish shore ; where the Gadelians
Were fighting with the Britons fierce and cruel,

Who, with envenom'd arrows, certain death
Dispensed ; and many a brave Milesian
Languished with wounds incurable, till relieved
By a prevailing antidote, prescribed
By the wise Trosdane, of the Pictish race.
This learned Druid, exquisitely skill'd
In poison, did expel the subtle venom
By a warm bath of milk, which from the dugs
Of an hundred and fifty bald-faced cows distilled ;
The soldiers here soften'd their rankling wounds,
And washed, and to the fight returned unhurt.
Thus were the Britons routed in the field
And all their barbarous art defeated."

Fiachadh Muilleathan, king of Munster, appealed on one occasion to a Druid, named Modhrauith, to deliver his armies out of difficulties occasioned by the lack of water. The charm used by the Druid was an enchanted dart, which he flung into the air with all his force, and from the spot of ground upon which the arrow fell there sprang a fountain of the purest water sufficient to supply the wants of the whole army.

According to legendary lore, the Druids could, by their magical powers, create clouds and mists and bring down showers of fire and blood. St. Patrick, on his way to Tara one Easter Sunday morning, chanted a hymn beseeching God to protect him against the spells of women, smiths, and Druids. In a contest which the Druids had at Tara with the celebrated Irish apostle, they are said to have caused snow to descend by means of their magical incantations. The following account is given of an encounter between the Druidical magicians and St. Patrick :

" All these things being done between the magician and Patrick, the king says to them : ' Cast your books into the water, and he whose books shall escape uninjured we will adore.' Patrick answered, ' I will do so.' And the magician said : ' I am unwilling to come to the trial of water with this man, because he has water as his god '—he had heard that baptism was given by Patrick with water. And the king [Laogaire] answering, said : ' Allow it by fire ' ; and Patrick said : ' I am ready ' ; but the magician, being unwilling, said : ' This man alternately, in each successive year, adores as god, water and fire.' And the saint said : ' Not so, but thou thyself shalt go and one of my boys shall go with thee into a separate and closed house, and my vestment shall be on thee and thine on him and thus together you shall be set on fire.' And this counsel was approved of ; and there was a house built for them, the half of which was made of green wood and the other half of dry ; and the magician was sent into that part of the house that was green and one of the boys of St. Patrick, Bienus by name, with the vest of the magician into the dry part of the house. The house, then being closed on the outside, was set on fire before the whole multitude, and it came to pass in that hour, by the prayers of Patrick, that the flame of fire consumed the magician, with the green half of the house, while the garment of St. Patrick remained untouched, because the fire did not touch it. But the fortunate Bienus, on the contrary, with the dry half of the house, according to what is said of the three children, was not touched by the fire, neither was he annoyed, nor did he experience any inconvenience : only the garment of the magician which he had about him was burned."

In the *Life of Senan* mention is made of the use of charms and spells by the Druids. Coel, a brother of Senan, was ordered by King MacTail of Hui Figente to command his brother to leave his territory. Coel met with death while on his way to perform his errand. When MacTail heard the news he was angry, but his Druid said to him : " Thou needest not to be anxious about this, for I will take a charm with me to him, and he shall either die or leave thy land in possession." The victory, however, did not come to the Druid.

In the story of *The Retreat of the Sons of Mile* we read :
" The sons of Mile submitted to the judgment of Amairgen. They returned by the way they had come, and, going on board their ships, withdrew from the shore to the mysterious distance of nine waves, in accordance with the judgment of Amairgen. As soon as the Tuathá dè Danann found them launched upon the sea, their Druids and the people began to chant magic poems, which caused a furious tempest to arise, so that the fleet of the sons of Mile was driven far out to sea and dispersed."

" Mannanan-Beg-Mac-y-Lheirr (Little Mannanan), " Son of the Sea," the first person who held Man (the Isle of Man), was the ruler thereof, after whom the land was named ; he reigned many years, and was a paynim (pagan). He kept the island under a mist by means of his necromancy. If he dreaded an enemy, he could cause one man to seem a hundred, and that by magic art." Thus runs one of the legends of the Isle of Man. Little Mannanan is said to have been converted to Christianity by St. Patrick in A.D. 447.

St. Patrick could meet charm with charm. It is said that when the Druids sought to poison him he wrote the following words and placed the paper on which they were written over the liquor in which the food had been placed :
" Tubu fis fri ibu, fis ibu anfis
Fris bru natha, ibu lithu, Christi Jesus,"

*Druidical Festival
at Stonehenge.*

and declared that whoever pronounced these words over poisoned liquor would sustain no injury.

According to the *Senchus Mor* :

" When the men of Erin heard of the killing of the living and the resuscitation of the dead, and all the power of Patrick since his arrival in Erin ; and when they saw Leghaire with his Druids overcome by the great signs and miracles wrought in the presence of the men of Erin, they bowed down in obedience to the will of God and Patrick."

Part of the ancient hymn known as *Ninine's Prayer*, referring to St. Patrick, runs :

" He fought against hard-hearted Druids,
He thrust down the proud men with the aid of our Lord of fair heavens,
He purified the great offspring of meadow-landed Erin,
We pray to Patrick, chief apostle, who will save us at the judgment from doom to the malevolence of dark demons,
Against snares of demons,
Against black laws of heathenry,
Against spells of women, smiths, and Druids."

There was a Druid whose Irish slave Columba was anxious to release. The Druid refused to listen to Columba's request, whereupon an angel broke the glass cup out of which he was drinking, which caused him to be cut severely. Columba healed the Druid's wounds by means of a magic pebble which floated on water. Another act attributed to Columba was the turning into blood of milk said to have been drawn from a bull by a Scottish Druid.

There is a poem attributed to Columba, part of which runs :

" I adore not the voice of birds,
Nor a sreod, nor a destiny on the earthly world ;
Nor a son, nor chance, nor woman,
My Drui is Christ, the Son of God."

Another verse, bearing reference to the practice of divination among the ancient Druids, runs :

" Our fate depends not on sneezing,
Nor on a bird perched on a twig,
Nor on the root of a knotted tree,
Nor on the noise of clapping hands ;
Better is He in whom we trust,
The father, the One, and the Son."

There is a Gothic manuscript of the twelfth or thirteenth century, if not earlier, part of which reads as follows :

" Columba went once of a time to the King of Curithne (Picts), *viz.*, to Brude, son of Milcoin, and the door of the dun (castle) was shut against him and the iron locks of the town were opened readily through the prayers of Columba. Then Maelcu, the King's son, came to his Druid to resist Columba through Paganism."

We know from Adamnan that there were magi in the palace of Brude, near Inverness. They were called *Geintighecht* by the Christian writers.

Among other achievements, the Druids have been credited with the power to drive a man insane simply by flicking a wisp of straw, which was called *Dlui fulla*, in his face.

At the famous battle of Culdreimne (Coolcrevny) in A.D. 560, according to the *Annals of Ulster :* " Fraechan, son of Temnan, it was that made the Druids' erbe for Diramit. Tuatan, son of Diman, it was that threw overhead the Druids' *erbe.*" The same author is responsible for the statement that in A.D. 738, " Fergus Glutt, king of Cobha, died from the envenomed spittles of evil men."

The belief that magical powers were in the possession of certain individuals was retained, as will be seen, until well on in the Christian era. Sopater, the philosopher, and friend of Constantine, was accused of binding the winds in an adverse quarter by the influence of magic, so that warships could not reach Constantinople, and, in response to ecclesiastical clamour, the Emperor was compelled to issue the order for his decapitation.

Belief in witchcraft can be traced to Druidism, and some of the practices attributed to witches after all traces of Druidical worship and customs were supposed to have died out are nevertheless exact, or almost exact, reproductions of the practices attributed to the Druids by earlier authorities. More than one writer has stated that the Scottish witch is the direct descendant of the Druidess, and, according to Pomponius Mela, the Druidesses of the Isle of Sena could grant fair winds or raise tempests, and, in 1792, the author of the *Statistical Account of the Hebrides* stated that in the island of Gigha it was believed that by performing certain ceremonies at a fountain there, persons thus initiated into its mysteries could cause the wind to blow from any quarter desired.

Concerning Druidesses, however, much controversy has arisen, some even disputing their existence. Most writers, however, agree that there were Druidesses and that they were divided into three classes, but none performed priestly duties. The members of the first, or highest, class took vows of perpetual virginity, and were regarded as the elite of the order. Their duty was to attend to the sacred fire, and they were known as *Inghean an Dagha*, " daughters of fire," but sometimes as *Breochuidh*, " fire keepers." The members of this class lived together in communities, separated from the world. The second class married, but spent the greater part of their time in religious work. They wove the hangings of the groves, made the vestments of the priests, took part in certain of the ceremonies, and performed the ordinary duties of the household. The third class consisted of such as performed the most servile offices about the temples and the priests' households. In Gaul, the second class, though married, were vowed to continence, remaining always within the temple enclosure, emerging only once a year to consort with their husbands for the purpose of procreation. The third lived at home with their husbands, training their children, but devoting their leisure to work in the temple. Although there, as in Britain, they were dependents and subordinates of the Druids, they, in fact, superintended entirely the divine mysteries and sacrifices, entrance to certain parts of the temples being interdicted to men. Druidesses appear also to have formed part of the Irish ecclesiastical organization. Toland, in his *History of the Druids*, speaks of Gealcossa, a Druidess, who resided near Gealcossa's Mount, in Inisoen, in the county of Donegal. Her name, he says, " is of Homeric strain, signifying ' white-legged.' On this hill is her grave, and hard by is her temple, being a sort of diminutive Stonehenge, which many of the old Irish dare not at this day in any way profane."

Every Druid wore around his neck, encased in gold, what was known as the *anguinum*, or " Druid's Egg." Pliny, in his *Natural History*, gives the following account of it :

" There is, besides, a kind of egg held in high esteem by the inhabitants of Gaul, unnoticed by the Greek writers. It is called ' the serpents' egg '; and, in order to produce it, an immense number of serpents, twisted together in summer, are rolled up in an artificial folding by the saliva of their mouths and the slime of their bodies. The Druids say that this egg is tossed on high with hissings and that it must be intercepted in a cloak before it reaches the ground. The person who seizes it flies on horseback, for the serpents pursue him till they are stopped by the intervention of some river. The proof of this egg is, that, though bound in gold, it will swim against the stream. And, as the magi are very artful and cunning in concealing their frauds, they pretend that this egg can only be obtained at a certain time of the moon, as if this operation of the serpents could be rendered congruous to human determination. I have indeed seen that egg of the size of an ordinary round apple, worn by the Druids in a chequered cover resembling the enormous calculi in the arms of a polypus. Its virtue is highly extolled for gaining law suits and procuring access to kings ; and it is worn with so great ostentation that I knew a Roman knight by birth, a Vocentian, who was slain by the Emperor Claudius for no cause whatever except wearing one of these eggs on his breast during the dependence of a lawsuit."

It is not improbable that this egg and the alleged marvellous manner of its production had connection with some primary dogma which Pliny never fathomed. Hughes, in *Horæ Britannicæ*, says that in the writings of the ancient Bards several allusions to what he terms the " mummery " are to be found, one of which he quotes as follows :

> " Lively was the aspect of him, who, in his prowess, had snatched over the ford that involved ball which casts its rays to a distance ; the splendid product of the adder, shot forth by serpents."

The Druids themselves were called *Nadredd*, or snakes, by the Welsh Bards ; and the whole of the tale mentioned by Pliny has a mystical reference to the difficulty of attaining Druidical secrets and the danger of disclosing them. There is, of course, no doubt that this famous object of Druidic superstition was merely artificial. The art of making these trinkets being known only to the Druids, they availed themselves of the credulity of the common people, to magnify the virtues of them and to give them a mysterious import.

The serpent was a sacred reptile among the Druids. They supposed its spiral coils to represent the eternal existence of the Almighty. Camden tells us that in many parts of Wales and throughout all Scotland and Cornwall it is an opinion held by the people that about Midsummer Eve the snakes meet in company and that by joining heads together and hissing, a kind of bubble is formed, which, by continually being blown upon, passes through the body, when it immediately consolidates and resembles a glass ring, which, whoever finds, shall prosper in all his undertakings. The rings thus generated are called *Gleinunadroeth*, or " snake stones." Wirt Sikes, in *British Goblins*, says that the snake stone is a striking Welsh tradition associated with Midsummer Eve, and there is a Welsh saying respecting people who lay their heads together in conversation that the talkers are " blowing the gem."

Any water poured on the serpents' eggs is said to have had wonderful life-giving power and become able to produce life. It has also been asserted that the Druids were wont to place live serpents at the foot of the altar during the time of sacrifice.

In Scotland, the Druids' egg was known as an adder stone, and it was in great reputation for the foretelling of events, the working of miracles, the curing of disease, and the gaining of law suits.

In the Scottish Museum there is a bead of red glass, spotted with white ; another of dark brown glass, spotted with yellow ; others of pale green and blue glass, plain and ribbed ; and two of curiously figured patterns, wrought with various colours interwoven in their surface.

These glass baubles were badges and passports that the bearers were initiated, and whoever purloined or carried one without authorization was pursued by the deadly vengeance of the Brotherhood. The amulet was variously shaped. Sometimes it was like a round bead of glass ; at others, like a crescent with a glass boat ; sometimes it was a glass circle, and sometimes it resembled a glass house. In every case it was regarded as a powerful talisman. Camden has thus described these magical appendages :

> " These geminæ anguinæ are small glass amulets, commonly as wide as our finger rings, but much thicker ; of a green colour usually, though some of them are blue, and others curiously waved with blue, red, and white."

Specimens have frequently been found in the Isle of Anglesea. Smaller consecrated beads—white for Druids, blue for Bards, and green for Ovates—were carried by the individuals and interred with them at death. A number of these beads were found in an excavation made at Quarrington in 1828. Taliesin, speaking of a warrior's amulet, says : " Beautiful is the circle with its enriched border."

The anguinum was not known in Ireland, the reason given by Llhwyd, the antiquarian, being :

> " The Druid doctrine about the *Glain Neidr* obtains very much throughout all Scotland, as well lowlands as highlands ; but there is not a word of it in this kingdom (Ireland), where, as there are no snakes, they could not propagate it. Besides snake-stones, the highlanders have their small snail stones, paddock stones, etc., to all which they attribute their special virtues and wear them as amulets."

In another letter, referring to the same subject, he says :

> " The Cornish retain a variety of charms, and have still towards the Land's End the amulet of Mael Magal and Gelin Nedir, which latter they call a Milpreu, or Melpreu, and have a charm for the snake to make it, when they have found one asleep and struck a hazel wand in the centre of her spires."

Edwards supposes that the Welsh Bardic title of Nadredd is to be traced to the belief in transmigration. The serpent, which sheds its skin annually and appears to return to a second youth, may have been regarded by them, as well as by other people of that time, as a symbol of renovation, and this renovation or reincarnation was the great doctrine set forth by the Arkite mysteries and by the symbolical egg.

Mason, in *Caractacus*, has described the ceremony of securing the anguinum in the following words :

> " The potent adder stone
> Gender'd 'fore th'autumnal moon :
> When in undulating twine

> The foaming snakes prolific join;
> When they hiss and when they bear
> Their wondrous egg aloof in air,
> Thence, before to earth it fall
> The Druid, in his hallow'd pall,
> · Receives the prize,
> And instant flies,
> Follow'd by th' envenom'd brood
> Till he cross the crystal flood."

The Druids represented the wren as the king of all the birds and the Welsh for king is *bren*. At one time the raven was regarded by the Greeks as the greatest of soothsaying birds. One of the Druidical proverbs ran as follows:

> He that takes a wren's nest
> Will have no health all his life.

The well-known song, "The Three Ravens," is a survival of a Druidic chant:

> There were three ravens sat on a tree,
>   *Down-a-down! hey down! hey down.*
> They were as black as black might be
>   *With a down!*
> Then one of them said to his mate
> Where shall we now our breakfast take,
>   *With a down, down, derry, derry-down.*

Every Druid carried a wand. The wand of the British Druids was made from oak, but that of the Irish Druids was made from yew. At the present day, in some Roman Catholic churches, it is a practice, when the faithful approach the confessional, for them to receive a touch on the head from a wand which the priest holds in his hand. In this way also the priests of Isis blessed and exorcised. In Scotland the Rowan, or Mountain Ash, will always be found near holy places and circles or Clachans. It was essential that on Belrane, or May-day, all sheep and lambs should pass through a hoop of the Rowan-tree, and that on all occasions Scottish shepherds should be careful to drive their flocks to the hills with a Rowan wand. In the Scottish isles, where malign influence is feared, it is the custom to place a Rowan branch over the doorposts. Many Highlanders at the present day plant the Rowan, or Mountain Ash, near their dwellings or fields for the purpose of warding off evil spirits. If heather and flowers be added to Rowan wands, important beneficial services on the part of the spirits may be expected, particularly if all be carried thrice round the fires kindled on the May festival.

The gift of prophecy was also believed to be a power in the possession of the Druids. They claimed to be able to predict future events, not only from holy wells and running streams, but also from rain and snow water, which, when settled and afterwards stirred, either by oak leaf or branch, or magic, might exhibit appearances, which would convey information to the far-seeing Druid, or appear to do so to the credulous inquirer, while the priest was at full liberty to represent the appearance in whatever manner he thought most suited to his purpose. The cauldron of Ceridwen was said to contain the water of inspiration and science. A few drops of this water allowed to fall upon the finger of a person and then put into his mouth would open up futurity to his view. This, however, could only be done on the completion of the course of initiation, when the testing of this water was an essential rite.

Several instances of the exercise of this prophetic power are related in ancient Irish writings, and many of them are similar to the recorded instances of modern clairvoyant predictions. D'Arbois de Jubainville says that the various Lives of St. Patrick and the other works of Christians who regarded the Druids as adversaries testify to the fact that even those Christians believed in the prophetic power of the Druids.

We read in Josephus (*Antiquities*, xviii) that the Jewish Agrippa fell into the displeasure of Tiberius, who put him into bonds. As he stood leaning against a tree before a palace, an owl perched upon that tree. A German (some versions say " a German Druid "), one of the Emperor's guards, spake to him to be of good cheer, for he should be released from those bonds and arrive at great dignity and power ; but bid him remember that when he saw the bird again, he should live but five days. All this, we are told, came to pass. He was made king by Caligula. St. Paul preached before him, and Josephus speaks of his death agreeably to the prediction.

Before St. Patrick went to Ireland, his advent was foretold by the Druids Lucait Mael and Luccra, or Lochru, in the following lines :

" Adzheads (tonsured heads) will come over a furious sea ;
    Their mantles (cowls) hole-headed :
    Their staves (croziers) crock-headed :
    Their tables (altars) in the east of their houses :
    All will answer ' Amen.' "

An interesting Druidical prophecy is told in the *Life of St. Brigit*, as follows :

" Once upon a time, Dubthach (father of Brigit) and a bondmaid (Broicsech), whom Dubthach married, along with him, went in a chariot past the house of a certain wizard (Druid). When the wizard heard the noise of the chariot, he said : ' My boy, see who is in the chariot, for this is noise of chariot under king.' Quoth the boy : ' Dubthach is therein.' The wizard went out to meet him and asked whose was the woman hiding in the chariot. 'Mine,' said Dubthach. Now Maithgen was the name of the wizard and from him Ross Maithgin is named. The wizard asked if she was pregnant by any one. 'She is pregnant by me.' said Dubthach. Said the wizard : 'Marvellous will be the child that is in her womb : her like will not be on earth.' 'My wife compels me to sell this bondmaid,' said Dubthach. Said the wizard, through grace of prophecy : 'The seed of thy wife shall serve the seed of thy bond-maid for the bondmaid will bring forth a daughter, conspicuous, radiant, who will shine like a sun among the stars of heaven.' Dubthach was thankful for the answer, for hitherto no daughter had been born to him."

The birth of Ciarán, of Clanmacois, an Irish saint, was foretold by Lughbrann, the Druid attached to the court of King Crimthann, who predicted concerning him :

> " He healed Oengus' steed
> When he lay swaddled in a cradle,
> From God that miracle to Ciarán
> Was given."

The story then goes on in prose as follows :

" On a certain day the horse of Oengus, son of Crimthann, died, and he felt great sorrow. Now when Oengus slept, an angel of God appeared to him in a vision and said this to him : ' Ciarán, the son of the wright, will come and bring the horse for thee to life.' And this was fulfilled, for, at the angel's word, Ciarán came and blessed water, which was put over the horse, and the horse at once arose out of death."

An ancient work, entitled *The Etymology of Names*, says that Lughaidh, who ruled over Ireland, *circa* A.M. 3490, was one of five brothers, all of whom bore the same name. The reason for this is explained by the statement that a certain Druid, who had the skill of prophecy, told the father, Daire Domtheach, that he should have a son whose name should be Lughaidh, who should one day sit upon the throne of Ireland. Daire, it seems, afterwards had five sons, and the more effectually to bring this prediction to pass, he gave the same name to each one as he was born. When the five brothers reached a mature age, Daire took advantage of an opportunity that presented itself and called upon the Druid. He inquired of him which of his sons would have the honour of being the monarch of Ireland. The Druid, instead of giving him a direct answer to the question, ordered him to take his five sons with him on the morrow to Tailteau, where there was to be a general convention of all the nobility and gentry of the kingdom. While the assembly was sitting he would see a fawn or young deer running through the field, which would be pursued by all the company ; his five sons would likewise run among the rest, and whosoever of them overtook and killed the fawn, the crown should be his and he should be the sole monarch of the island. The father followed the direction of the Druid with great exactness, and, accordingly, the next day, set out with his five sons for Tailteau, where he found the assembly sitting. Looking about him, he espied the fawn running over the fields, and the whole assembly suddenly left their debates and pursued her, following her close until they came to Binneadirr, afterwards called the Hill of Meath. Here a mist that was raised by enchantment separated the five sons of Daire from the other pursuers and they continued the chase and hunted her as far as Dail Maschorb, in Leinster, where Lughaidh Laighe, as the Druid foretold, overtook the fawn and killed her. The word *Laighe* in Irish, signifies " a fawn."

When the Caledonians were expelled from Scythia, they met with great difficulties on the water and, uncertain which way to steer their course, they appealed to Caicer, a renowned Druid, for advice. He, by means of his prophetic knowledge, informed them that there was no country ordained for them to inhabit until they arrived upon the coast of a certain western isle, which was Ireland. The Druids, even in those days, were accredited with being men of extraordinary learning and wisdom. They were attendants of the Gadelians, and settled with them in Ireland.

A Druid is said to have prophesied to Modha Nuagat, king of Ireland, A.D. *circa* 125, a seven years' famine to follow seven years of plenty, and advised him to build storehouses and to buy in all the corn of the country. Modha Nuagat was so convinced of the integrity of the Druid that he gave credit to his prediction and for seven years he and his subjects lived upon flesh and fowl, securing the corn and other necessaries of life in granaries, sending factors all over the kingdom who bought up all the provisions exposed for sale. The famine is said to have occurred exactly as predicted.

This power of prophecy was shared also by the Druidesses. It was a Druidess that foretold to Diocletian, when he was a soldier in Gallia that he would be Emperor of Rome. Diocletian was amusing himself one day in casting up his accounts, when his hostess, said to be a well-known Druidess, thus addressed him : " In truth, sir, you are too covetous." " Well," replied Diocletian, " I shall be liberal when I come to be emperor." " You shall be so," answered his hostess, " when you have slain a boar." Diocletian, struck with this answer, applied himself from that time principally to the slaughter of boars, without, however, securing the throne ; but, at last, bethinking that the equivalent Latin word for " boar " might refer to Aper, Numerian's father-in-law, he put him to death, and was chosen emperor.

It is also said that it was a Druidess who said to Alexander Severus as he was setting out on his last campaign, the expedition in which he was assassinated by his own soldiers : " Go on, my lord, but beware of your soldiers." Before setting out on the great expedition against Ulster, Medb, Queen of Connaught, went to consult her Druid, and just before the famous heroine, Derdriu, or Deirdre, was born, Caithbu prophesied what sort of woman she would be. Claudius also, it is stated, consulted female Druids on the question as to whether the empire would continue in its prosperity, and he was told that no name would be more illustrious in the republic than that of the posterity of Claudius.

Toutain, in *Les pretendues Druidesses Gauloises*, examines the question of these Druidesses very thoroughly, and throws doubt on their existence and, therefore, on their predictions. He points out that the term used for Druidess is *Dryas*, which means " nymph of the woods," but Greek and Latin writers never use this term when speaking of the Druids. The Greeks always write *druides* or *druidai*, with, as variant, *drouidas*, and the Latin *druidæ*, very rarely *druides*. These forms would not give the feminine as *dryas*. Moreover, these predictions are said to have taken place in that part of Gaul adjacent to Germany. The geographical indications in the account given by Lampridius of the death of Alexander Severus are very confused. He appears to be ignorant of the exact locality where Severus was killed ; he does not know whether it was Brittany or Gaul. But it is known from other sources that he was killed close to Mayence, at the extreme east of Gaul. The text of the life of Aurelian does not give any particulars as to locality. But in the case of Diocletian, it is known for certain that the incident took place in the country of the Tungri, in the neighbourhood of the Mause. Also, says Toutain, it would be astonishing to find Druidesses in the third century A.D., since no authors of the first century knew of their existence. Neither Cæsar, Diodorus of Sicily, or Strabo mention Druidesses. The women who made such a desperate resistance at the taking of Anglesea, as described by Tacitus, were female fanatics. No historian makes any reference to Druidesses.

Mela, however, says that in the Isle of Sena, off the coast of Armorica, there resided nine consecrated virgins, called Gallicenæ, who could raise up storms and tempests by their songs, cure all diseases, predict the future, and transform themselves into all shapes of animals. They are said to have solemnised in that isle the bloody orgies of Bacchus.

The Druids were also experts in the science of psychotherapy. Lady Wilde, in one of her works, says :

" The priests and magi of the ancient Druids possessed a wonderful faculty of healing. They were able to hypnotise the patients by the waving of the wand, and, while under the spell of this procedure, the latter could tell what was happening afar off, being vested with the power of clairvoyance. They also effected cures by stroking with the hand, and this method was thought to be of special efficacy in rheumatic affections. They also employed other remedies which appealed to the imagination, such as various mesmeric charms and incantations."

Vervain was much used in magical operations and many virtues were ascribed to it. By rubbing themselves with it, the Druids claimed to obtain anything they desired : it banished fevers, cured all sorts of maladies, and reconciled the hearts of those that were at enmity one with another ; sprinkled by way of aspersion upon guests, it had virtue to make those who were touched with it more gay and better pleased than the rest of the company. The medical practitioners held a high and influential place in the Order and occupied a distinguished place at the royal tables, next to nobles, and above the armourers, smiths, and workers in metals. They were also entitled to wear a special robe of honour at the courts of kings, and were always attended by a large number of pupils, who assisted their masters in the diagnosis and treatment of disease and the preparations necessary for the curative potions.

The Druids were inordinately attached to augury and divination, one of their methods being the practice of casting stones into water and counting the number of circular ripples thus formed. Other methods were the Druid's wheel, sneezing, examination of tree roots, the howling of dogs, and the singing of birds, particularly the croaking of the raven and the chirping of the wren. When St. Kellach, Bishop of Kellala, was about to be murdered, the raven croaked and the wise little wren twittered. After the deed was perpetrated, the birds of prey came scrambling for their share, but every one that ate the least morsel of the saint's flesh dropped dead. Both Pliny and Cicero bear testimony to the Druidical practice of sortilege or divination. They would foretell the future by the flight of birds and by the inspection of the entrails of victims. All the people would obey them unquestioningly, and it was an established custom among them that no one should offer sacrifice if a philosopher were not present. It was claimed that no one could offer sacrifices acceptable to the gods except through the intermediary of these men who knew the divine nature with which they were supposed to be in communication.

Tacitus, in *Germania* (c. x.), speaks of a full-grown tree from which a branch was severed and afterwards divided into small cuttings which were marked and then flung upon a white cloth, and, as the sticks fortuitously fell, the diviner interpreted fates.

According to Dèchelette, the Druidical teaching with regard to numbers is of more ancient origin than the Pythagorean. The Pythagorean philosophy flourished in the fifth and sixth centuries B.C., and it is supposed that at this time the Celtic civilization became subject to Grecian influence, and coming from meridional Italy, this was an influence not only on industry, but also on morals, and the Celts are supposed to have modified their funeral customs through contact with the Italian people.

Odd numbers were appropriated to the celestial and even ones to the infernal deities, and in all the occurrences of life, the former were accounted fortunate. A predilection in favour of odd numbers still persists among most peoples. Thus, in domestic concerns, a hen is usually set on an odd number of eggs. Palladius says that the same thing was done in his time. Druidic divination also consisted in watching the direction of smoke from fire. Sometimes the Druid would chew a bit of raw flesh, muttering at the same time an incantation and an invocation to the gods, when he claimed that generally the future would be revealed to him. Sometimes he would place his hands upon his cheeks and fall into a divine sleep : this was known as " illumination by the palms of the hands." Fionn was in the habit of biting his thumb continually when he was seeking superhuman knowledge. According to Dr. Joyce, the Irish Druids made their divinations from observations of the clouds.

Diodorus Siculus gives the following account of one of the Druidical methods of divination :

" On great occasions they practise a very strange and incredible manner of divination. They take a man who is to be sacrificed and kill him with one stroke of the sword above the diaphragm ; and, by observing the posture in which he falls, his different convulsions, and the direction in which the blood flows from his body, they form their predictions, according to certain rules which have been left them by their ancestors."

" And, leaning o'er the victims as they died,
Explored the future in the gushing tide.
Oft as the blood, impelled with various force
To right or left, directs its headlong course,
They saw some bless'd event, or traced with skill
Divine, some signal of impending ill."

Mallet, in *Northern Antiquities*, says that when the Swedes offered up animals in sacrifice, they speedily killed them at the foot of the altar ; they then opened their entrails to draw auguries from them, as among the Romans.

Belief in fairies was also Druidical. The hero, Cuchulainn, on his return from the land of the fairies, was unable to forget the fairywoman, Fand, who had enticed him thither. He was given a potion by some

Druids, which not only banished all memory of his adventures, but rid his wife, Emer, of the pangs of jealousy. Another story runs that Elain, the wife of Eochaid Airem, high king of Ireland, was, in a former existence, beloved of the god Mider, who again sought her love and carried her off. The king had recourse to the Druid Datan, who asked for a year in which to discover and hunt up the couple. By means of four yew wands inscribed with Ogham characters, he was successful in his mission. Dr. John Rhys, in his *Lectures on the Origin and Growth of Religion as illustrated by Celtic Heathendom*, says that Cúchulainn was educated at the school of which Cathbad, a Druid, was the master, though what the teaching consisted of is not known. Incidentally, however, it has been ascertained that he told his pupils of lucky and unlucky days. One morning, for instance, he informed an elder pupil that the day then beginning would be a lucky one for anybody who should take arms on it for the first time, which Cúchulainn, overhearing, at once carried out, to the surprise of his teacher and king, both of whom he outwitted in the matter. To be able to make the declaration ascribed to the Druid would seem to imply that he began the day with augury or some other kind of divination. Years later, when Cúchulainn was asked as to his education, he is represented as enumerating among the advantages he had enjoyed, that of having been taught by Cathbad, the Druid, which had, he said, made him a master of inquiry in the arts of the god of Druidism, or magic, and rendered him skilled in all that was excellent in visions. With regard to this latter statement, it is well known that the Druids were always ready to interpret a dream, which was probably done according to the canons they had elaborated for their use.

St. Columba is said to have striven against the Druids at a well in the country of the Picts. He exorcised the heathen demon of the well, which, thereafter, as a holy well, cured many diseases.

The dolmens of St. Pol-de-Leon, Brittany, are said to be haunted by dwarfs and fairies, who are believed to be the spirits of ancient Druids and Druidesses.

Trial by ordeal was known to and practised by the Druids. O'Curry, in his *Manners and Customs of the Ancient Irish*, gives one example of this practice : " A woman to clear her character had to rub her tongue on a red-hot adze of bronze, which had been heated in a fire of blackthorn or rowan-tree." Walking on red-hot coals was a frequent practice at their annual festivals and we are told by Marcus Verro, a Roman author, that the Druids had an ointment with which they besmeared their feet, when they walked through the fire. It was customary for the lord of the place, or his son, or some other person of distinction, to carry the entrails of the sacrificed animal in his hands, and, walking barefoot over the coals three times after the flames had ceased, to carry these straight to the Druid, who waited close by the altar. If the nobleman escaped harmless, it was accounted a good omen, but if he received any hurt, it was deemed unlucky, both to the community and himself.

The Druids of later times—the men who claimed to possess the power of making themselves and others invisible, who inscribed characters upon pieces of wood and distributed them as charms against sickness and other ills, who for money would curse the enemies, or bless the friends, of those who sought their aid—had no connection whatever with the Druids of more ancient times, who performed their mystic rites in the caves of the earth, the groves of oak, or the stone temples open to the heavens.

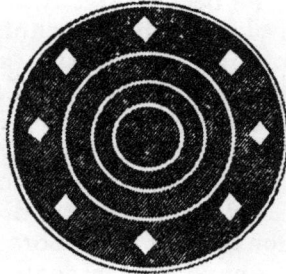

CHAPTER VI.

DRUIDICAL TEMPLES AND REMAINS

"The Druids met, Oh ! not in kingly hall or bower,
But where wild Nature girt herself with power ;
They met where streams flashed bright from rocky caves,
They met where woods made moan o'er warriors' graves,
And where the torrent's rainbow spray was cast,
And where cark leaves were heaving to the blast.

.   .   .   .   .

And the oaks breathed mysterious murmurs round."

The schools of the Druids were situated invariably in groves of trees, while the priests and other officials of the temples lived in houses erected in the woods and on the mountain slopes. Guards were placed at the stone entrances of the consecrated groves to bar the entrance of the uninitiated, in a manner similar to that of the Cutters or Tylors, who were stationed at the entrances of the Egyptian temples and as the Tylers are at the present day placed as Outer Guards to Masonic Temples and Lodges.

In this connection the following extract from the Rev. G. Stanley Faber's well-known work, *The Origin of Pagan Idolatry*, will be of interest. He says :

"In whatever mode the Mysteries were celebrated, we invariably find a certain door or gate viewed as being of primary importance. Sometimes it was the door of the temple ; sometimes the door of the consecrated grotto ; sometimes the hatchway of the boat within which the aspirant was enclosed ; sometimes a hole, either natural or artificial, through or between rocks ; and sometimes a gate in the sun or the moon or the planets. Through this the initiated were born again, and from this the profane were excluded. The notion evidently originated from the door in the side of the Ark through which the primary epoptæ were admitted, while the profane antediluvians were shut out.

"This circumstance gave rise to the appointment of an officer, who certainly bore a conspicuous part in the British orgies, and who probably was not unknown to the Mysteries of other countries. He was styled ' the door-keeper of the partial covering ' ; and, since he was considered to be the mystic husband of Ceridwen, he was certainly the representative of the great father Hu or Noe.   Hence he must have sustained the same character as Janus, when viewed as Thyreus, or ' the god of the door ' ;   while Ceridwen similarly corresponds with Venus or Ceres in her capacity of Prothyrea, or ' the goddess of the door.'   This personage was stationed before what Taliesin, in exact accordance with the prevailing ideas of the Mysteries, denominates ' the gates of hell ' ;   and he was armed with a bright, gleaming sword, whence he had the additional title of ' the sword bearer.'   His office was at once to exclude the profane, who might sacrilegiously attempt to gain admittance ;   and to punish, even with death, such of the initiated as should impiously reveal the awful secrets committed to them.   The same penalty, and (I apprehend) from the hand of a similar officer, awaited those who should too curiously pry into or divulge to the profane the wonders of the Eleusinian Mysteries.   Yet, notwithstanding every care that could be taken, we repeatedly find an adventurous epopt, who was content to run all risques rather than lose the pleasure of communicating a secret. . . .

" Whether the curiosity of the profane may be gratified at some future period by a similar disclosure of the portentous secret of Freemasonry remains yet to be seen.   I have frequently been inclined to suspect that this whimsical institution, which some have deduced from the Mithras or Buddhic Manicheans through the medium of the Knights Templar, is nothing more than a fragment of those orgies which have prevailed in every part of the world ; and the peculiar rites of the British Ceres, as their nature may be collected from the poems of the Bards, have served to strengthen my suspicion.   Not being one of the initiated myself, I can only speak from report ;   but the Masonic sword-bearer, who is said to be the guardian of the door during the celebration of those wonderful Mysteries, seems nearly allied to the similar character in the Orgies of Ceridwen ;   while the astronomical representations of the heavenly bodies, which are reported to decorate the cell of our modern epopts, bear a close analogy to the parallel decorations of the ancient cell or grotto or adytum.   The very title which they bear, when they throw aside the jargon respecting King Hiram and the temple of Solomon, affords no obscure intimation of their origin.   As professed masons or artisans, they connect themselves with the old Cabiric Telchines, as described by Diodorus, with the metallurgical Pheryllt of the Druidical Mysteries, with the architectural Cabiri of Phœnicia, with the demiurgic Phtha of Egypt, and with the great artisan Twashta of Hindostan.   All the most remarkable buildings of

Greece, Egypt, and Asia Minor were ascribed to the Cabréan or Cyclopian masons ; and in the present day, the Freemasons, with all their formalities, are wont to assist at the commencement of every public edifice. Finally, their affectation of mysterious concealment closely resembles the system of the Epopts in all ages and countries, particularly that of the Bards, when their religion no longer remained paramount. These last are probably the real founders of English Freemasonry."

The early generation of historical man had neither temples nor statues for their gods, but worshipped in the open air. Livy mentions that the ancient Latines used to hold their chief assemblies in a sacred grove. So deeply rooted was the opinion in the minds of the people that supplications to the Deity could not be made in any place so appropriately as from an eminence in the open air that down to the close of the eighteenth century a numerous sect existed in the south of Scotland called " Hill Folk," from their assembling on the hills to perform their devotional exercises under no canopy but that spread out by the hand of nature.

In exactness none of the Druidic temples can be so named from a strict etymological point of view, and they taught that there were but two habitations of the Deity : the soul, invisible ; the Universe, the visible temple. The inner enclosure of a Druidical circle always consisted of rough, unhewn stones. Similarly, the Israelite, if he erected an altar of stone was commanded (Exodus xx., 25, 26) that he should not build it of hewn stone : " for if thou lift thy tool upon it, thou hast polluted it." This prohibition was repeated at the passage over Jordan (Deuteronomy xxvii., 5, 6). Distinct mention is also made of unhewn stones, as applied to sacred uses, in the Edipus at Colonus, of Sophocles. Pausanias says that unhewn stones had the honour of gods and were worshipped among the Grecians, and that near the statue of Mercury there were thirty large stones which the people worshipped and gave to every one of them the name of a god. Tyrius states that he scarcely knew what god the Arabians worshipped, for that which he saw amongst them was only a white stone.

The Druids believed that the Eternal could not be locally limited to a house, the work of men's hands. They believed that the Universe was filled with His presence and they looked upwards to the heavens as His throne. Fergusson claims that " there is no passage in any classical author which connects the Druids, either directly or indirectly, with any stone temples or stones of any sort," a view also adopted by Dr. Stuart, but contested strongly by many writers. Dr. Stukeley was the first to suggest that the rude stone monuments in Britain were erected as temples by the Druids, but there is nothing in any of the ancient writers to support the suggestion. It may, however, be regarded as certain that their religious rites were performed within these circles. The circle played an important part in Druidical worship, which is the oldest form of religion known in Britain, but similar circles have been discovered in various and distant parts of the world, regions where probably the name of Druid was never heard. Clarke observed them in Ida and the Lebanon; Ouseley in Persia; Heber and Cox in Sweden and Norway; and others in Siberia and Africa.

There was doubtless a time when the Scandinavians worshipped their divinities only in the open air, and either knew not or approved not of the use of confined temples. Mallet, in *Northern Antiquities*, says:

"We find at this day here and there in Denmark, Sweden, and Norway, in the middle of a plain, or upon some little hill, altars around which they assembled to offer sacrifices and to assist at other religious ceremonies. The greatest part of these altars are raised upon a little hill, either natural or artificial. Three long pieces of rock set upright, serve for a basis to a great flat stone, which forms the table of the altar. There is commonly a pretty large cavity under this altar, which might be intended to receive the blood of the victims; and they never fail to find stones for striking fire scattered round it: for no other fire but such as was struck with a flint, was pure enough for so holy a purpose. Sometimes these rural altars are constructed in a more magnificent manner; a double range of enormous stones surround the altar and the little hill on which it is erected. In Zeeland we see one of this kind which is formed of stones of a prodigious magnitude. Men would even now be afraid to undertake such a work, notwithstanding all the assistance of the mechanical powers which in those times they wanted. What redoubles the astonishment is that stones of that size are rarely to be seen throughout the island and that they must have been brought from a great distance."

These engineering feats of the ancients formed the subject of an address recently by Mr. George H. Pegram, President of the American Society of Engineers, from which the following is quoted from the *Scientific American Supplement*:

"No works of modern times compare in magnitude with those of the ancients. Consider a reservoir, to impound the waters of the Nile, covering an area of 150 square miles, with a dam 30 feet high and 13 miles long. The pyramids of Gizeh had granite blocks which were five feet square and thirty feet long, and were transported 500 miles. One of the temples of Memphis was built of stones which were 13 feet square and 65 feet long, and laid with close joints. The Appian Way from Rome to Capua was so well built that after a thousand years its roadway was in perfect condition, and even now, after two thousand years, with slight repairs, is in use. The modern engineer would question the possibility of such work, without these great examples. If one could imagine cessation of life on this continent, and our works subjected to the destructive forces of time and nature for a thousand years, what evidences of civilization would remain ? We look in vain for the application of mechanical power by the ancients, whose works seem almost impossible without its assumption, but the stone reliefs showing the movement of large weights by manual power indicate that probably the other did not exist."

Haslam, in his book, *The Cross and the Serpent*, after referring to the Egyptian pyramids, the Babylonian walls, the city of Memphis, the Indian temples, the Chinese pagodas, and the American tescalli, says :

" Even yet a mystery of human labour remains untold ; many of the structures I have referred to are constructed of gigantic blocks of stone, varying from sixty to three hundred tons in weight. In Egypt single stones of this enormous weight have been traced to quarries five and six hundred miles from the pyramids into which they are built. . . . Our progenitors, the Scandinavian and Cymry, were not much behind the other races in this respect. Their temples consisted of gigantic stones set on end, in circles on hills and mountains ; and their cromlechs were composed of even larger stones, three being usually fixed into the ground, and the fourth laid upon them in the form of a table, pointing, and the surface, bowing a little, towards the east."

Stukeley divides the Druidic temples into three classes :

1. Rounds or Circles ;
2. Circles in serpentine form, as at Abury ;
3. Circles with the forms of wings annexed.

The remains of the first kind are most numerous. The groves of oaks were generally selected on the tops of mountains or hills, while caves were chosen for the instruction of youth and for initiatory rites. Prince Hywel, who died in 1171, was accustomed to invoke the Deity in the following words : " Attend Thou my worship in the mystical grove, and whilst I adore Thee, maintain Thy own jurisdiction."

According to Delta Evans, the following procedure was adopted at the " Meetings of the Circle " :

A huge flat stone, called *Gorsedd y Beirdd*, or " The Bard's Throne," was placed in the centre of a Cyclolith, or a circle of twelve smaller stones, with three others placed outside towards the rising sun, to represent two forecourts or porches. Through one of these porches the Chief Bard entered the Circle. He would be robed in a sky-blue gown and carry with him his Coelbren, or Bardic wood-memorial writing-frame. On entering the Circle he would recite a prayer to the Most High, of which the following is an example :

> Impart, O God, Thy strength,
> And in that strength, reason ;
> And in that reason, knowledge ;
> And in that knowledge, justice ;
> And in that justice, the love of it ;
> And in that love, the love of everything ;
> And in the love of everything, the love of God.
> Grant, O God, Thy refuge,
> And in refuge, strength ;
> And in strength, understanding ;
> And in understanding, knowledge ;
> And in knowledge, a perception of rectitude ;
> And in the perception of rectitude, the love of it ;
> And in that love, the love of all existences ;
> And in the love of all existences, the love of God and all
>   goodness.
> Grant, O God, Thy refuge,
> And in refuge, reason ;
> And in reason, light ;
> And in light, truth ;
> And in truth, justice ;
> And in justice, love ;
> And in love, the love of God ;
> And in the love of God, all blessedness and all goodness.
> God, impart Thy strength,
> And in strength, the power to suffer,
> And to suffer for the Truth ;
> And in truth, Light ;
> And in Light, blessedness ;
> And in blessedness, love ;
> And in love, God ;
> And in God, all goodness ;
> For in Him all terminates.

After the recital of the prayer any weapons of war within the assembly had to be surrendered. Two of the number present were invited to accompany the Chief Bard to within the Inner Circle to represent the three primitive Bards of Britain. These were, according to tradition, as stated, Gwyddon Ganhebon, the first man in the world who composed poetry ; Hu Gadarn, who first adapted poetry to the preservation of records and materials ; and Tydain Tad Awen, who first developed the art and structure of poetry and the due disposition of thought. From the labours of these three personages sprang Bards and Bardism, and the regulation of their privileges and the establishment of their discipline was accomplished by the three primary Bards, Plennydd, Alawn, and Gwron. Plennydd is a name for the sun, or Apollo ; Alawn means " harmony " ; and Gwron means " energy." The three representatives of the primitive Bards then addressed the assembly, after which followed the calling of the roll. This ceremony was known as *Cynal Gorsedd*, or " holding a throne."

STONEHENGE.

" A wondrous pyle of rugged mountaynes standes,
Plac'd on eche other in a dreare arraie,
It ne could be the worke of human handes,
It ne was reared up bie menne of claie.
Here did the Britons adoration paye
To the false god whom they did Tauran name,
Dightynge hys altarre with greete fyres in Maie,
Roastynge theyr vyctualle round aboute the flame,
'Twas here that Hengist did the Brytons slee
As they were mette in council for to bee."

Chatterton.

Of Stonehenge it has been asserted that nearly every prominent historical and mythical personage from the Devil onwards has, at one time or another, been credited with its erection. Inigo Jones maintained that it was erected by the Romans, and Dr. Charleton, with equal vigour, accredited it to the Danes, while, according to a calculation made by Prof. Norman Lockyer, the circles are, at least, 3,600 years old. His figures received some tangible confirmation in 1901 by the discoveries then made, when excavations were dug near the great monoliths, of some rude flints, axes, hammers, and other tools of the pre-bronze age, *viz.*, 1500-2000 B.C. Geoffrey of Monmouth asserts that Stonehenge was a monument erected in the reign of Aurelius Ambrosius, by Ambrose Merlin, to perpetuate the treachery of Hengist, the Saxon general who, having desired a friendly meeting with Vortigern at the monastery of Amesbury, assassinated him with 460 of his barons and consuls. A well-known Theosophist, Mr. A. P. Sinnett, asserts that Atlantean immigrants who came to the country a good deal later than the migration to Egypt—perhaps about 100,000 years ago—were really the engineers of Stonehenge, and they deliberately adopted the stern, rugged simplicity of its design because they were out of patience with the extravagant devotion to luxury and ornamentation then prevailing among the degenerate Atlanteans themselves.

I

Forlong, in *Rivers of Life*, says :

"It is generally acknowledged that this was a shrine to Apollo, or Belenus, and younger than that of Abury, which is thought to be more the shrine of ophiolaters and fire-worshippers than Solarists. The morticing of the Stonehenge blocks points to Phœnician art, which latterly set aside the ancient rules as to using only undressed stones. No one who has studied phallic and solar worship in the East could, I think, make any mistake as to the purport of this shrine, although I confess the many accounts of it which I have read, had not awakened my attention to the real facts, so misleading are many European writers on this, to them, unknown lore. Here stand upright stones, forming, as it were, a circular shaft within a perfect *argha*, or spoon-like enclosure, and there, to the eastward, the holy 'Pointer' in the *Os-Yoni*, over whose apex the first ray of the rising god of the midsummer Solstice (21st June) shines, right into the centre of the sacred circle. His eastward path is denoted by a long avenue, which diverges into two lines of wavy trench and embankment as it approaches the Lingam Pointer, around which and the circle it sweeps in an oval form. On all sides of this sacred spot are to be seen, scattered over a now bare, undulating country, large and small barrows or earthen mounds, the receptacles, no doubt, of the ashes, if not bones, of the dead, who once worshipped at the hallowed shrine, for it is clear the population of these days, like that of our fathers, loved to be buried around their church ; they were, perhaps, wiser than we, first burning the corpses, and only collecting the innocuous ashes to repose in these cellular caskets. The occurrence of such, all round the temple, reminds us of the holy spots which surround the Hindoo shrines, and to which visits must be paid by every devotee, after he or she has worshipped at the central holy place. If zealously pious, this is done, as elsewhere described, on hands and knees, and under a scorching mid-day sun, and always with many offerings to each holy spot, for without these, no priest can bestow his saintly blessing. In May, 1874, I made some very careful drawings of the Stonehenge shrine, and in the 'Pointer' at once distinguished 'the ever-anointed one.' He faces towards the circle, and in spite of every allowance for the accidents of weather-wear, etc., no one who has at all looked into Swaik lore will hesitate for a moment in pronouncing him a veritable Maha-Deva."

Stonehenge came into the market in 1915, when it was sold for £6,600 by Sir Charles Antrobus to Mr. C. H. E. Chubb, of Bemerton Lodge, Salisbury. In 1913 it had come under the Ancient Monuments Act, from which date it was impossible that it could be injured or destroyed by neglect or design, or be removed from its place at the will of any private owner. These limitations materially reduced the price which such a possession could command. In September, 1918, Mr. Chubb generously decided to present this historic monument to the nation, and this gift of the remains of a bygone civilization was accepted by the Government with the utmost satisfaction. Mr. Chubb expressed a wish that during the continuance of the war, the income from Stonehenge should be handed over to the Red Cross Society, whose work at that time was of such great national value, in which suggestion the Treasury willingly concurred. The property was thereupon transferred to the Ancient Monuments Board.

The conjectures as to the origin and construction of Stonehenge are many and varied. Mr. Herbert supposes that Stonehenge, Avebury, and other megalithic monuments of England were erected after the Romans had left the island. He supposes that the Bards and other adherents of the ancient religion returned from Ireland, whither they had been driven by the influence of Roman civilization, and that Druidism for a while regained its ascendancy and the enthusiasm awakened by the return to the old habits and feelings and by a sense of recovered independence led to the erection of these mighty structures. With the exception, as Dr. Edwin Guest points out, in *Origines Celticæ*, of Stonehenge, all the larger Druidical temples are situated in places where blocks of stone abound, or are known at one time to have abounded. Edwin Guest is of opinion that Stonehenge is of later date than Avebury and the other structures of unwrought stone ; that it could not have been built much later than 100 B.C., and, in all probability, was not built more than a century or two earlier. If its erection be fixed some eight or ten centuries before the Christian era, it would be difficult to advance any critical reasons against the hypothesis. W. S. Blacker, in his *Researches into the Lost Histories of America*, comes to the conclusion that the Apalachian Indians, with their priests and medicine men, must have been the builders of Stonehenge, and that that grand and marvellous creation, therefore, attests the truthfulness of Plato when he brings into Western Europe a great conquering people from beyond the Pillars of Hercules. Mr. Joseph Browne, who was for many years curator of the " Stones," used to expound his belief that Stonehenge stood before the Deluge, and would point out (to his own satisfaction) signs of the action of water upon the stones, even showing the direction in which the flood came rushing in.

Langtoft's *Chronicles* assert that the Monument was framed according to the most exquisite rules of architecture, of which the pitiful, naked Britons had no knowledge at all. The following twelve conclusions are arrived at :

      1. That Stonehenge was an old British monument ;

2. That it was a monument of a bloody battel foughten there ;
3. This bloudy battel produced a glorious Victorie ;
4. This victorie was wonne by the Cangi of Gladerhaf ;
5. The Cangi were Giants ;
6. Commanded by the famous Stanenges of Honnicutt ;
7. The Army conquered was King Divitiacus and his Belgæ ;
8. In this place, as soone as the Cangi had conquered, they triumphed ;
9. Where they triumphed they erected this monument as a trophie ;
10. This Trophie was a Temple ;
11. This Temple was consecrated to Anaraith, their Goddess of Victorie ;
12. In this temple the said Victors sacrificed their Captives and Spoiles to their said Idoll of Victorie.

The Cangi are said to have been " singers to instruments of Musick," and the westernmost inhabitants of the island.   Sir Thomas Elliott, in his *Dictionarie*, on the word " Cigas " says : " About thirty years since, I my self, being with my father, Sir Richard Elliott, at a Monasterie of Regular Canons (three or four miles from Stonage) beheld the bones of a dead man found deep in the ground, which being joyned together, was in length thirteen foot and ten inches, whereof one of the teeth my father had, which was of a quantity of a great wallnut.   This I have written because some men will believe nothing, that is out of the compass of their own knowledge."   He gives the foregoing as a reason for Stonehenge being known as " the Giants' Dance."

Wood, in *Stonehenge Explained*, gives an interesting theory concerning the stones.   He says :

" The two outward rows of pillars are the very emblems of the two first principles of the Magian religion : for the colour of the stones intimate good and evil ; and the lines which these stones form, being the peripheries of circles, or lines running into themselves, represent eternity.   But the two inward rows of pillars vary the principles pointed out by the former : for, notwithstanding the colour of the stones intimate good and evil, yet the imperfection in the lines which these stones form, as they are partly curved and partly straight, without returning into themselves, denotes created things, and exhibits the reformation which Zoroaster made in the Persian theology, by divesting the two first principles of it of eternity, and making light and darkness works of the Supreme God."

The word " Stonehenge " is supposed to have derived its name from the Anglo-Saxon and means literally " hanging stones."   In Yorkshire, pendulous rocks are called *Henges*.   Stonehenge was known formerly as

A Druid,
from an old engraving.

Choir Gaur, a Phœnician term meaning " a circular high place of the assembly or congregation." Stowe, in his *British Chronicle*, says that the Irish brought the stones with them from Africa ; that they were taken to England by Merlin from Mount Clare, and erected upon Salisbury Plain by Aurelius Ambrosius.

It may be taken for granted that the Druids were not the originators or builders of the circle, but that they used the place for the purposes of their ceremonies. Sir Norman Lockyer says :

"The cursus at Stonehenge and the avenues on Dartmoor may be regarded as evidences that sacred processions formed part of the ceremonial on holy days, but sacrifices and sacred ceremonials were not alone in question : many authors have told us that feasts, games, and races were not forgotten. This, so far as racing is concerned, is proved, I think, by the facts that the cursus at Stonehenge is 10,000 feet long and 350 feet broad ; that it occupies a valley between two hills, thus permitting of the presence of thousands of spectators, and that our horses are still decked with gaudy trappings on May-day."

In 1888 Sir Arthur Evans investigated the question of the age of Stonehenge in a lecture given at the Ashmolean Museum at Oxford, which was printed in the *Archæological Review* for January, 1889, and below is given, by permission, Mr. Falconer Madan's summary, which he quotes as an example of historical method, in his admirable guide, *The Bodleian Library at Oxford* :

1. Many of the barrows, two of which are in obvious connection with the great stones, are shown by their forms and contents to be of the largest types of Bronze Age barrows, known as Round Barrows (for instance, gold relics, glass beads, ivory and cremated remains are signs of lateness). This being so, it is significant that chippings of the stones brought *from a distance* to Stonehenge are found even in undisturbed barrows of this kind, where the action of earthworms and rabbits in introducing foreign elements is hardly possible. It is clear, therefore, that the building of Stonehenge was at least begun *late* in that period. There is the point also that, with the exception of two, the circumjacent barrows are *not* in any relation with the great circle, and are therefore not later.

2. The contents of the barrows earlier than Stonehenge have some imported articles which must have come from the Continent not before the fifth century B.C. One even is stated to have contained a socketed celt, pointing to the late fourth century. But late Celtic antiquities are wholly absent, which makes it hardly possible that the barrows should be as late as the second century B.C.

The skilful hewing and fitting of the huge blocks of Wiltshire

Sarsen stone are of the same stage in technical development as the triliths of Syria and Tripoli, and the great Doric temples of Segesta in Sicily, which latter was constructed about 415 B.C.

From these and similar indications he concludes that the gradual building of the great monument was probably between 300 and 150 B.C. He is now inclined to place the date earlier.

On 1st May, 1919, Sir Arthur Evans, in an address to the Society of Antiquaries, after referring to the recent presentation of Stonehenge to the nation, a subject of hearty congratulation, said he should continue to believe that the whole class of monuments to which Stonehenge belongs, grows out of a sepulchral cult. Its grand scale put it out of the category of ordinary funereal monuments and there was every reason to believe that it was associated with the higher cult. The bones of deer and oxen dug up in the interior, moreover, certainly pointed to sacrifices in such a connection. But that cult, he maintained, should be sought rather in the direction of the gods of the underworld than of any solar divinity. The stones seemed to him to have been set up gradually and might be taken also to include the commemoration of many individual chiefs of that bygone race.

In 1923 a missing eastern branch of the Stonehenge Avenue was discovered by means of air photography, and afterwards proved conclusively through excavations, superintended by Mr. O. C. S. Crawford, Archæology Officer of the Ordnance Survey, and Mr. A. D. Passmore. It is interesting to note that the measurements of Dr. William Stukeley (who was the butt of the ridicule of many of his contemporaries) were proved absolutely accurate. Mr. Crawford, in an article in the *Observer* of 23rd September, 1923, says :

It is a testimony to the accuracy of Stukeley, the pioneer field archæologist of the eighteenth century, that we found his figures correct to a foot : no unnecessary digging was required.

Several flints were found which had been chipped by human agency.

Mr. Crawford, continuing, says :

They resemble the flints found by Colonel Hawley at Stonehenge ; ours were clearly contemporary with the making of the ditch, since they were found right at the bottom ; and although flint was chipped and flint implements were used during the Iron Age and even in Roman times, it is more likely that these flints belong to an earlier epoch.

One result, and one of the highest importance, of the discovery of this avenue, which splits into two branches, one leading to a racecourse and the other to a river (and neither branch straight) cannot, says Mr. Crawford, be regarded as oriented to the rising sun for purposes of worship, so that it puts out of court once and for all the fanciful astronomical theories of Sir Norman Lockyer and others.

Stonehenge lies about two miles west of the village of Amesbury, in the middle of a flat area, near the summit of a hill and between six and seven miles from Salisbury.

The following description is adapted from the Ordnance Survey Report made by Sir Henry James :

The structure when complete consisted of an outer circle of thirty large stones, upon which thirty other stones were laid horizontally, so as to form a perfect continuous circle. The diameter within the stones was one hundred feet. The stones in the uprights have each two tenons on their upper surfaces, which fit into mortices cut into the under surface of the horizontal stones and by this mode of construction the whole circle was braced together. The average dimensions of the uprights in this circle are 12 ft. 7 ins. high out of the ground ; 6 ft. broad ; and 3 ft. 6 ins. thick. Those in the circle resting on the uprights are about 10 ft. long ; 3 ft. 6 ins. wide ; and 2 ft. 8 ins. deep. Within this circle there are five stupendously large trilithons, each consisting of two uprights with tenons on them, supporting a large horizontal lintel, in which two mortices are cut to receive the tenons. These trilithons are arranged in the form of a horseshoe, so that one of them is central as regards the other four. A horizontal stone which is called the altarstone lies in front of the central trilithons and the axial line of the structure is from N.E. to S.W.

All the stones in the outer circle and the trilithons are of an undulated tertiary sandstone, which is found upon the chalk in the neighbourhood, and particularly near Avebury and Marlborough, where they are known by the name of " Sarsen " stones and the " Grey Wethers."

The dimensions of the trilithons are nearly as follows :

			Breadth.	Thickness.
A.	Height of upright	22' 5"	7' 6"	4' 0"
	Lintel length	15' 0"	4' 6"	3' 6"
B.		17' 2"	7' 0"	4' 0"
		15' 9"	4' 0"	3' 7"
C.		16' 6"	7' 9"	4' 0"
		17' 0"	4' 0"	2' 8"
D.		22' 0"	8' 3"	4' 3"
		16' 0"	4' 0"	3' 6"
E.		16' 6"	7' 0"	4' 0"

The altar stone is 17 ft. long and 3 ft. 6 ins. wide.

In addition to these there was formerly a complete circle of thirty smaller upright stones about 6 ft. high, which was intermediate in position between the outer circle and the five trilithons. Within the trilithons

there was also a row of smaller stones about 7 ft. 6 ins. high, parallel
with the trilithons. In the opinion of Sir Henry James these were
probably monumental stones in memory of chieftains or priests.

Only seventeen of the thirty upright stones of the outer circle are
now standing and only six of the thirty lintels are now in their places.
Only two of the trilithons are perfect.

Geoffrey of Monmouth states that there was not one stone at Stonehenge which had not some healing virtue and that the water washed
over the stones was efficacious in healing the sick and curing wounds.

Dr. Charleton, who was a royal physician, was the author of a
treatise advocating the Danish origin of Stonehenge, but this theory is
overthrown by the fact that Stonehenge is mentioned by Nennius, who
lived about A.D. 620, and the Danes did not visit Britain until two
hundred years later.

> " Thou, noblest monument of Albion's isle,
> Whether by Merlin's aid, from Scythia's shore
> To Amber's fatal plain, Pendragon bore,
> Huge frame of giant hands the mighty pile,
> T'entomb his Britons, slain by Hengist's guile,
> Or Druid priests, sprinkled with human gore,
> Taught 'mid thy massy maze their mystic lore :
> Or Danish chiefs, enrich'd with savage spoil,
> To Victory's idol vast, an unhewn shrine,
> Rear'd the rude heap ; or, in thy hallow'd round,
> Repose the King of Brutus' genuine line ;
> Or here those Kings in solemn state were crown'd :
> Studious to trace thy pond'rous origin,
> We muse on many an ancient Isle renown'd."
>
> _T. Warton._

AVEBURY OR ABURY.

> " Near Wilton sweet, huge heaps of stones are found,
> But so confus'd, that neither any tie
> Can count them just, nor reason try
> What force brought them to so unlikely ground."
>
> _Sir Philip Sidney._

Avebury, which is situated about a mile from Beckhampton, on
the main road from London to Devizes and Bath, when perfect, consisted
of an embankment three-quarters of a mile in circumference, 12 ft.
broad and averaging 15 ft. above the natural surface of the land and a
deep circular ditch, now 15 ft. deep, but originally not less than 30 ft.
deep, containing an area of twenty-eight and a half acres. Inside the
ditch which, with the rampart, measured about 70 ft. in height, was a
circle of one hundred massive unhewn grey stones, generally about 20 ft.

in height, and within this principal circle were two smaller concentric circles formed by a double row of stones, each 7 ft. in height, standing side by side, the outer circle consisting of twenty and the inner of twelve stones.   From the outer embankment started two long winding avenues of stones, on each side at regular distances, one of which went in the direction of Beckhampton and the other in that of Kennet, where it ended in another double circle.   In the centre of one of these was a tall phallus 21 ft. in height and 8 ft. 9 ins. in diameter and within the other was a cell or adytum.   Each avenue being on an inclined plane, a person advancing towards the temple would have on all sides a very fine view of the site.

The temple formed the compound figure of a snake transmitted through a circle, an undisputed emblem of the Deity ;   the circle representing the Demiurgus or Creator, while the serpent symbolised the divine emanation to whose wisdom the government of the universe was entrusted.   Faber, in *Pagan Idolatry*, is of opinion that the ring represented the ark of Ceridwen, while the snake was the great god, Hu. In all there were 650 stones in the circles and avenues, but now only about twenty are standing, though some others still remain buried in the ground.

In its pristine glory Avebury must have been the most magnificent temple of its kind in the world.   The name has been derived from the Cabiri and signifies " the mighty ones."   It was regarded as so holy that no reptiles could live there and if any were taken into the sacred precincts they immediately died.   Celtic tradition affirms that it was within the circles of Abury that the institution of the Gorsedd had its origin, a national institution not known outside Britain.

John Aubrey, who was the first to examine Avebury with any care, expressed the opinion that " Avebury doth so much exceed Stonehenge in grandeur as a Cathedral doth an ordinary parish church," and Sir Richard Colt Hoare, in his work on *Ancient Wiltshire*, commences his chapter on Avebury with these words :   " With awe and diffidence I enter the sacred precincts of this once hallowed sanctuary, the supposed parent of Stonehenge, the wonder of Britain, and the most ancient, as well as the most interesting relict which our island can produce."

Stukeley considered the stones at Avebury to be at least twice the age of Stonehenge itself, and although it is perhaps the oldest monument of the British race in Britain, there is no record of it earlier than 1663, the year when Aubrey showed Charles II. over the site and afterwards, by royal command, wrote an account of the visit.

William Long says that

" the object for which the great work at Abury was constructed will probably for ever be involved in mystery.   We know so little of the Druids and their forms of worship that to more than conjectural approximations to the truth we can hardly hope to attain. An astronomical, a civil, and a religious purpose have each had their advocates. The erection, too, of circular stones like this and Stonehenge, has been assigned by different writers to different nations, to the Phœnicians, the ancient Britons, the Romans, the Saxons, and the Danes. There can, however, be little doubt that the temple at Abury dates from a period long anterior to the Roman occupation of Britain and that it was much older work than Stonehenge."

When the site was excavated by a committee of the British Association, fragments of mediæval pottery were found at a depth of from two to three feet from the surface ; fragments of Roman pottery from three-and-a-half to four-and-a-half feet ; and, below that depth, prehistoric pottery, flint chips, scrapers and antlers of red deer.

On the ancient Norman font in Abury Church there is a mutilated figure dressed apparently in the Druidical priestly garb, holding a crozier in one hand and clasping an open book to his breast with the other. Two winged dragons or serpents are attacking this figure on either side. It has been conjectured that this was designed to represent the triumph of Christianity over Druidism, in which there was much veneration entertained for the serpent.

Near Merrivale Bridge, on Dartmoor, a long avenue of rude stones, 1,140 ft. long, is terminated at each end by a sacred Druidic circle, whilst another circle stands in the centre. These circles consisted originally of nineteen stones—nineteen being a sacred number and indicated the meteoric or lunar circle, at whose completion the moon would resume her original position in the heavens. About one hundred yards to the east runs another avenue 800 ft. long and about 5 ft. wide. Somewhat to the north stands a rock pillar, 12 ft. in height and another sacred circle, 67 ft. in diameter, formed of ten stones.

At Vale Church, in Guernsey, is a Druidical altar which, when it was perfect and with the original conformation, must have been one of the finest in existence. It was first disencumbered of the drifting sand which had covered it, in 1811, but it was not until 1837 that it was thoroughly explored and exposed through the instrumentality of Dr. Lukis. The cromlech is 45 ft. long by 13 ft. wide and nearly 8 ft. in height at the western end, where it contracts gradually on each side, as it does at the top towards the eastern end. The space is covered by five larger and two smaller blocks of granite, which are not in contact. The western block is computed to weigh about thirty tons, it being nearly 17 ft. long, 18 ft. wide, and 4½ ft. thick, and it is thought that it was placed here by means of rollers. The second block is 16 ft. long, the third smaller, and so on, diminishing gradually until the seventh. On the floor, when it was opened in 1837, were found two layers, consisting of human bones, masses of coarse red and black clay, stone armlets, beads, bone-pins, etc.

The removal of some sand in the early part of the nineteenth century brought to light the remains of a Druidical structure at L'Ancresse Bay, 32 ft. in length with a greatest width of 12 ft. The largest stone weighed about twenty tons. A large stone closed the entrance to the temple, which was approached by a descent over some steps. About 18 ft. away from the temple were the remains of a circle of stones placed about a foot above the ground and about 2 ft. distant from each other. Another outer circle 42 ft. away from the temple, but of this fewer stones were remaining. These are the finest Druidical remains in the island. The roof is formed of six huge capstones graduated in size. Close by is the De Tus dolmen with three " side chapels." Both these temples were explored by Dr. Lukis.

Near Vale Church was a traditional stone *La Rocque dui Sonne*, which, according to the general local belief, formed a portion of a very extensive circle, of which one of the capstones was actually dug out in 1837. It is stated that the owner of the field in which this stone was situated began to build a house and broke up the stone for the supports and lintels of the doors and windows. No immediate judgment fell upon him, but in less than twelve months his house was burned down. He then rebuilt it, whereupon it was burnt down in a similar manner. With a persistency worthy of a better cause he sold the stones and shipped them to England, but the vessel containing the cargo foundered and all on board perished.

A Druidical temple was discovered in 1785 on the summit of a hill near St. Heliers, Jersey. It was covered with earth until then, when the Colonel of the St. Heliers Militia wanted to level the ground for the exercise of his corps. The workmen soon lighted upon the stones of the temple when the ground was cleared. It was assumed that the temple was covered up by the Druids to prevent its profanation by the people. It consisted of 45 large stones, averaging 7 ft. in height, 6 ft. in breadth, and 4 ft. in thickness, the whole being 56 ft. in circumference. The supposed entrance was in a subterranean passage facing the east and measuring 15 ft. in length, 4 ft. 2½ ins. in breadth, and 2 ft. in height. The medals were found in the passage, one being of the time of the Emperor Claudius, but the other was so worn as to be unidentifiable. Five graves were afterwards discovered on the same hill, about 170 ft. from the temple. Blindextre, who died in 1691, says that there were existing in the Isle of Jersey no fewer than fifty Druidical temples or altars, but Falle, in his *History of Jersey*, published in 1695, only mentions one Druidical altar.

There are the remains to-day of at least ten circles in the Isle of Man. One of the most striking of these remains is at Glen Darragy—" the Vale of the Oaks." The name would, on first consideration, appear to be a misnomer, as, instead of being a glen in the general acceptance of that term, the circle is situate several hundred feet above the sea level, on the side of a mountain near the village of Braid. It consists of one large oval lying due east and west. On the western side there are two distinct circles, one of which, consisting of twelve stones, most of which are from two to three feet high, is perfect. The other, on the southern side, which consists of about the same number of stones, is overgrown with brambles and some of the stones have apparently been thrown down, though it still preserves its circular form. Between the two appears to be what was formerly an avenue, the entrance to which was evidently at the eastern end. This also consists of twelve stones, two of which, namely, those at the entrance, are quite four feet broad and about three feet in height. When observed from the high road, about two hundred yards above the circle, the spectators cannot fail to be struck by the phallicism conveyed.

About a mile distant are three stones in a field known as Mager-y-chiarn, or " the holy field." This field is on the side of a mountain called Sleau-chiarn, or " the holy hill." The stones are known locally as St. Patrick's Chair, and at one time there was undoubtedly a sedalia underneath. The centre stone is higher than those on either side. The southernmost back slab has evidently been broken, as only a portion remains, but the centre and northernmost stones are still intact and have crosses engraved upon them. The broken stone evidently also had a cross engraved upon it, as the foot of a cross is still plainly to be seen. According to popular tradition, St. Patrick sat here and ordained the first bishop of the Isle of Man, and from here also blessed the people. Inside the circle a number of stones have been gathered and heaped up together.

In the parish of Marown, on the north side of the estate of Mount Murray, the visitor will find a perfect Druidical temple of large dimensions. The circle is of an unusually large diameter of forty-two feet, and is composed of perpendicular stones. Two terraces partially enclose the temple.

On the Mull Hills, in the extreme south of the island, near the village of Craighneich, there are two circles. One is at the summit of an elevation, almost directly over the popular watering-place of Port Erin. It consists of two circles, one within the other, the outside diameter being N. and S., 50 ft., and E. and W., 57 ft., and it is made conformable to the four points of the compass, and at each point there is an entrance to the centre of the circle. It is disputed whether the site marks a Druidical circle or a burying place. A little below are a number of stones and mounds, which are apparently the remains of an ancient town, believed by some to be of the Stone Age. This is corroborated by the fact that in a farm near by were found a large number of flint and other stone implements, including several querns or ancient stone grinding mills. One of these querns, together with samples of arrow heads and other flint implements, can be seen in a small refreshment hut, not a very great distance from the circle. A few years since, Dr. H. M. Léon found a flint arrow not very far from this place, which he has still in his possession. The other circle is near to Spanish Head and in close proximity to a very interesting spot known as " The Chasms," where great clefts appear in the rock extending downwards to between three and a hundred feet. In connection with these chasms there are certain caverns at the foot thereof, facing the renowned Sugar Loaf Rock, concerning which many interesting legends are related.

Another interesting stone circle, though of smaller size, can be seen in the parish of Santon. It is situate in a field about fifty or sixty yards from the main road and not very far from a granite quarry. It consists of fifteen stones in circular form.

In the north-west part of the island, between Douglas and Laxey, there is a stone circle called the Lonan or Cloven Stones. They are in the little village of Baldrine, a short distance from the main road. There are two large upright stones which seem to have been cleft asunder, and several smaller stones, and together they form a circle. There is an interesting legend in connection with these stones. It is said that the Druids were actually in the act of making a sacrifice of a human being upon one of these stones, when St. Maughold landed on the island from a leathern boat. St. Maughold arrived in the middle of the ceremony, and, sprinkling holy water upon the sacrificial stone, extinguished the fire and split the stone asunder, releasing the victim. St. Maughold is said to have crossed himself and said : " Avaunt ye fiends." Some of the water sprinkled upon the fire worked through the fuel and dropped on to the stone, thus causing it to split right down the centre, leaving it as it stands to the present day. The Druidical priests are said to have been so astonished at this miracle that they fled, leaving their intended victim behind. St. Maughold then cut the prisoner's bonds, released him and preached the Christian gospel to him, which faith he joyfully accepted. He was the first convert to Christianity in the Isle of Man, and he was baptized there and then, standing on the stone on which he was to have been sacrificed. He is said to have taken the name of Lonanus, become a priest, and subsequently Bishop of the Isle of Man in succession to St. Maughold, and, after his death, canonised, giving his name to the parish of Lonan. It is stated that after his conversion,

Lonanus desired to build a church upon the spot, but St. Maughold would not permit him to do so, saying it was better to let the stones remain as they were, in order that the Manx people might have always before their eyes the evidence of the miraculous power of holy water in the shape of the cloven stone, while the saint, at the same time, pronounced a dreadful curse against any one who should attempt to move those stones at any time thereafter.

St. Maughold is said to have been formerly a captain of banditti in Ireland, and as a punishment for his crimes was bound hand and foot, sent out to sea in a leathern boat, in which he was driven on shore at the north end of the island at a spot which now bears his name—Maughold Head. Being delivered from his perilous situation, he retired into the mountainous parts of the country and, devoting his life to religion, became so exemplary that, after the death of Germanus, whom St. Patrick had left in spiritual charge, prior to his departure for Ireland, he was elected bishop by the unanimous wish of the people.

On the western side of the island, in a bye road above Poor Town Quarry, is a group of stones known as the Giant's Grave, but which is apparently the remains of an avenue which once led to a circle which is no longer in existence.

Near Ballown or Crescent Cottage is a remarkable Druidical temple. The circle is thirty feet in diameter and is composed of irregular white quartz blocks. A large table of granite lies on the east side, which seems to have been removed from the interior of the circle and was probably used for human sacrifices.

Altogether there are about thirty-five distinct circles in the Isle of Man accredited to the Druids. It is also interesting to note that one of the principal valleys running almost to the foot of Snaefell is still known by the name of Druidale.

Buchanan, in his *History of Scotland*, says : " So highly were the Manx Druids distinguished for their knowledge of Astronomy, Astrology, and Natural Philosophy, that the kings of Scotland sent their sons to be educated by them. About the year 76, Dothan, the eleventh king of Scotland, left his three sons to be educated by the Druids in the Isle of Man."

On Rombald's Moor, close to Keighley, in Yorkshire, are some stones which are supposed to be Druidical remains. Brimham Rocks, in the vicinity of Harrogate, are credited by local tradition with having been the scene of Druidical worship. Brimham Rocks are scattered over an area of about forty acres and present at a distance the appearance of a ruined city. Three or four of them are so nicely poised as to rock on the application of the slightest force. The largest of these rocking stones is calculated to weigh one hundred tons. Some of the stones are perforated with singular regularity and have received from this circumstance the name of " Cannon Rocks." The bore of one of the rocks is twelve inches in diameter. Several tumuli may be observed in the neighbourhood of these stones, the larger of them being about 150 ft. in circumference. The place is called Graff-plain, or " the Plain of the Graves."

The Bridestones at Levisham in Yorkshire, a number of huge rocks fringing both sides of a deep glen, have a Druidical reputation.

There is a Druidical monument, known as " Long Meg and her daughters," which stands near Little Salkeld in Durham. It consists, according to Grose and Astle's *Antiquarian Repertory*, of 67 massy stones, of various sorts and sizes, ranged in a circle of nearly 120 paces diameter. Some of these stones are granite, some blue and grey limestone, and others flint. Many of them are ten feet high and fifteen or sixteen inches in circumference : these are called Long Meg's Daughters. On the southern side of the circle and about seventeen or eighteen paces out of the line stands the stone called Long Meg, which is of that kind of red stone found round about Penrith. It is so placed that each of its angles faces one of the cardinal points of the compass. It measures upwards of eighteen feet in height and fifteen inches in girth, its figure being nearly that of a square prism. It weighs about 16 tons. In the part of the circle most contiguous, four large stones are placed in a square form, as if they had been intended to support an altar ; and towards the east, west, and north, two large stones stand a greater distance from each other than any of the rest, seemingly to form the entrance into the circle. It is remarkable that no stone quarry is to be found hereabouts. The same ridiculous story is related concerning these stones as of those at Stonehenge, *i.e.*, that it is impossible to count them, and that many persons who have made the trial could never twice make them amount to the same number. These stones are mentioned by Camden, who either miscalculated their number or was misinformed, unless, which seems improbable, some have since been taken away. " At Little Salkeld," he says, " there is a circle of stones, 77 in number, each 10 ft. high, and before these, at the entrance, is a single one by itself, 15 ft. high. This the common people call Long Meg, and the rest her daughters, and within the circle are two heaps of stones, under which they say are bodies buried ; and, indeed, it is probable enough that this has been a monument erected in memory of some great victory."

These circles are now generally admitted to have been temples and places of judgment and not sepulchral monuments. Indeed, the editor of *Camden* has rectified the statement by making the following comment : " But as to the heaps in the middle, they are no part of the monument, but have been gathered off the plowed lands adjoining, and (as in many other parts of the country) thrown up here in a waste corner of the field : and as to the occasion both this and the Rollright Stones in Oxfordshire, are supposed by many to have been monuments erected at the solemn investiture of some Danish kings, and of the same kind as the Kingstolen in Denmark, and Moresteen in Sweden, concerning which several large discourses have been written." One tradition, by the way, states that Oxford itself was a Druid seat of learning and that the Bards held their mystic rites in the oak woods which still flourish in the neighbourhood.

Near to Keswick is an alleged Druidical monument, not mentioned by Camden and little known. It is said to have been discovered some years ago by Dr. Brownrigge, who resided in the neighbourhood. It stands on the flat summit of a hill, close under a mountain known as Saddleback, about two miles from Keswick and near to the Penrith road. It is composed of stones, mostly granite, of divers shapes and sizes, evidently collected from the surface of the earth, being rude and untouched by any instrument. They are ranged nearly in a circle, some standing and others lying. The diameter from east to west is about thirty yards and that from north to south measures nearly thirty-two yards. The stones at the north end are the largest, being nearly eight feet in height and fifteen feet in circumference. At the eastern end a small enclosure is formed by ten stones, in connection with those of that side of the circle. It is supposed to have been the Adytum, or Sanctum Sanctorum, into which it was not lawful for any but the Druids to enter. On the inside it measures about seven yards from east to west and three in breadth, and here, in all probability, the altar was placed. On the east side, opposite the Adytum, a single stone lies about three paces out of the circle. The entire monument consists of fifty stones, forty of which form the circle and the remainder are employed in the Adytum.

At Liverpool there is a perfect circle, near to Moseley Hill, known as Calder Stones. It has a diameter of thirty feet.

Four Druidical circles, each of nineteen stones, are to be seen in the vicinity of Penweth in Cornwall. Maurice thinks that they refer to the cycle of nineteen years, supposed to be of Druidical invention.

St. Patrick is believed to have visited Cornwall with twenty companions, when he preached to the people and founded a monastery. On elevations near the sea and on inland hills and tors, where bel-fires had long existed, churches and chapels were dedicated to St. Michael, the conqueror of the dragon.

" Each rocky spire
Of the vast mountain stood on fire,
Though now for ever gone the days
When God was worshipped in the blaze."

On the Mabe Road, five miles from Penryn, stood formerly the Tolmen or Holed Stone, on a bleak, bare steep, 690 ft. above the sea. This interesting memorial was 33 ft. long, 14 ft. deep, and 18 ft. broad. It rested upon two deeply embedded stones, in such a manner that a man might crawl under it and a superstition long prevailed that a person so crawling, upon certain holy days, could obtain instant relief from any malady from which he might be suffering. It was blown up some years ago by the owner of a neighbouring quarry. At Land's End, there is the Carn Leskez, or Carn of Light, where it is said Druids were wont to kindle the sacred fire ; and the Boxhednan Ring at Penzance is a sacred Druidical arch, 68 ft. in diameter and composed of eleven stones. The Hurlers at Liskeard are said to be the remains of three extensive Druidical circles, of which one only is now in tolerable preservation. A local legend, however, runs that the pillars represent the figures of some Sabbath breakers, who, while engaged in hurling—a Cornish ball game— were smitten into stone. There is a holed stone in the Vale of Lamorna, near to St. Paul, which is locally believed to have been used by the Druids for tying down their human sacrifices.

The Sacred Circle at Scorhill Down, above the confluence of the Wallabrook and North Teign, is by far the finest example of the shrines of Druidical worship in Devonshire. The two principal columnar masses stand at nearly opposite points of the circle, the highest rising nearly eight feet from the surface and the other standing upwards of six feet ; the lowest are about three feet high and the whole area is about 100 ft. in diameter. The whole of the enclosed area has been industriously cleared of stones.

The Grey Wethers, so called from their being easily mistaken for sheep at a little distance, are two Druidical circles, each about 60 ft. in diameter. They are on the higher part of Dartmoor, above Ladle Bottom, and directly under Sittaford Tor, and adjoin each other. They consist of thirty stones each, varying from 3 ft. to 5 ft. in height and are from 7 ft. to 8 ft. apart. Dr. Stukeley surmises that they were spewed out of the chalk by the centrifugal forces of the earth.

Quarnell Down contains a number of columns or circles, one enclosing a kistvaen or sepulchral chest.

On Buckland Down is a small circle of the same kind and there is another between Quarnell Tor and Shapitor.

There is a Druidical circle near Winterbourne Abbas, situated at the bottom of a deep valley, called the " Nine Stones," which are perfectly unwrought and vary in height from 1 ft. to 6 ft. The stones mark out a circle about 27 ft. by 25 ft. 6 ins. in diameter.

The circles at Stanton Drew, in Somersetshire, which are supposed by many to be of older date than that of Abury, are known as " the

K

wedding," from a tradition that a bride and her attendants were changed into these stones. Another legend says that they represent serpents converted into stones by Keyna, a holy virgin of the fifth century. There is also here the local tradition about the difficulty of numbering the stones and the danger of drawing them. A similar circle in Stafford-shire has the same name.

At Port Hellick, in the Scilly Isles, there is a Giant's Chair, where, according to tradition,

> " Sat the Arch-Druid, in his lonely pomp,
> With wistful eyes fixed on the rising sun."

There are also some rock-pillars, said to have been of Druidical origin, nine feet in height, at St. Agnes, Inangen Point. Tolmen Point, at Old Town, in the Scilly Islands, is so named from the perforated stone or Tolmen on its summit.

At Fountain Dale in Nottingham is a curious object, known as the Druid's Stone, a cloven rock, 14 ft. in height and 84 ft. in circumference, which crowns a national platform in a valley. Another similar stone stands a few yards distant. Both are regarded with veneration.

There are several Druidical remains in Derbyshire. Stanton Moor appears to have been a place much frequented by the Druids : here there are temples, caves, rock-basins, rocking stones, and cairns. Bateman, in his *Vestiges of the Antiquities of Derbyshire*, says :

> " At the south end of Stanton Moor, close to the village of Birchover, is a remarkable assemblage of gritstone rocks, which extends in length between seventy and eighty yards and rises to the height of about forty or fifty yards. This massive ridge would afford great facilities to the Druids for practising their deceptions upon the people, there being natural passages and cavernous hollows in various parts of the rocks, some large masses of which would require but little art and labour to convert them into moving or rocking stones ; in fact, oracles delivered from this ridge of rocks would be as much calculated to inspire awe in the breasts of the superstitious Britons, as those did from the temple of Apollo at Delphus, to the more polished but equally credulous Greeks and Romans."

Considerable excitement was caused among archæologists a few years since by the announcement in the public press that the Druidical circle known as Harborough Rocks, near Matlock, had been sold to a company with £75,000 capital, to be worked for its value as dolomite stone. The Harborough Rocks were at one time owned by the late Sir Joseph Whitworth, the founder of the firm of Armstrong, Whitworth, and he had intended to erect a mansion there, but changed his mind in favour of Stancliffe, at Darley Dale. The rocks include a Druid's chair, cut in stone, where, it is believed, the ritual was carried out. A short time prior to the sale some notable discoveries were made at Harborough by antiquaries, who excavated the floor of a cave in the rocks, formerly the home of cave-dwellers. They included the bones of animals long since extinct, and an ancient Cornelian ring.

About seven miles from Buxton, near to Middleton-by-Youlgrave, may be found the remains of a Druidical temple known as Arbor-Low, or Arbe Lowe, which recently was sold, much to the regret of archæologists. It consists of 38 stones, all in their proper order, but all prostrate on the ground, the stones inclined towards the centre and covering an area of from forty to fifty yards diameter. Round it is a deep ditch bounded by a high earthen bank turfed over. It is the most striking remains of antiquity in any part of Derbyshire. The temple is said to correspond more nearly than any other in character and features, though far inferior in size, with the gigantic monument in Wiltshire. Bateman says concerning this that it is the most important, as well as the most uninjured, remains of the religious edifices of the early religion of the Britons to be found in the Midland counties.

"It lies on the left of the turnpike road from Buxton to Ashbourne, and its situation, though elevated, is not so high as some eminences in the neighbouring county, but it commands an extensive view. The solitude of the place and the boundless view of an uncultivated country are such as almost carry the observer back through a multitude of centuries, and make him believe that he sees the same view and the same state of things as existed in the days of the architects of this once holy fane."

Arbor Low also changed hands shortly before the sale of Harborough Rocks, though that monument is scheduled, and therefore protected from destruction. The fact that it is scheduled under the Ancient Monuments Protection Act of 1882 diminished interest in the result of the auction.

About a quarter of a mile from Arbor-Low, in a westerly direction, is a large conical tumulus, known as Gib Hill, which is connected with the vallum of the temple by a rampire of earth, running in a serpentine direction, not dissimilar to the avenue through the celebrated temple of Abury.

At Bradley Ross there is a small circle of nine stones known as the "Nine Ladies." It is eleven yards in diameter, the stones being 2 ft. 6 ins. high. At Hartle Moor there are the remains of a temple which presumably consisted formerly of nine stones, as the adjoining field is known by the name of the Nine Stone Close. The height of the tallest stone is 17 ft. Upon Harthill Moor, near to the road from Bakewell to Winster, is a small Druidical circle, about thirteen yards in diameter. Circles also exist at Brassington Moor, Abney Moor, Eyam Moor, Froggat Edge, and Hathersage Moor.

After the retreat from Anglesey the Druids are believed to have settled at Great Barr, near to Sutton Coldfield, on the eminence known as Barr Beacon. Sutton Coldfield was once a part of the Forest of Cannock, at that time one of the most extensive in the kingdom. At the north of Sutton Coldfield lies the village of Aldridge, and near here a small common to this day retains the name of Druidheath.

As might be expected, there abound numerous monumental remains of Druidism in Wales. In the vicinity of Harlech, on the ascent of a precipitous hill, as well as on the summit, there are several circles formed of loose stones, placed at intervals. Some are single, others concentric, one circle being inscribed within a second; in other places they intersect each other, forming nearly an ellipse. They do not, however, bear comparison with either Stonehenge or Avebury, either in magnitude or regularity of design. The largest is found at St. Nicholas, Glamorgan, and there are other important cromlechs at Newchurch, Monmouthshire; Createn Arthur, Pembrokeshire; and Arthur's Stone, Glamorganshire. At Meini Hirion, near Penmaenmawr, there is a circle, described as consisting of twelve stones, some $2\frac{3}{4}$ yards above the ground. There is also an inner circle consisting of eleven large stones, some eight feet high and three feet square, much weathered, with smaller stones placed between them. The outer circle is much broken in, but the inner one is nearly complete, and within this, again, there is the trace of a still smaller circle, not concentric, but touching the inner circumference, as if it had been the foundation of a circular dwelling-house. Sir John Wynn, an ancient baronet, whose spirit is said to haunt the Swallow Falls near by, said that there was a wall round the circle at the time he wrote, early in the seventeenth century. One of the largest stones represents a human figure and has been dubbed the Deity Stone, with the result that innumerable visitors have carved their initials upon it.

The most remarkable Druidical remains in Scotland are those of Callernish in Lewis, and Stennis in Orkney. The late Archdeacon John Sinclair, in *Old Times and Distant Places*, gives the following interesting account of an old Druidical temple in Orkney:

"The two most notable objects, however, on the mainland of Orkney are not in Kirkwall itself, but a few miles off. One of them is the Orcadian Stonehenge, or Stones of Stennis. They are thirty-seven in number, surrounded by a trench, and enclosing an area of two-and-a-half acres, in the midst of a vast barren moor. Sixteen of them still stand erect, varying in height from three to fourteen feet. They must now have encountered the storms of more than a thousand years. The general opinion is that the circle was erected as a place of sacrifice by the early Celtic inhabitants of Orkney ; and it is remarkable that the name of Steinness, or ' the promontory of the stones,' was applied to the adjoining headland by the earliest Scandinavian settlers, implying that the stones had existed in still older times. When I was at Steinness, an obelisk sixteen feet in height, called the ' Stone of Odin,' stood apart from the great circle. It had a large hole cut through it by means of which the victims intended for sacrifice were tied with cords, but in modern times it was devoted to a very different purpose. For lovers were in the habit of plighting their troth, either to other, by joining hands through this aperture, and the vow to Odin was held to be an obligation as sacred as the most solemn oath. I hear with regret that this curious relic of the olden time has since been wantonly destroyed."

Charles Cordiner, who wrote the *Antiquities of the North of Scotland*, in a series of letters to Thomas Pennant, speaking of the neighbourhood of Dunadeer, says :

" Remains of Druidical circles frequently attract one's attention on these hills, though the uniformity of their appearance yields but small recompense for encountering the rough ways that lead to them. I will only add one remark to the many you have made on the subject of these ancient places of worship : that the church of Benachie is included in one of them, which is not unfrequent in Scotland. This seems the effect of choice, not chance, and designed by the founders to tempt the pagan inhabitants to attend on the doctrine of revelation by building the churches on the spots on which they were wont to celebrate their ancient rites."

Near to the " Hill of the Seven Towers " in the neighbourhood of Ardmucknage, is a Druidical circle 26 ft. in diameter. About ten feet distant from the outside is an erect pillar 7 ft. high. In the opinion of Dr. Borlase, the officers of the Arch Druid may have stood there to command silence among the people, or some other person versed in the ceremonies may have acted as prompter by warning the officiating priest should part of the ceremonial escape his memory. Near Callernish is a group of old, grey, moss-grown stones which form a perfect Druidical circle. They are great boulders of gneiss, arranged in the form of a cross. The circle from which the limits of the cross are thrown out contains fourteen stones and is fourteen feet in diameter. The limits of the cross, running north and south, and formed by a double row of stones, extend to 392 ft. ; while those which run east and west are formed by a single row, and extend to 141 ft. In the centre of the circle there is an immense boulder about 15 ft. high and, in front of it, the remains of an altar, with hollow centre and conduit.

The structure at Turusachan—" the place of the pilgrimage "—is thirteen miles due west of Stornaway and consists of forty-eight large upright stones, standing upon a low hill, the highest point of which is 143 ft. above the main level of the sea. The temple is cruciform in plan, with a circle at the intersection of the shaft and arms, but with an additional row of stones on the east side of the shaft. The circle stands about 80 ft. above the level of the sea and is about 42 ft. in diameter. The circle itself is comprised of thirteen stones, the most prominent one in the centre being 17 ft. in height above the ground level, and 5ft. 6 ins. broad at the base. From the centre stone to the northern extremity or foot of the shaft, the cross is a distance of 294 ft., while the portion south of the circle is 114 ft., measured from the circle : the total length, therefore, is 408 ft. The extremity of the eastern arm is 73 ft., and that of the western 57 ft. from the centre. The total breadth of the cross, therefore, is 130 ft. The stones are all of unwrought gneiss, of which rock almost the whole island is formed. In October, 1857, Sir James Matheson, Bart., the proprietor of the island, cleared away the peat which had grown and accumulated round the stones to an extent of five or six feet. This brought to light the existence of a cruciform grave, lying east and west, and so placed that the centre stone is made to serve as a head stone. The grave is built of small stones excepting at the four internal angles, which are formed by large single stones. It had been covered with flat stones, but they had fallen in. It was built upon the natural surface of the ground, but the walls are supported by a bank of earth around them. Nothing was found in it when opened. " Clach an Druidean," a name in the island, means " the stone of the Druids."

There are twenty-five circles within the watershed of the Nairn and some twelve or fourteen between that and the River Ness, extending as far as Loch Ness. The principal stone circles and remains are at Tordarroch, Gask, Clava, Newton of Petty, Druid Temple, and Dorres. Another interesting series of stone circles exist in Badenoch and Upper Strathspey. The principal circles are at Delfoor, Ballinluig, Aviemore, and Tullochgorm.

Hood's Hill, Tarbolton, the scene of many incidents in the life of Burns, is said to have been, in former times, a Druidical place of worship. To this day the Baal fire is lighted there on Midsummer Eve.

The Druid Houses in the Isles are called by the natives *Tinan Druninich*. After the Druidical period they became the abodes or cells of Christian anchorites. In the island of Lewis, one of the Hebrides, there stands a huge stone, called the Thorshel, about 20 ft. high and almost as many broad. On the north side of Loch Carlvay there are similar stones, 12 ft. high, and there are many such throughout the island; but the most remarkable piece of antiquity of the kind is a group of pyramidal stones near the village of Classerness, 39 in number, from six to seven feet in height, which are all supposed to have been the erection of the Druids.

Burns made the following memorandum on Glenlyon :

" Druids' temple, three circles of stones, the outermost sunk; the second has thirteen stones remaining, the innermost eight, two large detached ones like a gate to the south-east—say prayers in it."

The sacred isle of Mona was known as *Ynys Dywyal*, or " the dark isle," because of the dark shade caused by its umbrageous oaks. The earliest name borne by Iona, so far as is known, was *Innas-nan-Druidneath*, or " Isle of the Druids," thus indicating that Iona was the seat of a Druidical college. According to the Rev. W. Lindsay Alexander : "The Druids retained their predominance in Iona and over the adjacent isles and mainland until A.D. 563 or 564, when they were supplanted and their superstitions overturned by the arrival of St. Columba, the apostle of the Highlands, by whom the inhabitants of that district were first led to profess Christianity."

In the Highlands one often hears the expression when invited to go to church : *Am bheil thu doe don chlachan*, or "Are ye go to the stones ?" and, on returning from church : " Have ye been at the stones ? " The belief prevails in Scotland to this day that no one who ever meddled with Druids' stones ever prospered in this world.

The remains of many alleged Druidical temples are to be found in many parts of Ireland. The tomb of Ollamh Fodhla, which is built in the form of a cross, is claimed as the site of a former Druidical temple. In the parish of Donoughmore, by Carmeen, there is a grove still standing on the top of a hill, and, at the base, there is a lake of considerable size. The remains of Druidical groves or temples are invariably found in close proximity to lakes, which figure largely in the initiatory ceremonies. The chief seat of the Irish Druids was at Tara, the residence of the chief kings of Ireland. Moorna, a district in the south of Ireland, once famous as the residence of an Arch-Druid, possessed a cavern supposed to have been haunted by the spirits of the Firbolg chiefs. Londonderry is said to have been originally a famous grove and school of the Druids. The word " Derry " is claimed to have been derived from *Doire*, which, in Erse, signifies " a grove of oaks."

The Giant's Ring at Belfast is a huge circle, 580 ft. in diameter, enclosing an area of 60 acres by a mound about 80 ft. broad. It was originally of a greater altitude than it now is, but in its present condition it is sufficiently high to prevent an ordinary man from seeing anything outside it except the summit of the neighbouring mountains. In the centre is an overthrown cromlech of more than ordinary dimensions, known as the Druids' Altar. It consists of a number of rude pillars supporting a top stone 7 ft. long by 6½ ft. broad. In 1841 Viscount Dungannon, the then owner of the land in the neighbourhood, erected a substantial wall around it.

At Ardpatrick, Limerick, are the remains, 11 ft. in height, of a round tower, which is mentioned in an ancient *Life of St. Patrick* as a hill sacred to the sun. Near by is a holy well efficacious in the cure of cattle disease. On Scattery Island is a Druidical circle, near the church and tower, and immediately adjoining is a holy well, now known as " Our Lady's Well."

On the summit of a hill, Baltony, about two miles from Raphoe, stands a Druidical temple. It consists of a perfect circle of large stones, set perpendicularly, varying from eight to nine feet in height, and, in many instances, of the same breadth. The circumference of the circle is 150 yards, comprised of 67 stones placed at irregular intervals. On the east side is an open space of seven yards, bounded by two large stones, which probably formed the entrance to the temple ; and on the opposite side are two of the largest, tallest, and broadest stones, filling up a space of equal breadth, against which the altar stood. Baltony, which is not an uncommon name in Ireland, is supposed to be a corruption of *Baal tinne*, or " the fire of Baal."

Between Galway and Outerard, and nearer to the latter, is a space which for about two miles is covered with the stone remains of an old Druidic temple of such dimensions that it has been designated by Mr. and Mrs. S. C. Hall " The City of the Druids." There are a number of circles of various sizes, some very small, but others so large as to be apparently half-a-mile in circumference.

Knock-a-dun, an island in Lough Gar, Limerick, has an extensive assemblage of Druidical remains. The eastern shore of the Lough abounds with mighty vestiges of Druidical power, and a chain of Druidical works extends into the county of Tipperary.

On the northern extremity of island Magee, Co. Antrim, is a Druid's altar, consisting of six large stones, standing upright and forming two rows, about two feet asunder, extending east and west. Four of the stones are on the north side and two on the south, each being fully three feet above the ground. On these rest a large flat slab upwards of six feet in length, fairly smooth on both sides, and nearly two feet thick. The breadth is unequal, its west end being nearly six feet, but sloping to the east to about half that breadth. In ploughing up the field in which this altar stands, in 1817, a spiral instrument of pure gold, eleven inches in length, was discovered, and a few years afterwards several detached parts of a gold collar were dug up near the altar. In March, 1824, several spiral golden ornaments, supposed to be armlets or bracelets, were found, the largest weighing 526 grains and the smallest 188 grains.

At Broadstone, Finvoy, Co. Antrim, are the ruins of a magnificent temple. The principal stone is ten feet in length, nine feet in breadth, and one foot thick. Beneath it there is said to have been formerly a chamber communicating with two smaller compartments extending northward and covered with stone. On the south is a large stone detached from its supporters, and on the opposite side stood former'y another of similar dimensions. Adjoining on the north-west are the remains of a stone circle, and vestiges of a similar erection are seen on the south-east. These, as well as the altar, appear formerly to have been encompassed by a circle of large stones 43 feet in diameter.

Near to the Rath of Mullinmast is a stone known as the Druid's Altar. It is eleven-and-a-half feet long, seven feet in circumference, and the local tradition runs that it was rolled from a place about seven miles away.

Caillin, Bishop, whose festival is observed in Ireland on 13th November, performed a famous miracle on the Druids, when Fergna, son of Fergus, King of Breitne, sent against him when he commenced the erection of Fiodhnach, on which occasion he turned the Druids into stones and as standing stones they are said still to remain. According to the legend the earth swallowed up King Fergna.

The name " Druid " in some form or another is still preserved in the names of several places in Ireland, *e.g.*, Loughnashandree, " the Lake of old Druids "; Knockadroon, " the Hill of the Druids "; Tobernadree, " the Well of the Druids "; Loughnadroon, " the Lake of the Druids "; Killadroy, " the Druids' Wood "; Gobnadruy, "the Druids' Point "; and Derrydruee, " the Druids' Oak Wood."

These circles are, however, to be found elsewhere than within the British Isles, and even in countries where it is not known with certitude that the Druidical religion was established. Bell, in *Wayside Pictures*, says that :

" The finest Celtic monument, the largest and most regular, within the limits of Brittany or Anjou, is to be seen near the village of Bagneux, about a mile from Saumur. This monument is of rectangular form, raised on the side of a hill and composed of enormous blocks of sandstone. It is 58 feet long, 21 feet wide, and 7 feet high from the ground. The disposition of the stones is perfectly uniform, four on each side for the walls, four for the roof, one on the left side near the entrance, and one on the west closing up the structure at that end. There are altogether seventeen of these immense blocks, all unhewn, and in thickness they vary from eighteen inches to two-and-a-half feet. On the top of the hill, not far from the neighbouring village of Riou, is a smaller monument, consisting of six great stones, also set to the east, and equally regular in form. The interior of the larger structure has the appearance of a vast subterranean sepulchre."

Lord Carlisle, in his *Diary*, published in 1854, mentions two sites of curious ruins at Crendi, in the island of Malta, about a quarter of a mile from each other. He says:

"They are probably those of some Phœnician place of worship, consisting of very large stones, of which the lowest are upright, and what may be called Druidical. Above them are four or five horizontal layers, a portion of them being as if tattooed with a circular pattern. There is no vestige of any roof. The timbers are of different sizes, with the apertures and large seats round the outer thresholds. Two or three altars seem to be in their places, and one of them has a very long flat slab of stone, which might have served for human sacrifices. Near, another opening indicates that a second chamber, large enough to admit the body of a man, which again may have served for oracular responses."

At Barozza, Spain, the stones known as Druidic, and similar in every respect to other Druidic memorials, are visited by every peasant girl for fifty miles around on her bethrothal. Such visit is said to bring good luck, and wishes made in the shadow of the stone are supposed to be ensured of fulfilment.

Porphyry relates how much the cavern mode of worship prevailed among the first nations, who believed that caverns and hollows were the residences of the gods. When in the process of time men began to erect temples, they determined the sites by the vicinity of these objects, which they included, wherever possible, within the limits of sacred enclosure.

At Pherae, in Achaia, there was a fountain sacred to Hermes, near which were thirty large stones, each of which was looked upon as the representative of some deity. Pausanias remarks that instead of images the Greeks in ancient times universally paid their adoration to rude, unwrought stones.

Miss Ellwood, in her *Journey to the East*, says: "There is a sacred perforated stone at Malabar, through which penitents squeezed themselves in order to obtain a remission of their sins."

Peter della Valle, in his *Travels in India*, mentions that there was a famous temple at Ahmedabad, wherein was no other image but a column of stone, after a pyramidal form, which they call Mahaden, signifying in their language God.

Clements Markham, also, states that the ancient city of the Incas covered a large area. It was built by highly-skilled masons, and with the use of enormous stones. One stone is 36 feet long, by 7 feet, weighing 170 tons; another 26 feet by 16 feet by 6 feet. Apart from the monoliths of ancient Egypt, there is nothing to equal this in any other part of the world. The movement and the placing of such monoliths point to a dense population, to an organised government, and consequently to a large area under cultivation, with arrangements for the conveyance of supplies from various directions. There must, he says, have been an organization combining skill and intelligence with power and administrative ability.

The explorations of the Ordnance Survey of 1869 proved the existence in Palestine and Arabia of circles " nearly identical in character with those which in England and Scotland are commonly called Druidical circles."

In 1911 an interesting paper on " Stone Circles in the Gambia " was read at the Royal Anthropological Institute by Messrs. J. L. Tolbach and G. B. Wolbach, in the course of which they said (quoting from *Man* of November, 1911) :

" The stone circles which have been seen in the Gambia by ourselves and by Mr. Ozanne occur principally on the north bank of the river. M. Lanzerac, the French resident at Maka, states that there are many circles in an area extending from the district of Saloum in the west to the Falémé river, an affluent of the Senegal river, in the east. On the north side of the river we have seen them from Maka in the east to N'Jau in the west, and in 1903 one circle and a few detached stones were seen on the south bank of the river near Kudang.

" During our recent expedition to the Gambia we asked in every town which we visited if there were circles in the neighbourhood. Places in which circles existed, or where natives knew of any, are mentioned below.

" In the district of Sandugu circles are said to exist at Changali, near Misera, in the territory of a chief called Gimmamang; other circles exist near them at Dasilimi. Near Lammin Koto there are several circles; we opened one of the largest of these. About 600 yards to the south-west of the circle excavated by us is another circle which was opened by Mr. Ozanne some years ago.

" Circles are said to exist at Kaleng, not far from McCarthy's Island, and single stones occur at Jamarli and also near Kai-ai.

" We saw two circles in the bush about half a mile to the north of Gassan. There are two stone circles not far from Jallokunda. Others are said to exist at Buntung, while there are said to be odd stones near Kussassa. Others again are said to be near Nianimaru and near Ballangar.

" The circles at Maka were peculiar amongst those seen by us, in that there were more single stones outside the circles than was usual.   M. Lanzerac has opened two of these circles and has found in them only traces of bone.

" None of the natives know anything of the origin of the stones. The Mandingo, who now inhabit the territory where they occur, say that the stones were in the country when the Mandingo first came to it.   There is no special name for the circles ; they are called by the ordinary Mandingo name for stones—that is, *Bero*. At present the circles and stones have absolutely no significance. The natives do not use them as places for praying nor for landmarks ; neither do they generally believe that they were used for tombs. Some persons, particularly among the better educated people, believe that the Portuguese made the circles, and that some of those who died in the Gambia are buried within them, together with their belongings.   When questioned concerning the circles, most of the natives say, God or the people of the olden times put them there.

" It seems probable that the stones were cut and placed by some race which held the land long before the Mandingo appeared. It is certain that those who placed the stones had more knowledge of stoneworking than the Mandingo have at present.   They also had considerable aptitude in transporting heavy weights, for, as at Lammin, it must have been necessary for those who built the circles to bring the stones composing them a distance of at least two miles.

" Suntokomo, the paramount chief of Lammin, told us that the people who preceded the Mandingo in the country often made " Jalang " sacrifices of black animals of goats, sheep, horses, or cattle, before going to war, and that years ago the Mandingo sacrificed animals in much the same way.   These sacrifices were sometimes made near, or on, one of the stones of a circle."

In many parts of the British Isles are to be found Logan or Rocking Stones, but seldom far removed from a stone circle.   These consist of one immense stone poised so nicely on the top of some other stone that the slightest touch or pressure of the hand will cause it to move or rock, while, at the same time, it is almost impossible to move it from its station. There are a few instances of fallen rocks which, in falling, have become poised in this manner on some projecting mass, but there are many more which appear to have been formed in a deliberate manner.   These Logan Stones have been found, amongst other places, particularly in Cornwall, Wales, Lancashire, Yorkshire, and Derbyshire.   At Walton, in Lancashire, there are five of these stones, so contiguous one to another

Aerial View of Stonehenge,
showing the outer ring.

that, if one is touched, the motion is communicated to the remainder.

There is a legend that Uranus contrived stones called Betulia, which possessed the power of motion as if they were instinct with life, and accounts are given in ancient writers of many of these rocking-stones. Pliny says that at Harpasa, a town of Asia, there was a rock of such wonderful nature that if touched with a finger it would shake, but it could not be moved from its place with the whole force of the body. Ptolemy Hephaestion mentions a gygonian near the ocean, which was agitated when struck by the stalk of an asphodel, but could not be removed by a great exertion of force. The word *gygonius* appears to be Celtic, for *duringog* signifies motion.

The term " Logan Stone " cannot be explained by the Cornish or Welsh language, although the name is still retained in Cornwall. *Logh*, however, was the Irish for " divine essence," and the Druids claimed that the divine essence descended into the Logh-onn, or stone. Stones which possessed the power of motion, as if they were instinct with life, says Sanchoniatho, were known as Betulia. *Beth-el* was the usual patriarchal name for sacred structures of this character.

It has been conjectured, and with much probability, that the Logan Stone was a species of ordeal or test by which the Druid who, in conformity with the patriarchal custom, was also the judge of the people, determined the innocence or guilt of those persons brought before him. Mason, in his *Caractacus*, supposes two young men brought before the Druidic tribunal on a charge of treason, when the Arch-Druid addresses them as follows :

" Thither, youths,
" Turn your astonished eyes ; behold yon huge
And unhewn sphere of living adamant,
Which, pois'd by magic, rests its central weight
On yonder pointed rock : firm as it seems,
Such is its strange and virtuous property,
It moves, obsequious to the gentlest touch
Of him whose breast is pure ; but, to a traitor,
Tho' ev'n a giant's prowess nerv'd his arm,
It stands as fixt as Snowdon. No reply ;
The gods command that one of you must now
Approach and try it : In your snowy vests
Ye priests, involve the lots, and to the younger,
As is our wont, tender the choice of Fate."

The result of an appeal of this nature was frequently to make the guilty person confess his crime. If it became necessary to resort to the ordeal, the insertion of a wedge, or even of a small pebble in the socket in which the pivot moved and on which the stone was poised was sufficient to render the stone immovable, and thus resist the pressure of the hand. In that case the accused would be adjudged guilty and condemned, and the credit of the test would be vindicated.

At Rudston there is a Logan Stone 25 ft. 4 ins. in height ; its width varies from 5 ft. 9 ins. in the west to 6 ft. 1 in. in the east ; and its thickness from 2 ft. 3 ins. in the south to 2 ft. 9 ins. in the north. This stone is almost overgrown with moss from top to bottom, but, in 1773, More Bosville, of Thorpe Hall, ordered a small cap of lead to be placed on the top in order to preserve it. The question as to how this stone was placed was partly solved in the autumn of 1869, when the Rev. Canon Greenwall opened various barrows in the parish and several stone hammers, axes and flint implements were dug out, by which the stone could have been hewn into shape and placed into position. The fact that this stone and other similar stones are found close to churches may, perhaps, be accounted for by supposing that, in order to facilitate the introduction of Christianity, the early missionaries erected their churches on the spot where the people had been accustomed to worship. The letter which Pope Gregory sent to the Abbot Miletus when he was setting out for Britain contained the following instructions : " That the temples of the idols of the nations ought not to be destroyed : let holy water be made and sprinkled in the said temples ; let altars be erected and relics placed."

This custom of erecting churches on the sites of heathen temples continued in Scotland until the tenth century. Patrick, Bishop of the Hebrides, desired Orlygiis to found a church wherever he should find upright stones.

At Treryn Castle, near to St. Buryan, is the celebrated Logan-rock —a mass of granite weighing nearly sixty-five and a half tons, being 17 ft. long and 30 ft. in circumference, which was formerly so poised upon its axis that it could easily be shaken and yet regain its equilibrium quickly. In 1824 it was overthrown by Lieutenant Goldsmith, a nephew of the poet, and some sailors under his command, by way of disproving the assertion of Borlase, the antiquarian, that no mechanical force could remove it from its situation. Great and many were the complaints raised against this rash seaman, and the Admiralty ordered him to replace the stone in its former position, a task which he accomplished by the aid of powerful capstans and scaffolding, and at an outlay which crippled the lieutenant's limited resources to the day of his death. It has never " logged " with the same ease since it was replaced.

At Rowtor there is a Logan Stone 15 ft. long, 12 ft. broad, and 4 ft. in thickness, which is easily shaken.

At the Giant's Castle, in the Scilly Islands, there is a Logan Stone 45 tons in weight, but so finely balanced that it will obey the motion of a lady's slightest touch. Borlase, by the way, asserts that the old British appellation of the Scilly Islands was *Sulleh*, or *Sylleh*, signifying " rocks consecrated to the sun."

There is a remarkable rocking stone in the island of St. Agnes in Sicily. The under rock is 10 ft. 6 ins. high, 47 ft. round the middle, and it touches the ground with not more than half its base. The upper rock rests on one point only and is so nicely balanced that two or three men with a pole can move it. On the top there is a bason hollowed out 3 ft. 11 ins. in diameter at the medium, but wide at the brim, and 3¾ ft. deep. From the globular part of this upper stone it is highly probable that it was rounded by human art, and perhaps even placed on the pedestal by human strength.

In Stithney parish, near Helston, in Cornwall, stood the famous Logan Stone, Men-an-Bar, or the Topstone. It was 11 ft. 6 ins. high and 4ft. broad, and so nicely poised upon another stone that a little child could move it. Shrubsal, Cromwell's governor of Pendennis, caused it to be undermined.

There is a rocking stone near Balvaird Castle, in the Ochill Hills. One near Rippen Tor, 16½ ft. in length, 4½ ft. in thickness, and nearly the same in breadth, is called the Nutcrackers, but its rocking power has long since disappeared. The whooping rock, near North Bovey, is so called from the noise it made in tempestuous weather. This was originally a Logan Stone, but many years ago it was wantonly removed from its balance.

Mr. Rock, in *Archæology*, gives the following description of the logan stone at Brimham Craggs, in Yorkshire :

" It rests upon a kind of pedestal and is supposed to be about one hundred tons in weight. On examining the stone it appears to have been shaped to a small knob at the bottom to give it motion, though my guide, who was about seventy years old, born on the moors, and well acquainted with these rocks, assured me that the stone had never been known to rock ; however, upon my making trial round it, when I came to the middle of one side, I found it moved with great ease. The astonishing increases of the motion, with the little force I gave it, made me very apprehensive that the equilibrium might be destroyed, but on examining it I found it was so nicely balanced that there was no danger of it falling. The construction of this equipoised stone must have been by artists well skilled in the power of mechanics."

In Wales logan stones are known as *Maer Sigll*, or the Shaking Stones. Vallancey takes the word from the Irish *logh*, meaning divine power or spirit, which the Druids claimed was infused into the stone, which caused them to consult it as an oracle.

In 1808 Mr. Joshua Gosselin discovered a large Logan Stone at L'Ancresse Bay, Guernsey, which could be rocked easily by a child. It was afterwards destroyed.

Some Druidical remains near Halifax were discovered some years ago by the Rev. John Watson, then rector of Stockport. A rocking stone forms the boundary mark between the two townships of Golcar and Slaightwait, on Golcar Hill, and gives the name of Hole Stone Moor to the adjoining grounds. It is 10 ft. 6 ins. long, 9 ft. 5 ins. broad, and 5ft. 3 ins. thick. It has been damaged somewhat by some masons who endeavoured to discover the principle on which so heavy a weight could move so easily.

On the side of a lofty hill at the Gap of Dunloe, in Kerry, is a Logan Stone about 24 ft. in circumference, called by the peasants " the Balance Rock." Moore likens it to the poet's heart, which :
" The slightest touch alone sets moving
But all earth's power could not shake it from its base."

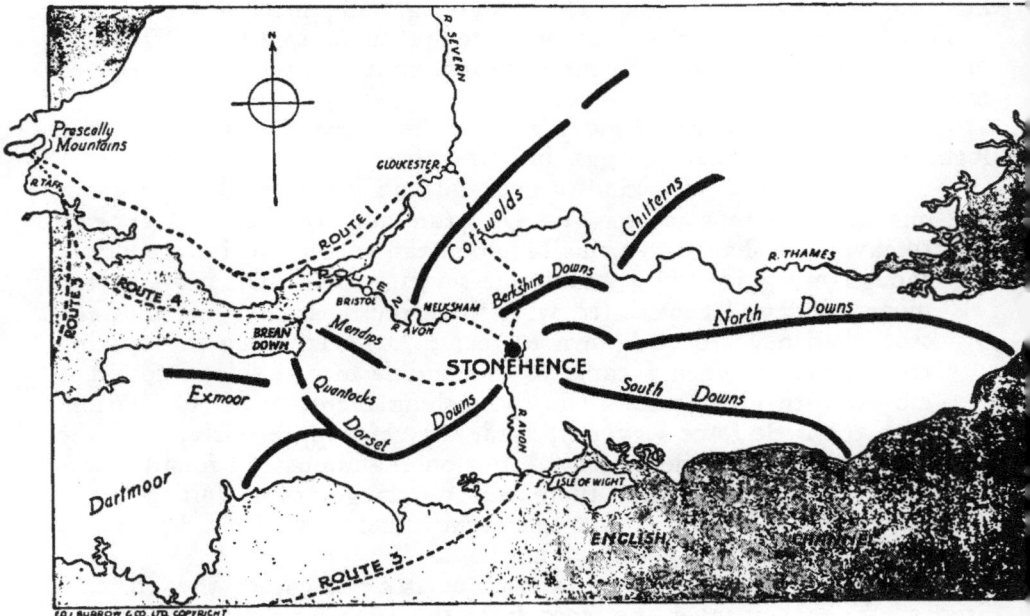

Hill ranges converging on Stonehenge, and Routes by which some of the Stones may have been brought to the spot.

CHAPTER VII

DRUIDICAL FESTIVALS
AND CUSTOMS

Druidism, in common with most other religions, set aside one day in each week for the special observance of religious ceremonies, while, in addition, they kept annually four great festivals, *viz.*, May Day, Midsummer Day, the first of November, and the tenth of March, this last-named being New Year's Day, although some writers accord that honour to the first of May. The Gaelic name for the month of May is still *ceituin*, or *ceuduin*, or " the first month of time."

Vallancey, in his *Collectanea de rebus Hibernicis*, cites Cormac, Archbishop of Cashel in the tenth century, as saying in his *Irish Glossary* that : " In his time four great fires were lighted up on the four great festivals of the Druids, *viz.*, in February, May, August and November."

Many hills were used in those days for beacons, and a telegraphic system was carried to considerable perfection. Intelligence was conveyed by means of a fire at night and a smoke by day ; and on urgent occasions by the simple expedient of shouting to each other from the summit of these beacon hills, which frequently were dedicated to Teut. Many, indeed, are called Teut, or Toob hills to this day. There is a hill with this name at Little Coates, near Grimsby. It consists of a magnificent mound thrown up on the summit of a lofty eminence, which commands a very extensive view of the surrounding country. Cæsar noted the practice and referred to it in the fifth book of *De Bello Gallico*. He says that the system was carried to such perfection that on urgent occasions the people might be raised within twelve hours through a tract of country 160 miles in extent.

May Day, the day on which the sun entered Taurus, was ushered in by a festival commencing on the eve, which was instituted in commemoration of the exit of Hu, the Mighty, and his family from the Ark. It was the principal time of the year for the initiation of aspirants for the priesthood. Maurice says he has little doubt that May Day, or, at least, the day on which the sun entered Taurus, has been immemorially kept as a sacred festival from the creation of earth and man, originally

149

L

intended as a memorial of that event. The ceremonial preparations for the May festivities really commenced at midnight on the 29th of April, and when the initiation ceremonies had been concluded on May eve, fires were kindled on all the cairns and beacon hills throughout the kingdom, and were kept alight throughout the night as an introduction to the sports and festivities of the following day. They were lighted in honour of Beal, or Bealan, a name Latinised by the Roman authors into Belenus, by which name the Gauls knew the sun. Beal is a compound word formed from *Be*, is, and *All*, universal, that is, the Universal Is, or the Universal Being. The other gods and even all visible things were regarded as mere emanations of this great spirit. Another name of Beal in the Celtic is Alla, or Allah, which seems to be formed from *All*, universal, and *Hea*, a vocal inflection of *Ta*, is, meaning again the Universal Is. The name Beal, or Bealan, corresponds with the Phœnician Baal, the Indian Bhole, the Chaldean Bel, and the Hebrew Bahal. The Irish and Scottish Druids knew the day by the name of *La Bealtine*, or " the day of Belen's fire." May Day is known in the Manx language as *Shenn Laa Boaldyn*. The day is still regarded in the Isle of Man as an unlucky one on which to lend anything and especially to give fire. So, even to-day, in the remote districts of Ireland if the fire goes out in the house of a peasant before the morning of the first of May, the tenant repairs to the priest's house in order to beg a lighted turf to re-kindle it. The " crosh cuirn " in the Isle of Man is a cross made of mountain ash, which is kept throughout the year behind the door and renewed every May Day. It is a belief there that no evil thing can pass in where the " crosh cuirn " is kept. It is interesting to note that one of the many titles by which the Druids were formerly known was Maysons, or Men of May. Prof. Veitch, in *History and Poetry of the Scottish Border*, writes very positively as to Beltane Day being the second day of May and not the first, as is generally supposed. The Royal Charter granted to the Burgh of Peebles for holding a fair or market on Beltane Day is given in the Burgh Records of Peebles, p. 85, as follows : "As also of holding, using, enjoying, and exercising within the aforesaid Burgh weekly market days, according to the use and custom of the said Burgh, together with three fairs, thrice in the year, the first thereof beginning yearly upon the third day of May, called Beltane Day, the same to be held and continued for the space of forty-eight houre thereafter." In a book of Scotch proverbs, published in 1721 by James Kelly, occurs the following :

"You have skill of man and beast
You was born between the Beltans."

In all countries in which Druidism was the prevailing religion the observances of the day included choral dances, performed in honour of the deliverance of Hu. May Day is still known by the name of Bealtine by many of the highlanders of Scotland. To this day, also, in some parts of Ireland the custom prevails of kindling a fire in the milking-yard on May Day, when men, women and children pass through or leap over it, and cattle are drawn through flames of burning straw, which custom is held to be an efficacious means of preserving them from accidents that would otherwise befall them before the return of May. The expression " to call over the coals," meaning to reprimand severely, had its probable origin in this passing through Bel's fire. This passing between two fires was not a remnant of any sacrificial practice, but was regarded merely as a means of purification. Leaping over the fire is mentioned in Ovid's *Fasti* as among the superstitious rites in vogue at the Palilia, or the feasts instituted in honour of Pales, the goddess of shepherds, on the calends of May.

Pennant, in his *Tour in Scotland*, published in 1771, gives a lengthy account of the Druidical festival of Beltine, or, as he calls it, Bel-tein, in which he says :

"They cut a square trench in the ground, leaving a turf in the middle ; on that day they make a fire of wood on which they dress a large caudle of eggs, butter, oatmeal, and milk, and bring, besides the ingredients of the caudle, plenty of beer and whiskey, for each of the company must contribute something. The rites begin with spilling some of the caudle on to the ground, by way of libation ; on that, every one takes a cake of oatmeal, upon which are raised nine square knobs, each dedicated to some particular being, the supposed preservers of their flocks and herds, or to some particular animal, the real destroyer of them. Each person then turns his face to the fire, breaks off a knob, and, flinging it over his shoulder, says : ' This I give to thee, preserve thou my horses,' or ' This to thee, preserve thou my sheep,' and so on. After this, they use the same ceremony to the noxious animals : ' This I give to thee, O fox, spare thou my lambs,' or ' This to thee, O horrid crow,' or ' This to thee, O eagle.' When the ceremony is over, they dine on the caudle, and, after the feast is finished, what is left is hid by two persons deputed for that purpose, but on the next Sunday they reassemble and finish the reliques of the first entertainment."

Ellis also gives a detailed account of the May Day festival and ceremonies in Scotland, in the course of which he says :

"That the Caledonians paid a superstitious respect to the sun, as was the practice among other nations, is evident, not only by the sacrifice at Baltein, but upon many other occasions. When a Highlander goes to bathe, or to drink water out of a consecrated fountain, he must always approach by going round the place from east to west on the south side in imitation of the apparent diurnal motion of the sun. This is called in Gaelic, going round the right or lucky way. And if a person's meat or drink were to affect the windpipe, or come against his breath, they instantly cry out ' disheal,' which is an ejaculation praying that it may go the right way."

Beiltin, it may be added, is still the Gaelic name for Whitsunday.

Dr. Norman Macleod, in *Reminiscences of a Highland Parish*, states that when a boy in his father's manse in the Highlands, the parishioners all came to it on New Year's Day and performed *deas-iul* round the house to bring good luck to the minister and his family for the ensuing year. Miss Constance F. Gordon Cumming, in *From the Hebrides to the Himalayas* says that one place where the deisul is still kept up is at Kilbar, in the Isle of Barra, where, on St. Barr's Day (25th September), all the Roman Catholic population attend Mass in the chapel in honour of their titular saint, and then ride across the island to Kilbur, the ancient burial-place of the M'Neils. Each rough pony carries not only his rough unkempt master, but also his master's sweetheart or wife, who, in her turn, carries a bunch of wild carrots. This quaint procession marches thrice round the ruins to secure luck for the island for the coming year.

The following account is extracted from the *Survey of the South of Ireland*, where the customs were very similar to those of Scotland :

" The sun was propitiated here by sacrifices of fire ; one was on the first of May, for a blessing on the seed sown. The first of May is called in the Irish language, *La Bealtine*, that is, the day of Baal's fire. Vossius says it is well known that Apollo was called Belinus, and for this he quotes Herodian and an inscription at Aquileia, Apolini Belino.

Sir John Sinclair, in his *Statistical Account of Scotland*, published in 1794, gives the following account of a Baal custom :

" The people of this district (Callander, Perthshire), have two customs, which are fast wearing out, not only here, but all over the Highlands, and therefore ought to be taken notice of while they remain. Upon the first of May, which is called Beltan, or Baltein Day, the boys in a township or hamlet meet on the moors. They cut a table in the green sod, of a round figure, by casting a trench in the ground of such circumference as to hold the whole company. They kindle a fire, and dress a repast of eggs and milk in the consistence of a custard. They knead a cake of oatmeal, which is toasted at the embers against a stone. After the custard is eaten up, they divide the cake into so many portions, as similar as possible to one another in size and shape, as there are persons in the company. They daub one of these portions all over with charcoal until it be perfectly black. They put all the bits of the cake into a bonnet. Every one, blindfolded, draws out a portion. He who holds the bonnet is entitled to the last bit. Whoever draws the black bit is the devoted person who is to be sacrificed to Baal, whose favour they mean to implore, in rendering the year productive of the sustenance of man and beast. There is little doubt of these inhuman sacrifices having once been offered in this country as well as in the East, although they now pass from the act of sacrificing, and only compel the devoted person to leap three times through the flames, with which the ceremonies of the festival are closed."

In the same volume the minister of Logierait, in Perthshire, writes concerning the May Day festival as follows :

"On the first of May a festival called Beltan is annually held here. It is chiefly celebrated by the cowherds, who assemble in scores in the fields to dress a dinner for themselves of boiled milk and eggs. These dishes they eat with a sort of cake, baked for the occasion, and having small lumps, in the form of nipples, raised all over the surface. The cake might, perhaps, be an offering to some deity in the days of Druidism."

For many centuries subsequent to Druidic times the Welsh were accustomed to hold a festival on May Day morning, in commemoration of the Deluge. Oxen were placed near a lake, in the centre of which was an island, regarded as holy, where a shrine or ark was kept. This was drawn through the shallow water on to dry ground by the oxen, by means of a chain, whilst the best singers in the district sang a chant known as *Cainc yr Ychain Banawg*, a melody said to resemble the lowing of kine and the rattling of chains. The principal character in the procession which was formed after the ark had been drawn safely to land was supposed to represent the Arch Druid bearing his magical wand, after which came about two hundred Druids and Bards, the latter carrying harps, followed by the ark of Ceridwen, borne upon the shoulders of Ovates and discipuli. Immediately in front of the ark went the hierophant, who represented the Supreme Creator ; a torch-bearer, who represented the sun ; and the herald-bard, who was regarded as the special official of the moon. The rear was made up by a large body of singers and dancers, who, with wreaths of ivy upon their heads, surrounded the car of the diluvial god. Some of these blew horns, others carried double pateras, while many clashed their shields with crooked swords. Ultimately the procession entered a temple erected in the centre of a grove of oaks.

One of the royal palaces erected by Tuathal, king of Ireland, A.D. 79 to 100, was in the province of Connaught, where a general convocation of all inhabitants of the kingdom was summoned each year on 1st of May. It was known as the convocation of Visneach, and sacrifices were offered to the god Beul, in whose honour two fires were kindled in every territory of the kingdom. It was a solemn ceremony at this time to drive a number of cattle between the fires.

Cormac's *Glossary* mentions an annual convention which took place at Uisneach, in Meath, in the month of May, where the men of Ireland were wont to exchange their goods and their wares and jewels.

"And at it they were wont to make a sacrifice to the Arch God, whom they adored, whose name was Bel. It was likewise their usage to light two fires to Bel in every district in Ireland at this season, and to drive a pair of each herd of cattle that the district contained between these two fires, as a preservative, to guard them against all the diseases of that year. It is from that fire thus made that the day on which the noble feast of the apostles, Peter and James, is held has been called Bealtine, *i.e.*, Bel's Fire. The origin of the proverb 'between two fires' is also ascribed to the passing of beasts about to be sacrificed between these two sacrificial fires. This deity, however, according to many authorities, appears to have been the principal deity in the Druidical calendar, and not the fourth in point of importance, as claimed by some."

Fire ceremonies, however, are not the exclusive property of any one nation or religion : they belonged to many, and, even at the present day, they may be witnessed frequently in India, Japan, and other Oriental countries. Hindoos also hold a festival on May Day known as Bhavani ; it is kept by all Hindoos who possess horned cattle for use or profit. May Day was also observed formerly as a phallic festival in Egypt and India. A somewhat similar festival is kept by the Persians towards the end of April. The domestic fires are everywhere extinguished, nor would any true believer rekindle them save by a taper lighted at the dwelling of the priests. A similar custom also exists at Jerusalem, where, annually, at the time of Easter, a sacred fire is supposed to descend into the holy sepulchre, and a considerable traffic is done by priests with tapers lighted at its flame. Until recently it was the custom of the poor people in the counties of Somersetshire and Devonshire to beg fire at the doors of the rich on the last day of October.

Stubbs in his *Anatomie of Abuses*, declaims against the May Day celebrations in the following language :

"Against Maie-day, every parish, town, or village assemble themselves, both men, women, and children ; and either all together, or dividing themselves into companies, they goe some to the woods and groves, some to the hills and mountains, some to one place and some to another, where they spend all the night in pleasant pastimes, and in the morning they return bringing with them birch boughs and branches of trees to deck their assemblies withal.   But their chiefest jewel they bring from thence is the maie-pole, which they bring home with great veneration, as thus : they have twenty or fourty yoke of oxen, every one having a sweet nosegaie of flowers tied to the tip of his horns, and these oxen drawe home the maypole, which they cover all over with flowers and hearbes, bound round with strings from the top to the bottome, and sometimes it is painted with variable colours, having two or three hundred men, women, and children following it with great devotion.   And thus equipped is reared with handkerchiefs and flaggs streaming on the top ; they strawe the ground round about it, they bind green boughs about it, they set up summer halles, bowers, and arbours hard by it, and then fall they to banquetting and feasting, to leaping and dancing about it as the heathen did at the dedication of their idols. I have heard it credebelie reported, by men of great gravity, credite and reputation, that of fourtie, threescore, or a hundred maides going to the wood, there have scarcelie the third parte of them returned home again as they went."

The maypole was denounced in England by an Act of Parliament passed in 1644, but a tall maypole still stands at Slingsby, and at Cawood, in Yorkshire, the maypole is still preserved as a memorial of old customs that have passed away.   Parade Square, at Hugh Town in the Scilly Isles, now enclosed, was formerly the scene of the Maypole dance and of midsummer night frolics.

Forlong, in *Rivers of Life*, says that the maypole was once no trumpery matter, for it was the symbol of the " Lord of Life."   It was called the *Column of May*, the great standard of justice, a term only applied to Toths or Jupiterstators.   The maypole marked the boundary of the year, the confines of summer and winter, and around it contended two troops of youths, one in winter and the other in spring costume, the latter, of course, winning with their triumphal branches of May flowers.   As the fires of love had to be renewed every Midsummer by a ray from Sol himself, young men and maidens had to see that their Maypole was so firmly set in its place that it would stand there immoveable and upright throughout the whole year.   Some insisted that it should be as high as the mast of a vessel of one hundred tons and be worshipped with garlands and dancings round it by the youths of both sexes every day throughout May.   It equally had its place, and was as important as the parish church or the parish stocks ; and if anywhere one was wanting, the people selected a suitable tree, fashioned it, and

brought it triumphantly and erected it in the proper place, there from
year to year to remain. London was very famous for its maypoles;
the parishioners of St. Andrew-under-Shaft set up every May morning
a shaft that was higher than the church steeple, and after the usual
observances put it carefully away under the eaves of the houses, which
were built so as to protect it. The Puritans cut this to pieces, as they
did all other maypoles they could discover.

We are not without remnants of the old "Nature-worship" amongst
us, says Forlong. On the 1st of May in every year all the choristers
at Magdalen College, Oxford, still meet on the summit of their tower,
150 feet high, and sing a Latin hymn as the sun rises; whilst the fine
peal of ten bells simultaneously welcomes the gracious Apollo. In
former days High Mass was held here, and the rector of Slimbridge, in
Gloucestershire, it appears, has still to pay £10 yearly for the due performance of sundry pieces of choir music at 5 a.m. on the top of this
tower. This May music, Christian priests explain, is for the repose of
the souls of kings and others, which, of course, is quite an afterthought.
Early Mass used also to be held in the College chapel, but it is now
explained that this having been forbidden at the Reformation, music has
since been performed at the top of the tower! Formerly after the
singing of the hymn the choristers used to throw down eggs upon the
crowd beneath and blow long loud blasts to Sol through bright new tin
horns. Long before daybreak, also, the youths of both sexes used to
go to great distances to gather boughs and flowers, reaching home at
sunrise to deck all doors, windows and selected spots. This May fete
is said to be the most ancient of all and formerly to have been accompanied with all manner of obscenity and lewdness.

The festivities of the second great festival of the Druidical year—
Midsummer Day—also commenced on the preceding eve, and also was
observed principally in the lighting of fires on eminences all over the
country. These fires were particularly numerous in Gloucestershire,
Cornwall, Cambridgeshire, Devonshire, Lancashire, and the northern
parts of England. Mr. Samuel Laing, who was born in 1810, relates
in *Human Origins* that when he was young these fires were lighted on
the highest hills of Orkney and the Scottish mainland. "As a boy,"
he says, " I have rushed with my playmates through the smoke of these
bonfires without a suspicion that we were repeating the homage paid
to Baal in the Valley of Hinnom." In many country villages and even
in towns and cities, it was the custom, until quite recently, for old and
young to meet together and make merry over a large fire kindled in the
open street, over which they would frequently leap, the younger members
playing at various games, such as wrestling, running, and dancing."

The ancient custom of lighting Baal fires on St. John's Day is still maintained in Northumberland. A modern writer, the Rev. J. Walker, has described the custom which is observed in the remote hamlet of Whalton, in Northumberland, in the following words :

"As Midsummer approaches, much wood is marked out for bonfire, sometimes with the consent of the local farmers. When this has been cut it is brought into the village with a certain amount of formality. On the evening of 4th July, a cart is borrowed and loaded with branches of faggots, some of the men get into the shafts, more are hooked on by means of long ropes, and then, with a good deal of shouting and horn-blowing, the lumbersome vehicle is run down into the village.

On Midsummer Day until recently a pleasure fair was held annually at Pelynt, in Cornwall, where from time immemorial a bonfire has been lighted on the evening of that day. Bonfires were also formerly lighted on the evening of Midsummer Day at Penzance. The fisher-folk of the villages near Penzance have transferred the observance of the fire festival of Midsummer Eve to the feast of St. Peter, the fisherman's patron saint, but the Cornish townsfolk still adhere to Midsummer Eve and celebrate the night with bonfires and fireworks.

To-day, on Midsummer Eve, people in the West Country betake themselves to some high ground where they watch for a sight of the first fire lighted. If first beheld in the east it is regarded as a good sign. Until recently there was in Cornwall a stone at Escals, known as the Garrick Zans, which was about nine feet in diameter, three feet high, and with a level top. A bonfire was made upon it and danced around at Midsummer. When petty offences were committed by unknown persons, those who wished to prove their innocence and to discover the guilty were accustomed to light a furze fire on the Garrick Zans. Each person who assisted took a stick of fire from the pile and those who could extinguish the fire in their sticks by spitting on them were deemed innocent : if any handling a fire-stick failed to do this they were declared guilty.

Wirt Sikes, in *British Goblins*, published in 1880, gave an elaborate description of the festival, as observed in his time, in the following words :

"Midsummer Eve, or St. John's Eve (23rd June) is still one of the ancient Druidic festivals, still liberally honoured in Wales. The custom of lighting bonfires survives in some of the villages, and at Pontypridd there are ceremonies of a solemn sort. Midsummer Eve in 1878 fell on a Sunday. Upon that day the Druids and Bards at Pontypridd held the usual feast of the summer solstice in the face of the sun. There is a breezy common on the top of a high hill overlooking the town where stands a logan stone and a circle of upright stones constituting the temple of the Druids.

Here it is the custom of the present day adherents of the ancient religion, beside which Christianity is an infant, to celebrate their rites 'within the folds of the serpent,' a circle marked with the signs of the zodiac. The venerable Arch Druid, Myfyr Morganwg, stands on the logan stone, with a mistletoe sprig in his buttonhole and prays to the god Kali, 'Creator of sun, moon, stars, and universe.' Then the white-bearded old man delivers a discourse, and new members are initiated into the 'Mysteries.' Occasionally these new members are Americans from over the sea, and they include both sexes. Large crowds gather to witness the impressive spectacle—a shadow of the ancient rites when from Belenian heights flamed high the sacrificial fires. It was a former belief that fires protected the lands within their light from the machinations of sorcery, so that good crops would follow and that their ashes were valuable as a medicinal charm."

To the present day there is a yearly pilgrimage to Stonehenge by many who journey thither to watch the sun rise above the Friar's Hill Stone, which many contend was erected by the Druids to assist them in locating the seasons.

In the old Cornish dialect Midsummer was known as Goluan, or "light," and the Druidical festival became transformed ultimately into a Christian festival, the day being dedicated to St. John the Baptist, a bright and shining light, the herald of the Christ.

The Midsummer Day festival was to implore the friendly influences of heaven on the fields and that on the eve of the 1st of November was to return thanks for the favourable season and the fruits of the year.

At one time the annual festival of the Grand Lodge of English Freemasons was always held on St. John the Baptist's Day, and that day is still reserved by many Lodges in all Constitutions as the day for the installation of Masters. It will be remembered that the Grand Lodge of England—the Mother Grand Lodge of the World—was founded on "St. John's Day in Summer." 1717.

Archdeacon John Williams, in his *Essay on the Non-Hellenic Portion of the Latin Language*, says that the Cambrian or Welsh form of *Vates* is Ovid, and suggests that probably the name Ovidius is a derivative of this.

The fire ceremony was undoubtedly of Aryan origin, since it is found in countries other than those in which Druidism prevailed. The festivals are continued to-day in the Christian Church. One of the festivals has become the festival of St. John the Baptist, the summer solstice, whilst the winter solstice has become the festival of Noel, the festival of the birth of the Saviour. Thus bishops and archbishops were enjoined by Diocletian to have no scruple in preserving the festivals and almost all the rites which they found, transforming them into Christian practices and customs.

In Ireland the greatest festival of the year, when all the kings paid homage to the supreme king, was the festival of Beltene, which was held triennially at Tara on the 24th June. Then assembled the five provincial kings and three or four hundred chiefs of clans representative of the *elite* of the nation. The fire of Beltene was regarded as a sacred fire. Every Irishman looked upon it as a duty to kindle the home fire for the year from it in order to secure the protection of the gods. It was at the triennial assemblies at Tara that the laws were revised. The gathering was not only religious but also political and social.

From the *Life of St. Patrick* we learn that he found this custom established in the court of King Laogaire, whose hospitality he accepted, although he knew that he was still a pagan. He arrived on the eve of the festival, and, according to his custom, lighted the candles in his little oratory, for which he was taken severely to task. A royal decree existed throughout Ireland extinguishing all fires that day under very severe penalties, and fires were only to be re-kindled from the sacred fires of Tara.

The full story is told by Patrick Kennedy, in his *Fiction of the Irish Celts*, as follows :

"At the moment when the high pile of brushwood, crowned with flowers, was about to be lighted by the hands of the chief Druid, the king's eyes sparkled with rage, for eastward a weak but steady light was beheld glimmering. 'Who,' said he, ' has dared to commit that sacrilege ? ' 'We know not,' was the answer from many voices in the assembly. ' O King,' said the Chief Druid, ' if this fire be not extinguished at once, it will never be quenched. It will put out our sacred fires, and the man who has enkindled it will overcome thee, and he and his successors rule Erinn to the end of time.' ' Go then,' said Leoghaire, ' quench his light, and bring him hither.' ' We go,' was the answer, ' but let all in the assembly turn their backs towards the magic blaze. Meanwhile, let our own sacred fires be kindled, and all the dwellers in Erinn rejoice in this light. When we have brought this stranger into the presence, let no one rise to do him homage.'

" So saying, the Chief Druid set fire to the pile, and, accompanied by two other Druids and some guards, proceeded till he came to where the saint and his assistants, in their white robes, were chanting their hymns. ' What mean these incantations ? ' cried the Druid, curiously glancing at the books, so unlike their wooden staves and tablets ; ' and why this flame on the eve of Bealteine, contrary to the orders of the Ard Righ and the Arch

Druid ? Accompany me to the assembly at Tara, and account for your disobedience ; but first extinguish that ill-boding light.'

"Of all that sat or stood in the presence of the King, no one stood to show respect to the newly-arrived, but Dubthach, an aged Druid, and the young poet, Fiech, who thus braved the King's displeasure. He, fixing his eyes stern on the saint and his followers, sharply addressed them : ' Know ye not the law of this land, that whosoever on the eve of Bealteine kindles a fire before the blaze is seen from Tara is devoted to death ? '

"Patrick then commenced by declaring the unity of the Godhead in a Trinity of Persons, the Creation and the Fall of Man, the necessity of a Mediator, the Incarnation of the Son of God, and our redemption thereby, the necessity of true Christian belief, and the rejection of all creature worship, not excepting that of the genial, life-cherishing Baal. He then alluded to his former captivity and the object of his present mission, and besought the king and people not to resist the good impulses which would be vouchsafed by God's goodness to every one who did not wilfully offer opposition to them.

"The hearts of the king and the greater part of the Druids remained obdurate, but such persuasive strength was vouchsafed to the words of the saint that very many hung on his lips with veneration and enthusiasm. The Ard Righ observed this with regret, but his power was much restricted, and he did not venture to express open dissatisfaction. He ordered apartments to be reserved for Patrick and his companions, and appointed him to argue with his Druids on the morrow.

"Thousands were assembled next day on the wide plain, and the stern-looking Druids, filled the greater part of the space enclosed for the disputants. After some explanations and arguments were adduced by the missionary which told heavily on the priests, the Chief cried out in an arrogant tone : ' If the Son of God has redeemed the human race, and if you are sent by Him, work a miracle to prove your mission.' ' I will not seek to disturb the order of Providence to gratify mere curiosity,' modestly answered the saint. ' Then will I approve the truth of Druidic worship by effecting what you fear to attempt,' cried the infuriated pagan ; and beginning to describe lines in the air with his wand, and to chant spells, a thick veil of snow shut out the light and heat of the sun, and covering the ground for several feet. An intense cold was felt, and the teeth of everyone in the assembly chattered. Cries of discontent arose, and the saint addressed the Druid : ' You see how the assembly suffers ; banish this snow and cold, and admit the warm sunshine.' ' I cannot do so until this hour on to-morrow.' 'Ah, you are powerful for evil, not for good. Very different is the gift bestowed on me by the messenger of the Giver of All Good.' He made the sign of the Cross, invoked the aid of the Holy Trinity, and the snow sank in the soil, the grass again emerged green and dry, and the blue air again appeared warmed by the bright and comforting sunbeams. All the people invoked blessings on the head of the beneficent apostle.

" 'To convince you all,' cried the Druid, ' of our power and that of our gods, behold what I am empowered to do.' In a few seconds darkness such as seldom shrouds the earth fell on the assembly, and they groped about and murmured. Again was the thick black cloud dispersed by the prayer of the apostle, and thousands of tongues blessed him."

Fiech, the poet mentioned in this narrative, was converted, and was afterwards canonised

A similar fire-lighting ceremony was formerly observed at Rome on the first day of March, which was at one time the first day of the year. Philostratus (*Heroica*, I, p. 40) refers to a like custom that prevailed on the isle of Lemnos. In the Highlands of Scotland, and in Sweden also, the sacred fire was lighted in the same manner. The kings of France did not disdain to kindle the fires of St. John. It is on record that Louis XI. kindled the fire at Paris in 1471 and that Louis XIV. once, at least, assisted at the ceremony. As these fires are to be found in countries where Druidism was not the prevailing religion and was in all probability unknown, it is possible that they were the outcome of Aryan teaching anterior to the introduction or development of Druidism.

The following is an extract from Bossuet's *Catechism :*

Q. Why does the Church exhibit such joy at the birth of St. John the Baptist ?

A. She only perpetuates the joy which the angel foretold.

Q. How ?

A. The angel Gabriel predicted to his father, Zacharias, that he would rejoice at the birth of his son, saying, ' Thou shalt call his name John, and he shall be a joy.'

Q. Is that the reason why fires of rejoicing are kindled ?

A. Yes.

Q. Does the Church take part in these festivities ?

A. Yes, because in several dioceses, and particularly in this, several parishes make the fire in what is termed an ecclesiastical manner.

Q. What is the reason for making this fire in an ecclesiastical manner ?

A.   In order to banish the superstition attached to the kindling of the fire.

Q.   What are these superstitions ?

A.   Dancing around the fire, playing, feasting, singing songs, behaving indecently, throwing herbs into the fire, and preserving brands, cinders, and other things drawn from the fire throughout the year following.

Charlotte Elizabeth, in *Personal Recollections*, after describing the blazing bonfires which take place in Ireland on St. John's Eve, goes on to say :

" But something was to follow which was to puzzle me not a little. When the fire burned for some hours, and got low, the indispensable part of the ceremony commenced. Every one present of the peasantry passed through it, and several children were thrown across the sparkling embers, while a wooden frame of some eight feet long, with a horse's head affixed to one end, and a large white sheet thrown over it, concealing the wood and the man on whose head it was carried, made its appearance. This was greeted with loud shouts of ' Oh ! the white horse ! ' and having been safely carried by the skill of its bearer several times through the fire with a leap, it pursued the people, who ran screaming and laughing in every direction. I asked what the horse was meant for, and was told that it represented ' all cattle.' "

In Tom Taylor's translation of Hersart de la Villemarque's *Ballads and Songs of Brittany* (published in 1865) we are told that at that date the festival of St. John, the Christian substitute for the Druidic sen-feast, was still celebrated. Beal-fires blazed on every hillside, round which the peasants danced all night, in their holiday clothes, to the sounds of the *biniou*—a kind of rustic hautboy—and the shepherd's horn, or of a rude music drawn out of reeds fixed across a copper basin. The girl who danced around nine St. John's fires before midnight was sure to marry within the year. In many parishes the curé himself went in procession with banner and cross to light the sacred fire, a brand from which was preserved with reverence and placed between a branch of box blessed on Palm Sunday and a piece of Twelfth Night cake, and this was supposed to preserve the cottage from evil by thunder. The flowers of the nosegay which crowned the fire heap were powerful talismans against bodily ills.

In many places in France it was the practice to throw into the fire of St. John hampers and baskets of wickerwork containing animals —cats, dogs, foxes, and wolves. In several French villages even in the eighteenth century, the mayor or someone else in authority would cause a dozen or two dozen cats to be sent in a basket to be burnt in the

" St. John Joy Fire." This custom existed even at Paris and was not suppressed until the reign of Louis XIV.

In remote parts of Brittany a festival, evidently of Druidical origin, is held every June. The youths and maidens from the surrounding country over the age of sixteen and still unmarried assemble around a moss-grown dolmen. The youths decorate their hats with green ears of corn and the maidens wear in their bosoms posies of the flowers of flax. These are deposited on the dolmen in the superstitious belief that so long as the objects of their affections remain faithful, the ears of corn and the flowers of flax will remain unwithered. The festival is opened by a youth who is generally chosen for his beauty, commanding height, and gay dress. He wears in his buttonhole a favour of blue, green and white ribbons. He selects a partner, on whose finger he slips a ring, and with her opens the dance round the dolmen, a song meanwhile being sung. In former times the dance was opened by the parish priest, who wore a tri-coloured vestment of blue, green and white, and it is a local tradition that in Druidical times the dance was opened by the Arch Druid himself.

In several parts of the country huge bonfires are lighted every year on St. John's Eve, as the holy flame is considered essential to the cattle as a preservative from contagious disorders.

In the South Harz and in Thuringia the so-called St. John's fires are common. In Edersleben, near Sangerhausen, the proceeding is as follows : A high pole is set up, on which a tar barrel is placed, having a chain drawn through it which reaches to the ground. When it is on fire they swing the barrel round the pole amid great rejoicing. In this neighbourhood of Baruth, down to recent times, St. John's fires were lighted, as well as in the Catholic parts of Westphalia.

In heathen mythology the summer solstice was a day dedicated to the sun, and was believed to be a day on which witches held their festivities. St. John's Wort was their symbolical plant, and people were wont to judge from it whether their future would be lucky or unlucky ; as it grew they read in its progressive character their future lot. The Christians dedicated this festive period to St. John the Baptist, and the sacred plant was named St. John's Wort, or toor, and became a talisman against evil. In one of the old romantic ballads, a young lady falls in love with a demon, who tells her :

" Gin you wish to be Leman mine
Lay aside the St. John's Wort and the vervain."

When hung up on St. John's Day together with a cross over the doors of houses it kept out the devil and other evil spirits. To gather the root on St. John's Day morning at sunrise, and retain it in the house, gave luck to the family in their undertakings, especially to those begun on that day.

The most important of all Druidical festivals, however, was held on the eve of the 1st of November, when all the people throughout the country extinguished their fires and every master of a family was obliged to take home with him a portion of the consecrated fire and kindle with it the fire in his house. This sacred fire was lighted as a thanksgiving for the completion of the harvest. If any man had not paid his tithes by the last day of October in each year, he was not allowed to have even a spark from the holy fires, nor dare any neighbour give him a portion under the pain of excommunication, a punishment worse than death.

At the Hallowe'en festival, which, in many parts of the Highlands, still retains its Gaelic name of *Samh-in*, or " the fire of peace," the Druids met annually to adjust all disputes and to decide controversies.

Miss Catherine Sinclair, in *Hill and Valley*, says :

" The same animated celebration of All Saints' Eve takes place among the Welsh peasantry that Burns describes in his poem on Hallowe'en, and all superstitious ceremonies seem exactly similar to those in Scotland. Apples and tallow candles are hung alternately from the cottage ceiling so close together that those who leap up to catch them in their mouths can scarcely touch the one without tasting the other, though the greatest proof of skill and good fortune is to succeed in doing so."

MacLauchlan, in *The Early Scottish Church*, a work published in 1865, says :

" There are places in Scotland where within the memory of living men the *teine eigin*, or ' forced fire,' was lighted once every year by the rubbing of two pieces of wood together, while every fire in the neighbourhood was extinguished in order that they might be lighted anew from this sacred source."

It was not until 1220 that Loundres, Archbishop of Dublin extinguished the perpetual fire which was kept in a small cell near the church of Kildare, but so firmly rooted was the veneration for this fire that it was relighted in a few years and actually kept burning until the suppression of the monasteries. A writer in the *Gentleman's Magazine*, 1795, says that being in Ireland the day before Midsummer he was told that in the evening he should see " the lighting of fires in honour of the sun " at midnight.

Tuathal ordered a fire to be kindled annually on the eve of 1st of November at his royal seat at Tiachtga for the purpose of summoning the priests, augurs, and Druids in order that they might consume the sacrifices which were offered to the gods. It was established under the penalty of a heavy fine that no other fire should be kindled upon that night throughout the kingdom, so that the fire that was to be used in the country was to be derived from this holy fire; for which privilege the people were to pay a Scroball, amounting to threepence each year to the King of Munster.

These fires were a feature of Irish Druidism, although the Irish Druids had no particular veneration for the oak, and the mistletoe was unknown in Ireland until the nineteenth century. In an ancient tract called Dinnseanchus, there is a legendary account of Midhe, son of Brath, son of Detha, who is said to have been the first to light a fire for the sons of the Milesians on the hill of Uisnech in Westmeath, which continued to burn for seven years, and from this fire every chief fire in Erin used to be lighted. The successor of Midhe was entitled to a sack of wine and a pig from every house in Erin every year. The Irish Druids, however, said that it was an insult to them to have this fire ignited in the country, and all the Druids of Erin came into the house to take council, but Midhe had all their tongues cut out, and he buried the tongues in the earth of Uisnech and then sat over them, upon which his mother exclaimed: " It is uisnech (*i.e.*, proudly) you sit up there this night."

The third day of the Feis, or Convention, of Tara, instituted by Ollamh Fodhla, was devoted to the feast of Saman, or the moon. Saman, or Samhen, has also been rendered " heaven." At the conclusion of the festival the fire of Saman was lighted and the tutelary divinities invoked.

Vallancey says that among the Irish Hallowmas Day is known as La Samhna, that November was the month of mourning, being the season appointed by the Druids for the solemn intercession of the quick for the souls of the dead, or those who had departed this life within the space of the year. The first day of November was dedicated to the angel presiding over fruits, seeds, etc., and was therefore named *La Mas Ushal*, or " the day of the apple fruit," and being pronounced *Lamasool*, has been corrupted into " Lambswool," the name given to a composition made on this eve, of roasted apples, sugar, and ale. The festival lasted until the beginning of December, which month was named *Mi Nolagh*, or the month of the new born, from the Hebrew word *Nolah*, " to bring forth young," whence the French word *Noel* and the Irish *Nolagh*, or Christmas Day. The feast of *Murdad*, the angel of the ancient Persians, who presided over fruit, fell also on 1st November, and it is not impossible, says Vallancey, that the Irish name for agrimony, viz., *murdrad*, may have been derived from this source.

So great was the hold of these ceremonies upon the people that the Christian priests were unable to abolish them and therefore transferred them to Christian observances. Thus St. John the Baptist's Day came

M

to be observed by the building up of large fires of which bones formed part of the constituents, while the customs of driving cattle through the flames and of people leaping over them were still retained. The cattle were driven through the flames in substitution for the actual sacrifice and the bones were, in all probability, burned as substitutes for the actual cattle. From this custom sprang the term " bone fire," corrupted into " bonfire."

These fires were interdicted at the sixth Council of Constantinople, held in A.D. 680, in the following words :

" These Bonefires that are kindled by certain people on New Moones before their shops and houses, over which also they are ridiculously and follishly to leape, by a certain ancient custome, we command from henceforth to cease. Whoever therefore shall doe any such thing ; if he be a clergyman, let him be deposed ; if a layman, let him be excommunicated ; for in the fourth book of the Kings it is thus written : 'And Manasseh built an altar to all the host of heaven, in the two courts of the Lord's house, and made his children to pass through the fire.' "

Prynne, in his *Histriomastix*, says : " Bonefires therefore had their originall from this idolatrous custome, as this General Councill hath defined ; therefore all Christians should avoid them."

They were further interdicted by the Synodus Francisca under Pope Zachary when " the sacrilegious fires which they call Nedri (or Bonefires) and all other observations of the Pagans whatsoever " were further interdicted.

The observance of the Druidical New Year on the 10th of March was also accompanied by the usual lighting of fires on the elevations of the country.

The festival of the 25th of December also was celebrated by the Druids, both in Great Britain and Ireland, with great fires lighted on the tops of hills which were re-lighted twelve days afterwards on what is known as the feast of the Epiphany. The mistletoe was honoured by the Druids as a divine plant. It was known to them as the *Ollyach*, or the " all-heal," and the tree on which it grew, frequently, in Britain, the oak, was called the *pren awyr*, or " the celestial tree." The cutting of the mistletoe, with a golden knife, was the occasion of a special religious function.

The oak was reverenced by the Druids as a sacred tree, and oak leaves were used in many of their most solemn services. The growth of mistletoe upon an oak was, therefore, to the Druid a sign that the tree was particularly sacred, for mistletoe does not commonly grow upon the oak, and its presence enhanced the sanctity and mystery of the tree. There is an oak tree in Lord Henry Somerset's park at Eastnor, near Ledbury, at the western base of the Malvern Hills, on which the mistletoe grows, and at Rosenau, Datchet, on the bank of the Thames, mistletoe could, until quite recently, be seen growing on an acacaia. Pliny refers to the Druidical belief that whatever grew on an oak was sent from Heaven and was a sign that the tree had been chosen by the gods. Hence, when cut, it was not allowed to fall to the ground and become profane and thus lose its marvellous virtue.

Sir John Colbatch, a famous physician, was the author of *A Dissertation concerning Mistletoe, a most wonderful specific remedy for the cure of convulsive distempers*, and in some country places there is still a lingering belief in the magical powers of the mistletoe, particularly in curing animals of diseases. It was once known as *omnia sanane*. In the reign of George I. it was called *lignum sanctae crucis*. There are several references to it in English literature. In Holstein, the mistletoe is believed to confer the power of ghost-seeing upon its possessor. At Glastonbury, once possibly a stronghold of Druidism, which, according to tradition, contains the tomb of the great British hero, King Arthur, the mistletoe hangs in thick clusters.

The Druids had a remarkable veneration for the number three, and the mistletoe is said to have been regarded by them as sacred because not only its berries, but its leaves also, grew in clusters of three united to one stock. The mistletoe was invested with a character so holy that it was considered a profanation to touch it with fingers. The Arch Druid alone was deemed worthy to pluck the mistletoe, and he first carefully purified himself with consecrated water. The golden hook held in his left hand must never have been used before. Some doubt has been cast by Dr. Lort as to whether gold really formed the substance of the sickle, whether *aerea* should not be the word instead of *aurea*, and Virgil, in the *Aeneid*, iv, 513, expressly says that herbs for magical purposes were cut with brazen sickles.

The following catechism relating to the gathering of the mistletoe is taken from C. McIntyre North's *The Book of the Club of True Highlanders*:

Q. When is the sacred plant gathered?

A. At the new moon next the winter solstice, they thus gather the sacred plant: Having made all due preparation for the sacrifice and the banquet beneath the trees, they bring thither two white bulls, the horns of which are bound then for the first time. Clad in a white robe the priest ascends the tree, and cuts the mistletoe with a golden sickle, which is received by others in a white cloak. The chief Druid then says: ' The gift in the golden horn, the golden horn in the hand, the hand on the knife, the knife on the leader of the herd. Sincerely I worship thee, Beli, giver of good, and Manhogan the king, who preserves the honour of Bel, the Island of Beli.' They then immolate the victims, offering up their prayer that Beli will render this gift of his propitious to those to whom he has so granted it.

Q. Name some of the other sacred feasts.

A. The feast of Belteine, when the faithful offer sacrifices to Hu and Ked, when the king receives a horse and arms from each lord of the manor or chieftains of the lands. The day on which the great fire is kindled (according to O'Curry this was 31st of October) to summon the priest to consume the offered sacrifice; and every other fire in the country extinguished; so that the faithful use only the sacred fire to rekindle the house fire, and for which each pays a screpall. And the great feast which is held three days before and three days after Samhain, in every third year when, if any person commits a crime during this period, the penalty is instant death.

The oak has always and everywhere been the tree of the gods. In the North the oak was under the special protection of Thor, the hammer-wielding god, whose name is handed down to us in the word " thunder." The oaks of Zeus belted his oracle at Dodona.

Aubrey, in his *History of Surrey*, says :

" It has not been usually observed that to cut oakwood is unfortunate. There was at Norwood one oak that had mistletoe, a timber tree, which was felled about 1657. Some persons cut this mistletoe for some apothecaries in London, and sold them a quantity for ten shillings each time, and left only one branch remaining for more to sprout out. One fell lame shortly after; soon after each of the others lost an eye ; and he that felled the tree, though warned of these misfortunes of the other men, would, notwithstanding, adventure to do it, and shortly after broke his leg, as if the Hamadryades had resolved to take an ample revenge for the injury done to this sacred and venerable oak. I cannot omit here taking notice of the great misfortunes in the family of the Earl of Winchelsea, who, at Eastwell, in Kent, felled down a most curious grove of oaks, near his own noble seat, and gave the first blow with his own hands. Shortly after his countess died in her bed suddenly, and his eldest son, the Lord Maidstone, was killed at sea by a cannon ball."

Towards the end of the eighteenth century Mr. Philip Rashleigh found at the bottom of a mine near the River Powey, ten fathoms below the surface of the earth, a brass hook corresponding to the description given of the Druidical hook.

A bas-relief discovered at Autun has been described by Aubrey, in his *Antiquities of Autun*, in which a Druid is represented " crowned with oaken leaves." Another Druid, by his side, has in his hand a crescent resembling the moon at six days old. It was a rule among the Druids not to celebrate any ceremony in which mistletoe formed a part except on the sixth day of the moon. The Britons, according to Pliny, " began their months and years when the moon was six days old, because then she is thought to be of great power and force sufficient, but is not yet come to her half light and the end of her first quarter."

The power of the mistletoe, contended the Druids, made women fruitful.

Sir Walter Scott, in *Marmion*, refers to the mistletoe in :

" Forth to the woods did merry men go
   To gather in the mistletoe."

Gay, in *Trivia*, writes :

" Now with bright holly all the temple strew
   With laurel green and sacred mistletoe."

while Herrick in *Hesperides*, says :

" Down with the rosemary and days,
      Down with the mistletoe ;
   Instead of holly now upraise
      The greener box for show."

Shakespeare has only one allusion to the mistletoe, and that an uncomplimentary one :

" Trees, though summer, yet forlorn and lean,
   O'er come with moss and baleful mistletoe."

Watts thus apostrophies the plant :

" Hail, Hail to its leaves of rich green,
   With pearls that are fit for a queen."

Pliny, in his *Natural History*, gives a description of the plant and the mode of gathering it. He says (Book xvi, c. 44) :

" The Druids, for so call they their Magi, have nothing more sacred than the mistletoe, and the tree on which it grows, provided it be the oak. They select a particular grove of oaks and perform no sacred rites without oak leaves, so that from this custom they may seem to have been called Druids (Oakites), according to the Greek interpretation of that word. They reckon whatever grows on these trees is sent down from Heaven and a proof that the tree itself is chosen by Deity. But the mistletoe is very rarely found and when found is sought after with the greatest religious ardour, and principally in the sixth moon, which is the beginning of their months and years, and when the tree is thirty years old it is then not half-grown only but has attained its full vigour. They call it

All-heal (Ull-ice) by a word in their own language, and having proper sacrifices and feasts under the trees with great solemnity bring up two white bulls, whose horns are then first bound. The priest, clothed in a white surplice, ascends the tree and cuts it off with a golden knife, and it is received in a white sheet. Then they sacrifice the victims and pray that God would render his own gift prosperous to those on whom He has bestowed it. They reckon the mistletoe administered as a potion can impart fecundity to any barren animal and that it is a remedy against all kinds of poision."

The mistletoe was, and is, more rare even in Scotland than in England, where any variety of the plant is regarded as a rarity. In the *Statistical Account of Scotland* the minister of Kiltarility, in Inverness-shire, writes : " In Lovat's garden are a number of standard trees. On two standard apple trees here mistltoe (*sic*) grows, which is a very rare plant in this country." There are references in the writings of the Bards to the use of tallies or sprigs cut from a fruit-bearing tree, a custom which Tacitus ascribes to the Germans.

Among the Druidical ceremonies may be included the turnings of the body during the times of worship. The numerous round monuments in Damonium are said to have been formed for the purpose of this mysterious rite. In several of the Scottish isles the people never approached " the fire-hallowed kurne " without walking round it three times from east to west in accordance with the course of the sun. The Druids turned sun-ways in order to bless and worship the gods, and the opposite way when they wished to curse and destroy their enemies. On the point of facing the east in religious ceremonial, Hurd, in his *Ceremonies and Rites*, says :

" This ceremony was peculiar to all those heathen nations who lived westward of the Hellespont, as well as the ancient Britons ; and although they had all formed the most unworthy notions of the Divine Being, yet the hope of a great person being born in the East seems to have prevailed everywhere among them. This undoubtedly was handed down to them by tradition and there is great reason to believe that they expected (like Socrates in Plato) he would rectify all the abuses that had crept into their religion, and that he would reign for ever among men. Thus in every nation we meet with something of a traditional hope of the coming of the Messiah, although some are ignorant of the character he is to assume."

Plutarch says that the Druids observed a feast in honour of Saturn every thirty years, the time taken by the planet Saturn to complete its course round the sun ; and that the festival took place on its entrance into the second sign—Taurus—of the zodiac.

At St. Maughold's Well, in the Isle of Man, there was formerly a custom, believed to be of Druidical origin, of resorting thither on the first Sunday in August to drink of the water to which medicinal virtues were ascribed.

At St. Ives, in Cornwall, once every five years public games are held round the monument of one, John Kerill, a barrister, who died in 1791, and who caused to be erected in his lifetime a pyramid of granite to his own memory. A band of four matrons and ten virgins dressed in white silk walk in pairs to the summit of a hill, accompanied by musicians. They dance a merry measure, after which they chant a psalm "in imitation of the Druids round the cromlechs of the departed brave." Then the Mayor of St. Ives appears in his official robes, and wrestling, racing and rowing are duly accomplished by athletic competitors, the winners receiving appropriate rewards.

In 1792 an effort was made to revive the annual meetings of the Bards. On 2nd September of that year, the day of the autumnal equinox, some Welsh Bards resident in London assembled in congress on Primrose Hill, when the wonted ceremonies were observed. A circle of stones was formed, in the middle of which was the *Maen Gorsedd*, on which a naked sword being placed, all the Bards assisting to sheathe it. This was attended by a proclamation that the Bards of the island of Britain were the heralds and ministers of peace and never bore a naked weapon in the presence of any one ; nor was it lawful for any person to bear one, on any pretence, in their presence.

It was an unwritten law of the Bards that, as a community, their whole life and actions were to be governed by the principle that what is wrong in public must be wrong in private, and the proverb that governed the doings of their circles was : " In the face of the sun and the eye of Light." Hence one reason for holding their meetings in the open air and in the broad daylight.

In Switzerland the most important day of the summer is St. John's Day, 24th of June. Certain herbs only acquire virtue from being gathered on that date ; in Valais a bunch of nine different plants is then picked and fastened to the house to protect it. A bath on the night of St. John's Day has curative properties though in some places it is held to be dangerous, as St. John's night might claim a victim. " On this day three persons must perish, one in the air, one by fire, and one by water." Bonfires on the hills are restricted to French Switzerland.

In the Border counties on Hallowe'en, New Year's Day, and Midsummer Eve, and in Ireland on May Day Eve, the fire is not permitted to go out, for, if extinguished, none would be given or good luck would disappear.

James Napier, in *Folk Lore*, quotes from Train's description of a ceremony witnessed in 1810 while at Balnaguard, a village of Perthshire, as a charm to ward off the " Black Haunch," an infectious cattle disease. He says :

"All fires are extinguished between the two nearest rivers, and all the people within that boundary convene in a convenient place, where they erect a machine, as above described ; and after they have commenced, they continue night and day until they have forced fire by the friction of two sticks. Every person must perform a portion of this labour, or touch the machine in order not to break the charm. During the continuance of the ceremony, they appear melancholy and dejected, but when the fire, which they say is brought from heaven by an angel, blazes in the tow, they resume their wonted gaiety ; and while one part of the company is employed in feeding the flame, the others drive all the cattle in the neighbourhood over it. When this ceremony is ended, they consider the cure complete ; after which they drink whisky, and dance to the bagpipe or fiddle round the celestial fire till the last spark is extinguished."

CHAPTER VIII

THE AFFINITY OF DRUIDISM
WITH OTHER RELIGIONS

The Druidical religion and philosophy were so like to the Pythagorean system that some writers have arrived at the conclusion that the one was borrowed from the other, but the borrower is assumed generally to be Pythagoras, and not the Druids. Dr. Abraham Rees, in his *Cyclopaedia*, is of opinion that Pythagoras himself learned and adopted some of the opinions of the Bards, and imparted to these some of his own thoughts and discoveries. Milton states that : " The studies of learning in the deepest sciences have been so eminent among us that writers of good antiquity have been persuaded that even the school of Pythagoras and the Persian wisdom took beginning from the philosophy of this island." Borlase, in his *Antiquities of Cornwall*, expressed the belief that long before Greece could boast of her wise men, Britain was famous for learning, philosophy, and wisdom, and that the Greek philosophers were really beholden to our Bards whom they copied in many particulars. In the opinion of Toland, no heathen priesthood ever attained the perfection of the Druidical, which he describes as being " far more exquisite than any other system, as having been much better calculated to beget ignorance and an implicit disposition in the people, no less than to procure power and profit to the priests."

Both the Druidic and Pythagorean alphabets were Etruscan in character. The three Orders of Druidism correspond to the three orders of Pythagorics, Pythagoreans, and Pythagorists. Each cultivated the study of theosophy, metaphysics, ethics, physics, the magnitude and form of the earth, the motions of the heavens and stars, medicine, and magic. Pythagoras enjoined the rule of concealing philosophy from the uninitiated and forbade it to be written down.

The points of resemblance between Druidism and Brahmanism are very striking. In ancient times, according to Brahmanical lore, a great intercourse existed between India and the countries in the West, and the British Isles are said to have been described in the *Puranas* as *Breta-*

st'han, or "The Place of Religious Duty." Faber, in his *Cabiri*, gives expression to the opinion that the undoubted resemblance which existed between Brahmanism and Druidism originated probably from the Asiatic extraction of the Druids. The various Japhetic tribes which peopled Europe all came out of the widely-extended regions of Tartary ; and many of them, among whom were doubtless the Celtic Druids, came from the neighbourhood of the Indian Caucasus. The Brahmans made it a rule never to reveal to the uninitiated the secret doctrine of their religion and, in like manner, the Druids concealed from strangers and the uninitiated, even of their own country, the sacred mysteries of their religion. There was throughout India a veneration for the serpent, and amongst the Druids there was a superstitious reverence for the Anguinum, or serpents' egg, and many of their temples were constructed in serpentine form. The Druids regarded it as unlawful to eat ducks, hens, and other winged animals. The Brahmans, of course, looked upon the killing of any live animal as unlawful and abstained from eating anything that had been killed. The Brahmans carried a sacred staff and a consecrated wand or magic rod was carried by every Druid as a sign of his initiation. Brahma is generally represented as holding in his hand a wheel or circle, and the circle was regarded by the Druids as a symbol both of the sun and of eternity. Each had a veneration for white horses and for vast pyramidical heaps of stones. The Indian stone temples were, for the most part, uncovered or in the open, like Stonehenge, Abury and many other sites. Each had solemn rites of initiation ; in each religion the priests wore tiaras and white robes, not unlike the Persian Mithra. Just as the Brahmans were the most venerated caste in India, so the Druids were regarded as superior even to the nobility of Britain. Belief in the immortality of the soul was the basic article in each creed, combined in both with the belief in transmigration. Each had severities of discipline and penitential exercises. Maurice is of the opinion that " it is impossible to doubt that at some remote period the two orders were united, or, at least, were educated in the same grand school with the Magi of Persia and the seers of Babylon," while Sir W. Jones contends that a race of Brahmans anciently sat on the throne of Persia. Barrow, in Volume II. of *Asiatic Researches*, says : " That the Druids were Brahmans is beyond the least shadow of a doubt, but that they were all murdered and their sciences lost, is out of all bounds of probability : it is much more likely that they turned schoolmasters, Freemasons, and fortune-tellers ; and, in this way, part of their sciences might easily descend to posterity, as we find they have done."

Francklin, in his *Tenets and Doctrines of the Jeynes and Boodhists*, sums up the striking similarity in the following words :

" The similarity of the laws and customs of the Druids and ancient Brahmans has been remarked by a variety of writers, and it is beyond doubt that the hierarchy of the Druids was a ramification of the worship of the Hindoos : their offices and privileges were of a similar nature, they administered all the religious ceremonies, they managed the sacrifices, and instructed the people, by whom to the present day, among the Hindoos, they were considered as the oracles and depositaries of everything learned and instructive which belonged to the times ; above all, Abaris, or Bladud, the high priest of the Druids, who is said to have instructed Pythagoras, the Samian philosopher, was, in fact, no other than the Puttee Cooroo (lord of priests) of Hindoostan, and the Archimagus, or Peer-i-Moghaun of the Persians."

There is also a striking resemblance between Druidism and Judaism. Not only did each religion inculcate a belief in a Supreme Being, but the name given to that Supreme by each is akin. The Jewish name for the Supreme Being, Jehovah, means " The Self-Existent," or, to adopt the term employed by Maimonides, " The Eternal." Among the Druids, Bel was the name given to the Supreme, the meaning of which is " He that is." The name Ptah, also, it may be pointed out, means " I am all that has been, is, or shall be." The Hebrews were accustomed to worship the Eternal under the name of Baal. Thus we read in Hosea ii., 15 : "And it shall be at that day, saith the Lord, that thou shalt call me Ishi, and shalt call me no more Baal." This was because the Israelites had become idolaters and served other deities under the name of Baalim. Each possessed a priest vested with supreme authority, and had three classes or orders of sacred men. The Jews had their priests or judges, prophets, and scribes, while among the adherents of the Druidical faith there were the Druids, Bards, and Vates. Each measured time by night and day. Grove worship was common to both Israelite and Druid, and it is clear from the many references to the oak in the Old Testament that it was regarded as a sacred tree. The same Hebrew word which signifies " oak " also means " an oath," and the root of this word is " mighty," or " strong," the root of the name given to the Deity in many languages. The angel (or messenger) of the Eternal came and sat under the oak at Ophrah when sent to deliver a message to Gideon (Judges vi., 11). A similar incident is recorded in I. Kings xiii., 14. in Ezekiel vi., 13, and Hosea iv., 13, reference is made to the practice of offering up incense under the oak. It was at the oak of Moreh (Genesis xii., 6, R.V.) that the Eternal appeared to Abram, and it was there that Abram built an altar. Joshua (xxiv., 26) wrote particulars of the covenant in a book of the law of God and took a great stone and set it up under an oak tree, by the sanctuary of the Eternal. Amongst the Jews the oak was occasionally a burying-place. Deborah, Rebekah's nurse, was buried beneath Bethel, under an oak (Genesis xxxv., 8), and Saul and his sons were buried under an oak (I. Chronicles x., 12). Abraham planted a grove of trees as a retreat of silence and solitude and prayer, but, in latter times, the denunciations of heaven were launched against groves, because they were used by idolaters, or the followers of a different religion. The May Day festival was in honour of Spring, when the sun entered the sign of Taurus, the bull. Hence the calves or bulls adored by the Israelites were golden, because gold was a fitting representation of the benign sun, then beginning to shed his glittering beauties at the approach of Spring. By the ancient Britons, says Faber, in his *Pagan Idolatry*, the bull was not only reverenced in a very high degree, but he was likewise exhibited by them exactly in the same manner as he was by the Egyptians, the Hindoos, and the Greeks. He was the symbol of their great god, Hu, the whole of whose character and attributes prove him to be one with Osiris, Siva, and Bacchus, all of which deities were represented by living bulls. The oak also has ever been held in veneration by all nations and peoples. In Rome an oaken garland or crown was called *corona civica*, and was bestowed only upon him who had saved a citizen's life, though in process of time it came to be bestowed upon an official if he spared a Roman citizen when he had power to kill him. In Ovid's time the Emperor had always standing before his gates an oak tree, in the midst of two laurels, as an emblem denoting two worthy virtues, required in all emperors and princes ; first, such whereby the enemy might be conquered ; secondly, such whereby the citizens might be saved. In Sweden, the ancient inhabitants held in reverence and awe the sacred groves and trees, because they regarded them as given by the Supreme as ornaments to his noble creation, as well as to afford protection to the husbandman and cattle against the scorching heat of the midday sun. The Dryopes, who lived near to Thibet, are said to have been named from *drus*, an oak, and *ops*, the voice, and Pococke claims that they are identical with the Druids. Dr. Stukeley, as already noted, calls Abraham " the first Druid," in reference to the oak grove at Beersheba. Although Dr. Stukeley has been vindicated so amply by Mr. Crawford, care must be exercised in accepting some of his theories, which are rather fanciful.

The affinity between Druidism and the religion of the Persians is also strongly marked. The Druids held that the Supreme Being was too exalted to be confined within temples made with hands. Their open-air temples were circular in form, and in their worship they made use of the circle to intimate that God was to be found in every direction. Cyrus, in Xenophon, sacrifices to Jupiter, the sun, and the rest of the gods, upon the summits of mountains, " as the Persians were wont to sacrifice." The Persians taught that the celestial expanse was their Jupiter, whom they worshipped in the open air. In like manner to the Druids, the Persians forbade the introduction of images into their temples, for they held that the Supreme was too refined to be represented by any figure, a belief also taught by Mohammed and held firmly by all Moslems to the present day. The Druids were not idol worshippers, and they would not sanction the setting up of any image or statue, although certain stones, rough as taken from the quarry and consecrated according to ritual, are said to have been erected in retired spots to represent Isis, or Ceridwen, British divinities whose merits were eulogised by the Bards. Some of the Persian temples were caverns in rocks, either natural or artificial. They had likewise Puratheia, or open temples, for the celebration of their rites of fire. The Persians also venerated the serpent, which they regarded as a representation of their god Mithras, who, according to their teaching, was born from a rock. The Druids had their sacred fires and the Persians had their holy flame, to which they paid divine honours, and they, like the Druids, lighted festal fires at the return of the consecrated season. The Druids considered their fires to be antidotes against the diseases of cattle, and the Persians extended their powerful influence to the human body, placing their sick within the range of the gentle heat of the fire, in order that they might recover the more quickly. The Druids compelled the Britons at a certain season of the year, to extinguish all their fires and to re-kindle them from the sacred fire, a toll being exacted, and, with some trifling variations, a similar custom prevails in Persia to the present day. In the art of divination both the Druids and the Persians are said to have been proficient ; both also regarded the mistletoe as a sacred plant. The Druids regarded it as unlawful and a sacrilege to cut the mistletoe with anything but a golden scythe, and the Persians used a knife consecrated and set aside for that special purpose. Both knew the power of excommunication and cast out and expelled from their communion the abandoned and impenitent transgressors of their holy laws. In Mithraic worship there were ceremonial bull fights annually on the first of May, but the maypole festival was common to all ancient countries and is generally believed to have had a Phallic origin. Cicero says that none was qualified to be king of Persia who had not first learned the doctrine and science of the Magi. The Persians, even in ages when temples were common in all other countries, had no temples made with human skill, which was the reason, some think, why Xerxes burned and demolished the temples of Greece. Borlase, as did Strabo, saw much similarity between the Magi and the Druids ; each carried in the hand during the celebration of sacred rites, a bunch of plants : that of the

Magi was the *Hom*, or *Barsum*, which closely resembled the mistletoe.
Dr. Stukeley is of opinion that this parasite is the same as that mentioned
in Isaiah vi., 13. It is generally agreed by commentators that the
" tiel " tree of the translators should be rendered " oak," or a species
of sacred lime, having purple flowers, like those of the vine, growing
in bunches, with a fruit of ruddy purple, the size of a juniper berry.
It will be noticed that it is winter time with this tree, and Dr. Stukeley
maintains that the passage should be translated : "As an oak, whose
plant is alive upon it," which, says Isaiah, " shall be eaten," so that
here we have the same idea in regard to the all-heal, or mistletoe, as
was the case with the Hom.

A similarity also existed, both in belief and practice, between
Druidism and the religion of the Phœnicians. Pinkarton, in his *Enquiry
into the History of Scotland*, says that Druidism was palpably Phœnician,
and Sammes remarks that " the customs, religion, idols, offices, and
dignities of the ancient Britons are all clearly Phœnician."

There are many points of affinity between Druidism and the religion
of Greece. The Greeks worshipped their gods upon the tops of mountains.
Jupiter, in Homer, commends Hector for the many sacrifices he had offered
upon the top of Ida.

"My heart partakes the generous Hector's pain ;
Hector, whose zeal whole hecatombs has slain,
Whose grateful fumes the gods received with joy,
From Ida's summits and the towers of Troy.
                                        Pope.

They also worshipped in groves of trees, and looked upon the oak as
the oldest tree. It was so common to erect altars and temples in groves,
and to dedicate them to religious uses, that all sacred places, as we
learn from Strabo, even those where no trees were to be seen, were
called groves. The solitude of groves was regarded as creative of religious
awe and reverence in the minds of the people. Pliny says that in groves
the very silence of the place became the object of adoration. Ovid says :

" A darksome grove of oak was spread out near,
Whose gloom oppressive said : 'A god dwells here.' "

The number three was commonly observed in the religious ceremonies
of the Greeks. Thus, in Ovid :

" *Terque senem flamma, ter aqua, ter sulphure lustrat.*"

It was customary for the Greeks on some occasions to dance round
the altars while they sang their sacred hymns, which consisted of three
stanzas or parts, the first of which, called *strophe*, was sung in turning
from east to west ; the other, named *antistrophe*, in returning from west
to east ; then they stood before the altar and sang the *epode*, which was
the last part of the song. The Greeks practised divination by the entrails

of animals slain.   If the entrails were whole and sound, had their natural place, colour, and proportion, then all was well ; but if any part was decayed, or wanting, if anything was out of order or not according to Nature, evil was portended.   The palpitation of the entrails was a very unfortunate omen.   Pythagoras, the soothsayer, is said to have foretold the death of Alexander because his victim's liver had no lobes.   Among the Greeks the oak of Dodona was the seat of the oldest Hellenic oracle, whose priests sent forth their declarations on its leaves.

Carte, in his *History of England*, says that the Druids agreed so much with the Curetes of Greece in the rites and ceremonies of their religion, in the methods they used to raise the wonder and veneration of the people ; in the nature of their studies ; as well as in their manner of life, customs, and institutions, that Pezron makes no difficulty in pronouncing the Druids to be the immediate descendants of those Curetes, or, at least, their successors ; being admitted into their society, initiated into their mysteries, and charged with the care of religion in the Gomarian colonies settled in the western parts of Europe.

The Egyptians worshipped the sun and the serpent was sacred among them as representing the eternal existence of the Deity.   At the temple of Isis at Dendera there is a representation of a procession of men and women bringing to Isis and Osiris, who stands behind her, globes surrounded with bulls, horns, and mitred snakes.   The Egyptians had a Tauric festival and even went so far as to embalm cattle.   They were firm believers in the doctrine of metempsychosis.   They also offered up both human and animal sacrifices.

If not Druidism, it was a religion of a very similar character which was followed by the inhabitants of a considerable part of Italy.   The Sabin country lies about twenty miles to the north of Rome, on the west side of the Tiber.   On the top of the mountain Soracte, in that country, were the grove temples and carn of Apollo.   Hirpins was the name given to the race of people inhabitating that district, and they held annually a sacrifice similar in every respect to that of the Druids. It is thus referred to in Dryden's version of Virgil's *Aeneid* :

"O Patron of Soracte's high abodes,
   Phœbus, the ruling pow'r among the gods
   Whom first we serve, whole woods of unctuous pine
   Burnt on thy heap, and to thy glory shine ;
   By thee protected, with our naked soles
   Thro' flames unsinged we pass, and tread the kindl'd coals.
   Give me, propitious pow'r, to wash away
   The stain of this dishonourable day.

The priests of Moloch also walked through the fires they lighted in honour of their god.

John Keeson, in *The Cross and the Dragon*, relates how that the
Franciscan missionaries when they reached the court of the Prince of
Batou, situated on the Volga, had first to pass through two fires in order
to destroy any malign influence they might have brought with them.
Two lances erected by the side of these fires supported a stretched cord,
from which depended several pieces of rag ; and, beneath this cord, to
be purified, had to pass men, beasts and goods. Two females, one on
each side, sprinkled them with water at the same time, reciting certain
words in performing the act.

It was the custom among many ancient peoples to erect a stone
in commemoration or remembrance of any benefit received at the hands
of the Supreme. Such practice was particularly observed among the
Jews. Jacob, after his wonderful vision, " rose up early in the morning
and took the stone that he had put for his pillow and set it up as a pillar
and poured oil upon the top of it " (Genesis xxxviii., 18). He did the
same thing when he entered into a covenant with Laban (Genesis
xxxi., 45), and when he is said to have talked with God at Bethel
(Genesis xxxv., 14). Joshua built at Gilgal (a word which means a
circle) a temple composed of twelve stones, and when he had assembled the
children of Israel within this temple he told them that when their children
should ask them the meaning of the stones they were to make answer
that it was the acknowledgment of the power of the Eternal. The
custom of venerating baetyla, or consecrated stones, and worshipping
under oaks was diffused over both hemispheres in the remotest periods.
The existence of stone monuments, whose antiquity is undoubted by
archæologists, is proof that learning and culture existed in Britain long
prior to the Roman invasion, before even the foundation of Rome.
Stone circles are common in America, in the province of Coimbatoor in
India, and over all northern Europe, as well as in several of the islands
of the Mediterranean. Sir John Chardin says that he saw in Media a
circle of stones which the traditions of the people living near, in singular
conformity with Grecian and Celtic customs, ascribed to Caous, or giants,
who wishing once to hold a council respecting some matter, brought
each his official seat and left it, when the meeting broke up, as a wonder
to men. The explorations of the Ordnance Survey of 1869 proved the
existence in Palestine and Arabia of circles " nearly identical in character
with those which in England and Scotland are commonly called Druidical
circles." In Germany, as in England, the oak was long regarded as a
sacred tree ; solemn assemblies were held beneath it, and decrees were
often dated *sub quercibus* or *sub annosa quercu.* Scandinavian folk-lore
ascribed man's origin to the oak or ash, a myth also prevalent among
the Romans. The Arcadians believed their ancestors were oaks before
they became men.

Whenever possible the tops of hills were chosen by the Druids for their services and worship; their temples of initiation and the scenes of the performance of their secret and sacred rites being in caves. Mountain worship is referred to frequently in the Old Testament as being a patriarchal practice, just as afterwards it was adopted by non-Israelitish nations. The Persians also worshipped on mountain tops. When Philip II. made war against the Spartans he sacrificed on the mountains of Olympus and Eva. Cyrus sacrificed to the gods on the mountain just before his death. So, in China, 2,300 years before the Christian era, sacrifices were offered to the Supreme and Chan-Ti on the four great mountains with the four Yo. Cicero tells us that when Xerxes made his expedition into Greece, the Magi commanded that all the Grecian temples should be destroyed " because the Grecians were so impious as to enclose those gods within walls who ought to have all things round them open and free—their temples being the universal world."

The principal deity of the Germans was Mercury; they sacrificed human victims, they had open temples, they consecrated groves and venerated oaks, and computed by nights instead of by days, and this last-named practice was common to all the northern nations of Europe.

It has been a practice from time immemorial to build temples in the form of crosses. The crux ansata of the Egyptians was the hieroglyphic of life. A serpent joined to the cross symbolises the immortality of the soul.

The close affinity between the doctrines of the newly-established Christian faith, as taught by the early missionaries, and the beliefs of Druidism, will warrant the assertions of several writers that the followers of the doctrines of the old religion were without difficulty persuaded to embrace Christianity. It was a question really of merging of beliefs, rather than an entire change of faith. O'Donovan, in his *Annals of the Four Masters*, says: "Nothing is clearer than that Patrick engrafted Christianity on the pagan superstition with so much skill that he won the people over to the Christian religion before they understood the exact difference between the two systems of belief, and much of this half-Pagan, half-Christian religion will be found, not only in the Irish stories of the Middle Ages, but in the superstitions of the peasantry of the present day." The cross, as a symbol, was known to and revered by the Druids, and their mode of consecrating an oak tree was first to fasten a cross beam upon it if the two main horizontal arms were not sufficiently prominent. Upon this right branch they cut in the bark, in fair characters, the word " Hesus "; upon the middle or upright stem the word " Taramis "; and upon the left branch the word "Belenus." Over all, and above the branching out of the arms, they inscribed the

N

word " Thau " (see Ezekiel ix., 4), and, according to Schedius, " This tree so inscribed, they make their Kebla in the grove cathedral, or summer church, towards which they direct their faces in the offices of religion, as to the ambre-stone or the cove in the temple of Abury, like as the Christians do to any symbol or picture at the altar." St. Columb, when in Deacon's Orders, is said to have placed himself under the instruction of an aged Bard named Gemman. A miracle wrought by St. Brigit in the production of butter is given as the cause of her Druidical master becoming a Christian. Richards, in his *Poems Lyric and Pastoral*, published in 1794, says in the preface :

" The patriarchal religion of ancient Britain, called Druidism, but by the Welsh most commonly called *Barddas*, Bardism, although they speak of *Derwydditaeth*, Druidism, is no more inimical to Christianity than the religion of Noah, Job, or Abraham ; it has never, as some imagine, been quite extinct in Britain ; the Welsh Bards have, through all ages down to the present, kept it alive. There is in my possession a manuscript synopsis of it by Llewellyn Sim, a Bard, written in the year 1560 ; its beliefs are corroborated by innumerable notices and allusions in our Bardic manuscripts of every age up to Taliesin in the sixth century, whose poems exhibit a complete system of Druidism. By these (undoubted authentic) writings it will appear that the ancient British Christianity was strongly tinctured with Druidism. The old Welsh Bards kept up a perpetual war with the Church of Rome and therefore experienced much persecution. Narrow understandings might conceive that they were the less Christian for having been Druids. The doctrine of the metempsychosis is that which of all others most clearly vindicated the ways of God to man. It is safely countenanced by many passages in the New Testament and was believed in by many of the primitive Christians and the Essenes amongst the Jews."

Dr. Stukeley boldly asserted that Druidism and Christianity were identical. It is clear that Christianity assimilated Druidism to a great extent, but it is difficult to say how much the newer faith was indebted to the older religion. There is no evidence that the Druidical Britons gave other than a welcome, and, it may be, a hearty welcome to the exponents of the newer creed : in fact, Christian historians state that the Britons embraced the new teachings with more alacrity than any other nation. There is, indeed, a legend to the effect that Edwin was persuaded to embrace the Christian faith by Corfe, the chief of the Druids. At that time, also, it must be remembered, the Christian religion had not developed many of the corruptions and sacerdotal elements which have afflicted it in later times.

Hu, whether considered as the god of Arabia, India, or Greece, all of which countries have claimed him, is described as having been the first to teach his people to build, plant, and enter into societies, and also to have given them laws ; and Grecian mythology also represents him as having been exposed in an ark at sea, and miraculously preserved. Similar characteristics are also ascribed to Menu, the great patriarch of Hindustan, as also to Vishnu, in his ninth incarnation, under the name of Buddha. Buddha was worshipped in Japan under the name of Hudso, and Sir William Jones is of opinion that this deity was also the Odin or Woden of Scandinavia and the Fo-Hi of China. Buddha and Woden are likewise to be identified with the Mercury of the Romans and Greeks. Hence *Bhood-War*, Wednesday, and *Dies Mercurii* are used to denote the same say of the week. Hu is recorded not merely as having colonized Britain, but as having colonized it in equity and peace, rather than by means of bloodshed and violence. This praiseworthy distinction is also ascribed alike to Vishnu, Fo-Hi, and Manco Capac, while Phoroneus is also described by Bryant, in his *Ancient Mythology*, in the following words :

> " He lived in the time of the flood, he first erected altars, he first collected men together and formed them into petty communities, he first gave laws and distributed justice, he divided mankind by their families and nations over the face of the earth."

The same term was used in the Hebrew as one of the Divine names. " He " and " Hu " are also used in the Arabic version of the Scriptures, once for *El* (Psalm xcix., 2), and another time (Genesis xlix., 10) for *Shiloh.*

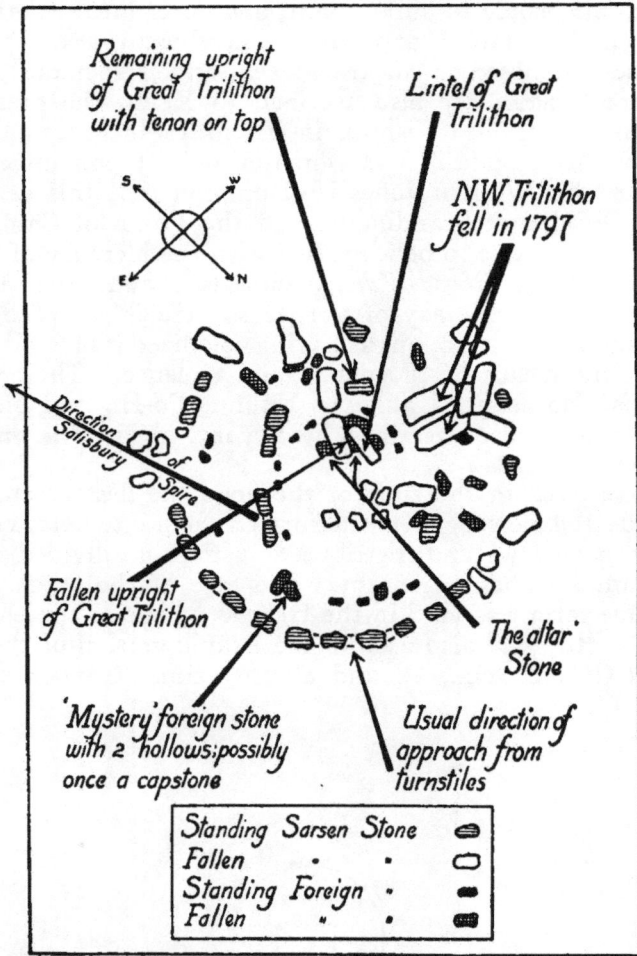

Remaining upright
of Great Trilithon
with tenon on top

Lintel of Great
Trilithon

N.W. Trilithon
fell in 1797

S W
E N

Direction
of Salisbury
Spira

Fallen upright
of Great Trilithon

The 'altar'
Stone

'Mystery' foreign stone
with 2 hollows; possibly
once a capstone

Usual direction of
approach from
turnstiles

Standing Sarsen Stone
Fallen
Standing Foreign
Fallen

[D.] BURROW & CO. LTD COPYRIGHT

DIAGRAMMATIC PLAN OF STONEHENGE.

BIBLIOGRAPHY

Adamnan	..	*Life of Columba.*
Anonymous	..	*Perambulations of Dartmoor.*
do.	..	*A Description of Stonehenge, 1809.*
do.	..	*Conjectures on Stonehenge, 1821.*
do.	..	*A Complete History of the Druids, 1810.*
do.	..	*A Guide to the Stones of Stonehenge, 1840.*
do.	..	*Stonehenge, its Origin, 1892.*
Antient Laws of Ireland		
Antient Laws and Institutes of Wales		
Appleyard, E. S.	..	*Welsh Sketches.*
D'Arbois de Jubainville	..	*Les premiers habitants de l'Europe.*
do.	..	*Irish Mythological Circle.*
Archæologia		
Armstrong, R. R.	..	*Gaelic Dictionary.*
Astle, Thomas	..	*Origin and Progress of Writing*
Aubrey and Jackson	..	*Wiltshire Collections.*
Avebury, Lord	..	*Prehistoric Times.*
Barclay, Edgar	..	*Stonehenge and its Earthworks.*
do.	..	*The Ruined Temple, Stonehenge.*
Banier	..	*Mythology and Fables of the Ancients.*
Barnes, W.	..	*Notes on Ancient Britain.*
Bateman	..	*Vestiges of the Antiquities of Derhys.*
Beauford, William	..	*Druidism Revived.*
do.	..	*Origin and Learning of the Irish Druids.*
Beaumont, Barber	..	*Suggestions on the Ancient Britons.*
Beauties of England and Wales		
Bertrand	..	*Archeologie Celtique et Gauloise.*
do.	..	*Nos Origines, La Religion des Gaulois.*
Betham, Sir William	..	*The Gael and the Cymbri.*
Bevan	..	*Guide to the Channel Islands.*
Black	..	*Guide to Cornwall.*
Boethius	..	*History of Scotland.*
Bonwick, J.	..	*Irish Druids and Old Irish Religion.*
Borlase	..	*Antiquities of Cornwall.*
Bottrell, William	..	*Stories and Folk Lore of West Cornwall.*
Bouché, J. B.	..	*Druides et Celtes.*
Bowles, W. L.	..	*Hermes Britannicus.*
Brand	..	*Popular Antiquities.*
British Association Report, 1916		
Britton	..	*Beauties of Wiltshire.*
Brown, Thomas	..	*Dissertation about the Mona of Cæsar and Tacitus.*

Bryant, Jacob	..	*Ancient Mythology.*
Burke, Oliver J.	..	*The South Isles of Arran.*
Burton	..	*History of Scotland.*
Bury, J. B.	..	*Life of St. Patrick.*
Calendar of the Saints of Ireland		
Cambrian Journal		
Cambrian Quarterly Magazine		
Cambridge Mediæval History		
Cambro-Briton		
Campbell, J. F.	..	*Popular Tales of the West Highlands.*
Carew, R.	..	*Survey of Cornwall.*
Cashen	..	*Manx Folk-Lore.*
Catholic Encyclopædia		
Celtic Magazine		
Celtic Review		
Charleton	..	*Chorea Gigantum.*
Churchward	..	*Signs and Symbols of Primordial Man.*
Cicero	..	*On Divination.*
Coleman	..	*Hindoo Mythology.*
Cooke, William	..	*Inquiry into Patriarchal and Druidical Religion.*
Cordiner, Charles	..	*Antiquities of the North of Scotland.*
do.	..	*Remarkable Ruins of North Britain.*
Cormac	..	*Glossary.*
Cromwell, Thomas	..	*The Druid ; a Tragedy.*
Dalyell, Sir J. G.	..	*Darker Superstitions of Scotland.*
Davies, E.	..	*Celtic Researches.*
do.	..	*Mythology and Rites of British Druids.*
Déchelette	..	*Manuel d' Archeologié prehistorique.*
Diogenes Lærtius	..	*Lives of the Philosophers.*
Duke, E.	..	*Druidical Temples of Wiltshire.*
Dottin	..	*Manuel pour servir a l'etude de l'antiquite celtique.*
Dublin Penny Journal		
Dudley	..	*Naology.*
Elton	..	*Origins of English History.*
Evans, D. Delta	..	*The Ancient Bards of Britain.*
Faber, G. S.	..	*Origin of Pagan Idolatry.*
Fergusson	..	*Rude Stone Monuments.*
Forlong, J. G. R.	..	*Rivers of Life.*
Francklin	..	*Jeynes and Boodhists of India.*
Frazer	..	*Golden Bough.*
Giles, J. A.	..	*History of the Ancient Britons.*
Gomme, G. L.	..	*Ethnology in Folk-Lore.*
do.	..	*Village Community.*
Gordon, E. O.	..	*Prehistoric London.*
Gough	..	*Camden.*
Greenwell, W. and Rolleston G.		*British Barrows.*
Gregory, Lady	..	*A Book of Saints and Wonders.*
Guest, Edwin	..	*Origines Celticæ.*
Haddon and Stubbs	..	*Councils.*
Hall, Mr. and Mrs. S. C.	..	*Ireland, its Scenery, Character, etc.*
Hardy	..	*Christianity and the Roman Government.*

Henry	..	*History of Great Britain.*
Herbert, Algernon	..	*Cyclops Christianus.*
do.	..	*Essay on neo Druidic Heresy.*
Heron	..	*Celtic Church in Ireland.*
Higgins	..	*Celtic Druids.*
Hughes, John	..	*Horæ Britannicæ.*
Hutchinson, W.	..	*History of Cumberland.*
Identity of the Religions called Druidical and Hebrew		
James, Sir Henry	..	*Druidical Structure at Callernish.*
do.	..	*Plans and Photographs of Stonehenge.*
Jamieson	..	*History of the Culdees.*
Jones, Edward	..	*Musical and Poetical Relics.*
Jones, George	..	*Druidism Historically Considered.*
Jones, Inigo	..	*Most Noble Antiquity of Ancient Britain.*
Jones, Owen	..	*Myfrian Archaiology.*
Joyce, P. W.	..	*Social History of Ancient Ireland.*
Keane, Marcus	..	*Towers and Temples of Ireland.*
Keating, G.	..	*History of Ireland.*
Kennedy, Patrick	..	*Legendary Fictions of Irish Celts.*
Langtoft	..	*Chronicle.*
Ledwich	..	*Antiquities of Ireland.*
Leslie, Forbes	..	*Early Races of Scotland.*
Lockyer, Sir N.	..	*Stonehenge and other Monuments.*
Lang, Andrew	..	*History of Scotland.*
Lloyd, J. E.	..	*History of Wales.*
Long, William	..	*Abury Illustrated.*
do.	..	*Stonehenge.*
Lundy	..	*Monumental Christianity.*
M'Alpine	..	*Gaelic Dictionary.*
Macbain, Alexander	..	*Celtic Mythology and Religion.*
MacCulloch, J. A.	..	*Religion of Ancient Celts.*
Mackey and Singleton	..	*History of Freemasonry.*
Maclean, D.	..	*History of Celtic Language.*
MacLauchlan, T.	..	*Early Scotch Church.*
Malkin	..	*Scenery and Antiquities of Wales.*
Martin, Jacques	..	*La Religion des Gaulois.*
Maurice	..	*Ancient History of Hindoostan.*
do.	..	*Indian Antiquities.*
Meyrick	..	*History of Cardigan.*
Moore, A. W.	..	*Folk-Lore of Isle of Man.*
Morgan, Owen	..	*Light of Britannia.*
Myvrian Archaiology of Wales		
Napier, James	..	*Folk-Lore.*
Nash, D. W.	..	*Taliesin.*
O'Brien, Henry	..	*Round Towers of Ireland.*
O'Conor	..	*Dissertation on History of Ireland.*
O'Curry, Eugene	..	*Manners and Customs of Ancient Irish.*
O'Donovan, Dr. John	..	*Annals of Kingdom of Ireland by Four Masters*
O'Flaherty, Roderic	..	*Oxygia.*

Oliver, Dr. George	..	*History of Initiation.*
do.	..	*Existing Remains of Ancient Britain.*
O'Reilly, E.	..	*Irish-English Dictionary.*
Ossian	..	*Poems.*
Parsons, James	..	*Remains of Japheth.*
Pelloutier	..	*Histoire des Celtes.*
Petrie, Flinders	..	*Stonehenge.*
Pezron	..	*Antiq. de la Nat. et de la Langue des Celtes.*
Pictet Adolphe,	..	*La Mystere des Bardes de l'Ile de Bretagne.*
Pike, L. Owen	..	*The English and their Origin.*
Pokorny, Julius	..	*Origin of Druidism.*
Polwhele	..	*History of Cornwall.*
Poste, Beale	..	*Britannic Researches.*
do.	..	*Celtic Inscriptions.*
Potter, Dr. John	..	*Archæologia Græca.*
Pownall	..	*Treatise on Study of Antiquities.*
Pratt, John B.	..	*The Druids.*
Probert	..	*Ancient Laws of Cambria.*
Pughe, Owen	..	*Cambrian Biography.*
Reade, W. Winwood	..	*The Vale of Isis.*
Reinach, S.	..	*Cults, Myths, and Religions.*
do.	..	*Orpheus.*
Rhys, J.	..	*Celtic Britain.*
do.	..	*Celtic Folk-Lore.*
do.	..	*Celtic Heathendom.*
do.	..	*Origin and Growth of Religion.*
Richards, William	..	*Cambro-British Biography.*
Rowlands	..	*Mona Antiqua Restorata.*
do.	..	*History of Isle of Anglesea.*
Royston, Peter	..	*Rudston, its History and Antiquities.*
Rust, J.	..	*Druidism Exhumed.*
Sacheverell	..	*Survey of Isle of Man.*
Samnes	..	*Britannia Antiqua Illustrata.*
Schrader	..	*Reallexikon.*
Sibbald, Sir Robert	..	*History of Fife.*
Simpson, W.	..	*Circular Movements in Custom and Ritual.*
Skene	..	*Four Ancient Books of Wales.*
do.	..	*Celtic Scotland.*
Smiddy, R.	..	*Essay on the Druids.*
Smith, Dr. George	..	*Religion of Britain Historically Considered.*
Smith, Dr. John	..	*Choir Gawr of Stonehenge.*
do.	..	*Gaelic Antiquities.*
Stokes, Dr. Whitley	..	*Lives of Saints from Book of Lismore.*
Stone, Gilbert	..	*Wales.*
Stothard	..	*Traditions and Legends of Devonshire.*
Stukeley, William	..	*Stonehenge.*
do.	..	*Abury.*
Thackeray, Francis	..	*Ancient Britain.*
Toland	..	*History of the Druids.*
Toutain	..	*Les pretendes Druidesses gauloises.*
Train, Joseph	..	*History of Isle of Man.*

Trevelyan, Marie   ..   *Folk-Lore of Wales.*
Tripartite Life of St. Patrick
Turner, Sharon   ..   *Vindication of Ancient British Poems.*
Vallancey, Charles   ..   *Vindication of Ancient History of Ireland.*
   do.   ..   *Collectanea de Rebus Hibernicus.*
   do.   ..   *Grammar of Irish Language.*
Villemarqué   ..   *Popular Songs of Brittany.*
Walker, J. Cooper   ..   *Historical Memoirs of Irish Bards.*
   do.   ..   *Historical Essay on Dress of Irish.*
Ware, Sir James   ..   *Antiquities and History of Ireland.*
Weaver, Robert   ..   *Monumenta Antiqua.*
Wilde, Lady   ..   *Antient Cures, Charms, and Usages of Ireland.*
Williams, Edward   ..   *Poems, Lyric and Pastoral.*
Williams, J.   ..   *Barddas.*
   do.   ..   *Druidic Stones.*
Wilson, Daniel   ..   *Prehistoric Annals of Scotland.*
Wise, T. A.   ..   *History of Paganism in Caledonia.*
   do.   ..   *Traces of Elder Faiths of Ireland.*
Woodward, E. H.   ..   *History of Wales.*
Yeowell   ..   *Chronicles of Ancient British Church.*
Zeitschrift für celtique philologie

INDEX